Re-envisioning the Synagogue

Edited by
Zachary I. Heller

The National Center for Jewish
Policy Studies at Hebrew College

HEBREW COLLEGE
המכללה העברית

STAR

Synagogues:
Transformation and Renewal

Hollis Publishing Company
95 Runnells Bridge Road, Hollis, NH 03049
(t) 603.889.4500   (f) 603.889.6551
books@hollispublishing.com

Printed in the United States of America by Puritan Press, Inc., Hollis, NH.

This book is dedicated . . .

In loving memory of **Charles Schusterman**, whose passion for Jewish life lives on through STAR (Synagogues: Transformation and Renewal) and the other visionary initiatives of the Charles and Lynn Schusterman Family Foundation of Tulsa, OK. His legacy inspires us to follow in his footsteps.

In gratitude to **Rabbi Benjamin Z. Kreitman**, whose rabbinate and leadership have been devoted to the enhancement of the synagogue and its relevance. His life and career are an inspiration to us. His support of the original conference and this publication helped bring them to fruition.

CONTENTS

Editor's Preface. . . . . *Zachary I. Heller*   vii

Prologue: Re-envisioning the Synagogue:
    Challenges and Opportunities . . . . *David M. Gordis*   xi
    Zachary I. Heller
    David Kaufman

HISTORY: DESCRIPTIVE AND PRESCRIPTIVE

The Synagogue as a Mediating Institution . . . *David Kaufman*   3

A World Within a World: The History of the
    Modern Synagogue. *David B. Starr*   38

SYNAGOGUE DWELLERS AND SPIRITUAL SEEKERS

The Commanding Community and the
    Sovereign Self . . . . *Hayim Herring*   55

RE-ENVISIONING THE AMERICAN SYNAGOGUE

The Challenge of Renaissance. . . . . *Richard A. Marker*   111

The Synagogue as Counter-Culture:
    A Long Range View. *Riv-Ellen Prell*   119

Getting There From Here . . . . *Michael Hammer*   126

The Synagogue of Tomorrow:
    A Non-Prophetic Vision . . . . *Morris Allen*   133

MODELS OF FUTURE SYNAGOGUE LEADERSHIP –
HOW DO WE ENVISION AND PREPARE THEM?

Professional Leadership and the
    Future of the Synagogue. . . . . *Harvey Shapiro*   149

Rabbinic Education for An Evolving Community . . *David M. Gordis*   155

The Synagogue as a Home and the Role
    of the Rabbi . . . . *Avi Weiss*   162

The Cantorate: History as Precedent for
  Evolving Roles .... *Scott Sokol*   169

The Role of the Educator in Synagogue
  Transformation .... *Isa Aron*   187

MODELS OF LAY LEADERSHIP: A SYMPOSIUM

                                          Jerome M. Epstein   197
                                          Lee M. Hendler   202
                                          Terry Rosenberg   206

EPILOGUE

Re-envisioning the Synagogue:
  Some Closing Reflections.................. *David M. Gordis*   217

The Contributors 219

EDITOR'S PREFACE

Zachary I. Heller

For the past two millennia the synagogue has been the central point of engagement for Jews and continues to be the locus of religious, cultural, and educational expression that is a focal point for Jewish identity, education, cohesion and community. The synagogue is the core institution within the community that is uniquely positioned to provide content to Jewish life and helps us navigate the issues of faith and fate, personal experience and communal continuity. One objective emerging from many studies in this volume is that the synagogue must be open and inviting to all Jews, both for those who already are committed to Jewish tradition and find fulfillment in it as well as for those who find the language and symbols of the synagogue either unfamiliar or lacking in meaning.

The examination of synagogue history represented in this volume by the essays of David Kaufman and David Starr or the development of the role of the Hazzan set out by Scott Sokol provide an opportunity to explore the continuities with the past that root the contemporary synagogue in Jewish tradition and practice while at the same time suggesting how historic precedents and the evolution of roles give us the basis for considering new developments and formats. The study of history, therefore, is not just descriptive but prescriptive as we build on those insights in order to strengthen the synagogue for the future and project a trajectory for its continued evolution.

We live in an era of autonomy where personal identity and Jewish commitments are not necessarily based upon communal norms but often are choices made by individuals. Jewish identity, as analyzed by Hayim Herring, is not necessarily a unified framework

but rather a series of referents that are prisms through which individuals refract their personal Jewishness. The synagogue is challenged to meet these complex realities frontally, it must be
multi-faceted and multi-portal. Like the midrashic portrayal of the
tent of Abraham and Sarah that was open to travelers coming from
all directions, the synagogue must be welcoming to Jews and seekers traversing a range of intellectual, emotional and spiritual paths
who are searching for a spiritual and communal home whose doors
will be open and wide enough to accommodate them all.

Similarly, the nature of the rabbinate and Jewish professional
and lay leadership has been influenced by these same phenomena.
David Gordis and Avi Weiss each approach the question of rabbinic
training from different directions and analytic perspectives, the
former focusing upon the challenges emerging from the contemporary intellectual environment, and the latter focusing upon the
human condition. Both understand that the underlying issue is not
a matter of theory but praxis. The oft-cited *bon mot,* attributed to
one or another of several rabbinic leaders three quarters of a century ago, summed up the sentiment that in order to be a good rabbi
(leader) one had to love not only Judaism but Jews who must be
engaged wherever they are in their own lives. Gordis and Weiss are
joined by the discussants of lay leadership (Epstein, Hendler and
Rosenberg) in their emphasis on this sensitivity to people, meeting
them where they are intellectually and responding on their terms,
listening to their human concerns in order to draw them into community, and accepting them as they are in the hope that in time
they will share a common vision articulated by successful leaders.
As Isa Aron reminds us, the role of the educator in transforming
the synagogue is predicated upon similar principles of vision and
leadership.

While analysis of the details and degree of malaise of the contemporary synagogue may differ, there is a strong consensus that
it is in need of a new vision to meet not only the challenges of the
day but to attempt to anticipate future needs and directions to be
taken without any claims to prophecy. As Michael Hammer asks:
How do we get there from here? This rich discussion of Re-envisioning the Synagogue is shaped by the critical insights of Hayim
Herring, Richard Marker, Riv-Ellen Prell, Michael Hammer and
Morris Allen who discuss both goals and process, understanding
that a vision that does not include specific goal is a road that leads

nowhere. The essays in this volume attempt, individually and collectively, to articulate visions that can be translated into goals and guidelines that can become process.

The future shape of the synagogue will be defined not by its physical architecture but by its inner dynamics. Form will have to follow content and structure will be determined by new programmatic realities. Synagogue buildings will always reflect external societal influences and the aesthetic sense of unfolding eras, but the inner content must express that inner continuum of Jewish experience, faith and community as it encounters new challenges that are simultaneously new opportunities.

This volume, *Re-envisioning the Synagogue*, is the product of several processes in which the National Center for Jewish Policy Studies at Hebrew College, the successor to the former Wilstein Institute, has been involved. When the communal leaders and philanthropists Charles Schusterman (of blessed memory), Edgar Bronfman and Michael Steinhardt began their initiative that resulted in the creation of STAR (Synagogues: Transformation and Renewal) they asked the Institute to undertake an assessment of synagogue renewal projects on national, regional and local levels. The report of that study, conducted by David Gordis, Zachary Heller and David Kaufman, with the latter acting as principal investigator, also attempted to place those current activities in the context of a broad view of the history of the synagogue and varying perspectives on its vitality and relevance. The prologue of this book reflects some of those insights along with others developed more recently and David Kaufman's new paper is an extended development of one theme that he initially proposed in that report.

In November 2003, the National Center for Jewish Policy Studies and STAR organized a joint conference at Hebrew College in Newton Centre to explore the theme *Re-envisioning the Synagogue*. Many of the essays in this volume were first presented there, some have been revised by their authors in light of the discussion at the conference or to meet the needs of this format and a few have been written for it subsequently. This book, like the original conference, was organized around three major themes: a) the historic development of the synagogue and its contemporary challenges, b) re-envisioning the synagogue, and c) models of future synagogue leadership—how do we envision and prepare them?

It should be noted that this exploration transcends denominational bounds just as The National Center of Jewish Policy Studies and its host Hebrew College as well as STAR (Synagogues: Transformation and Renewal) are all trans-denominational, sharing a common concern for the vibrancy and effectiveness of all synagogues as central institutions of Jewish life, including synagogues that are affiliated with each of the denominations as well as those that do not identify with any of them.

May all who establish and maintain synagogues and those who enter therein to pray and learn, find inspiration and Jewish connection, be the beneficiaries of our efforts in promoting this exchange of ideas and presenting them to the community. *Re-envisioning the Synagogue,* is intended to examine the synagogue as it is and as it might be in the hope that it will be a stimulus to further private thought and public discussion that will help reinvigorate the synagogue as the epicenter of Jewish life in North America. If this discussion also resonates with Jews elsewhere, either in Israel or in other locales of Jewish habitation, we will be most pleased.

The editor wishes to express his appreciation to his colleagues, Dr. David M. Gordis who in addition to being President of Hebrew College is the founder and Director of the National Center of Jewish Policy Studies and to Dr. Hayim Herring, the Executive Director of STAR (Synagogues: Transformation and Renewal) who have both been intimately involved in the creative processes out of which this book developed. Their wonderful insights, continued encouragement, advice and support are reflected herein. Dr. David Kaufman, too, was involved in the original conceptualization of the conference from which this volume developed. We are grateful to each of the authors for their contribution to this far-reaching discussion and trust that in bringing their words to print we have been faithful to their text and not permitted any errors to distort their language or intent.

Our gratitude is expressed as well to Leslie Schweitzer for her invaluable assistance in both the administration of the conference and the preparation of the text of this book.

Erev Pesach 5765

PROLOGUE

David M. Gordis, Zachary I. Heller and David Kaufman

Re-envisioning the Synagogue: Challenges and Opportunities*

The reality of the synagogue in America does not begin to approach its potential. A common critique of the synagogue refers to its lack of influence, both in terms of quantity and quality. In the first case, the statistics can be deceptive. Whereas survey research tells us that about 80% of American Jews affiliate with a synagogue or have a relationship with one at some point during their lives, their engagement tends to be temporary and ephemeral and generally no more than 50% are members of synagogues at any one time. Interestingly, two recent surveys regarding actual synagogue attendance as opposed to membership reveal that monthly (or more) participation ranges from 16% (Harris Poll) to 27% (NJPS 2000/2001). At best, this indicates that only about ½ of the 50% of Jews who claim synagogue affiliation actually attend on at least a once a month basis.

(Prior to the development of STAR (Synagogues: Transformation and Renewal) in 2000, the then Wilstein Institute was commissioned by the partnering philanthropists to survey and assess the variety of synagogue renewal initiatives. Prof. David Kaufman, the principal investigator, worked closely with Dr. David M. Gordis and Rabbi Zachary I Heller, the Institute's Director and Associate Director. Their report, which has not been circulated, contained many observations on the wider issues of the synagogue that are germane to this discussion. Zachary Heller has presented some of these ideas here in a revised and expanded form along with some further observations developed since the original report was written.)

Many synagogues apparently do not retain their members in a lasting, meaningful way. A cadre of respondents in various surveys often claim that they find an unwelcoming atmosphere in the synagogue, complaining of a variety of negative experiences during their brief encounter. On the other hand, rabbis and other synagogue professionals are more likely to cite the low levels of knowledge and participation on the part of congregants. While seemingly active on a surface level, the depth of commitment and seriousness of engagement are lacking. As a result, the Jewish content of synagogue life—liturgical, intellectual, cultural, and spiritual—is too often shallow and, critics say, has been "dumbed down" in relation to a more authentic Jewish culture. In many cases, these discouraging trends are changing for the better, and we are currently seeing a reversal of some of the negative tendencies. Yet much work remains to be done.

One feature that reveals both the strength and weakness of the synagogue is its relative isolation within the greater Jewish community. Historically, the synagogue developed as an independent and autonomous institution. Each congregation was established as a totally separate entity from any other. This phenomenon occurred within the context of American religious voluntarism and denominationalism. The free marketplace of American religion created a situation of survival of the fittest—every congregation for itself. In American Jewish history, the disparate congregational entities were first woven together by the formation of congregational movements, i.e., the four major religious "denominations" of American Jewry: Reform, Orthodox, Conservative and then Reconstructionist Judaism.

Both ideologically and institutionally resourceful, the movements have certainly contributed to the success of the synagogue in American Jewish life. Nevertheless, this relationship between congregations and denominations is very complex and uneven. Denominations are only ideological nuances without the congregational bodies. Without a constituency, denominations do not exist, but congregations do exist by virtue of their membership even without denominational affiliation. Denominations help congregations in several ways: ideological definition, shared identity and bonds of affinity, and specific services. Concurrently, there are major tensions between congregations and denominations. Denominations need dues and allocations from congregations for their major financial base in order to maintain their infrastructure and provide the services that flow from national and regional sources. Their fiscal decisions are made at national and regional levels by denominational partisans who have risen to lay or professional leadership positions. The grassroots congregational leadership and membership often chafe at what they view as inordinate demands being placed upon them. Congregational leadership is jealous of the resources that they feel should be used for "local purposes" and not drained from them. The grassroots commitment to denominational ideology is often not strong enough on its own to elicit unwavering support. This will be verified by the experience of any regional director of a denominational organization. The real glue that holds the relationship of congregations and denominations together is not ideology but services and programs. For example, if a congregation's teenagers may be denied access to their movement's teen programs (NCSY, USY, NFTY) the synagogue leadership will be very hesitant to endanger the affliational relationship. Conversely, synagogues will affiliate with a denomination to secure the services of a rabbi or cantor. While individuals may identify with denominations by virtue of congregational affiliation, their choice of congregation may be based on multiple factors that are local. These include the general tenor of the congregation, its professionals, attractiveness of its religious services, educational programs, and personal social relationships. The choices are made individually by virtue of these local issues and are only partially influenced by national denominational ties. It is evident that there is an element of permeability across denominational lines with the exception of some adherents to Orthodoxy. Even in the latter case the rule is not hard and fast. The relationships between congregations and denominational structures therefore reflect both the positive features of shared ideological commitments and support network and the tensions that are inherent in diminished ideological concerns and heightened fiscal self-interest. The recent growth of non- or trans-denominational synagogues and the long-term effect of the *Havurah* movement that began in the 1960s—has yet to be evaluated properly.

However, a gap remains between the synagogue and other agencies of the Jewish community—Federations, Jewish Community Centers, schools, and other organizations. As presently constituted, the fragmented Jewish community wastes numerous opportunities for the sharing of resources and cross-fertilization of its culture. But a healthy Jewish communal life necessitates the integration of its diverse parts. As the Jewish community begins to view itself more organically, these schisms should begin to be healed. In the meantime, the synagogue remains in a weakened position by virtue of its isolation.

Another area in critical need of attention is the question of the unaffiliated. While some American Jews may never have any interest in synagogue life, and may be better served by alternative institutions, if at all, there remain large numbers whose current state of alienation may be reversed. This spectrum of uninvolved though potentially engaged Jews falls into two broad categories. First are the so-called "secular Jews," those we often hear say, "I am a Jew by culture, not by religion." This common self-image encompasses a wide swath of the American Jewish public, even including many who do belong to synagogues (which ought to provide us with some clue to possible solutions.) The persistence of this population raises the legitimate question as to whether they ought to be invited into the religious sphere of the synagogue at all, and if so, how can synagogues broaden their other spheres of activities to include those who define themselves as secular. As the late Egon Mayer and others have found in their studies, a significant cohort of those who define themselves as secular, nevertheless indicate that at times they have what may be defined as religious feelings including moments of prayer and even belief in supernatural miracles. The second group of disaffected Jews encompasses those individuals who may have a sincere interest in some form of spiritual experience, but, for various reasons, have not been able to find it in the synagogue. These seekers are prime candidates for synagogue involvement, yet they find the synagogue as presently constituted to be a turn-off rather than a safe haven. Conforming to the individualism (ironically enough) of American culture, they tend to avoid joining any formal group and instead search for spiritual fulfillment along a personal, internalized path. Again, many such Jews are ripe for synagogue engagement, but only once the synagogue is redefined and reconfigured so as to reach out to the unaffiliated and enable their re-entry into Jewish life.

Both the secularists and the individualists remind us of a key point in our analysis of the contemporary synagogue. As has been noted by numerous observers, American Jewish life is characterized by a series of tensions deriving from the duality of American society and Jewish culture. The former invites integration into a society premised upon freedom and individualism; the latter demands survival as a distinct religious group and ethnic sub-culture. Despite arguments to the contrary, opposing values between Americanism and Judaism abound.

As the central institution of American Jewish life, the synagogue is both affected by and continues to generate a number of tensions key to its functioning. In order to explore new directions for the American synagogue in the future, these essential tensions must be enumerated and understood.

1. **American individualism vs. Jewish communality**—The American synagogue responds to both of these imperatives, serving both as a place for personal expression, along the lines of contemporary American culture, and a setting for group participation, more in keeping with the norms of Jewish life. We see this, for example, in the two kinds of spiritual experiences the synagogue is asked to provide: spirituality through communal prayer and group study, on the one hand, and spirituality through personal meditation and individual insight on the other. As the power of individualism increases, however, the tension increases between constituents' demands for autonomy and the communal expectations of the synagogue. The synagogue of the future must continue to represent the traditional values of Jewish peoplehood, community and congregation, while also creating space for the equally cherished American values of self-expression and individualism. Turning (American) individuals into members of a (Jewish) group, while continuing to honor their independence and iconoclasm, is perhaps the central challenge confronting the American synagogue.

2. **Religious Judaism vs. Ethnic Jewishness**—The synagogue is a locus of Jewish religion. The synagogue is a center of Jewish community. Again, both statements are valid insofar as American Jews continue to display both forms of Jewish identification. This duality may be glossed over, as is often the case, or it may be embraced, as the legitimate and authentic expression of historical Judaism. That is, rather than seeing one side of the equation as simply the means to an end, both Jewish religion and Jewish peoplehood ought to be acknowledged as equally vital aspects of Jewish life. We

believe that the more this is actualized through education and programming, the more effective and energized the synagogue of the future will become.

3. **Tradition vs. Modernity**—Perhaps the most familiar of our dichotomies, it is also the most complex. As it relates to the synagogue, it centers on the tension between the need for continuity, i.e., maintaining the normative patterns of the past—whether we are speaking of the ancient norms of Jewish tradition or the more recently established norms of the American synagogue—and the equally important need for change, in direct response to the enlightened intellectual progress of the modern age and the most recent innovations of contemporary culture. Again, both imperatives are valid and desirable; and both are intrinsic features of the synagogue. The question, of course, is how to honor both on an equal plane and as they relate to each other. For example, tradition untempered by modernity is bound to become a stultifying and regressive culture; and will never attract any significant portion of the American Jewish public. On the other hand, modern innovation unimpeded by traditional norms will err to the extreme of a consumer-driven agenda and an efficiency-based approach. The contemporary synagogue will, by necessity, continue to reflect the values of the American environment; yet at the same time, it must carry on its sacred responsibility to generate the values representative of Jewish tradition. The task may seem paradoxical, though its completion is essential. Each of the religious streams confronts this issue in its own way from broadest accommodation on one hand to rejection at the other end of the spectrum. Nevertheless, whatever the nature of the response, there is an acknowledgement of this reality.

Though these three themes are the key tensions and hence the central challenges confronting the American synagogue, other relevant dilemmas include the tensions between uniformity and diversity; "mega"-synagogues and intimate *havurot*; professionalization and democratization; denominational identity and the trans-denominational tendency. These tensions are inherent in the American Jewish experience and though the synagogue may represent our best hope for some satisfactory resolution, no single institution can carry the load entirely on its own. Each of the enumerated tensions may in fact require other institutional and communal responses in addition to the current initiatives for renewal of the synagogue, and that certainly needs further study.

A meaningful community can only be created, however, within the context of an effectively functioning communal structure, one that works harmoniously. Yet, it is clear to us that the synagogue is, by definition, an integrated multi-faceted, religious, and social institution and that any attempt to effectively influence the functioning of one aspect alone will be futile. For the sake of both Jewish authenticity and transformational efficiency, any process must take a holistic approach to the synagogue and it's functioning. Nevertheless, as we examine visions of the synagogue and stress the need for multi-dimensional models, we are not suggesting a uniform approach and image. Each congregation must highlight those of its qualities that make it unique and therefore attractive to members of the community.

At present, many of our synagogues exhibit difficulties of poor administration, strained professional-lay relations, congregational apathy and uncertain relations between the synagogue as an institution and other communal institutions. Not surprisingly, many of the initiatives in the current movement for change center about such issues as professional roles, governance and congregational dynamics. In some ways, these are more pressing matters than content issues for the simple reason that the Jewish content of synagogues has historical foundations and traditional bases. But, what are the "sources" for best working relationships between rabbi, cantor, educator and administrator? What guidelines do we have for the relationship between these Jewish synagogue professionals? Where might we find precedents to determine the relationship between synagogues and other structures of the organized Jewish community? These are often pragmatic questions without either historic precedent or theoretical guidelines. Changes in the dynamics of governance, institutional relationships, and internal functioning are often spontaneous, uncoordinated and lacking foresight and direction. New eras produce new needs and changing professional and lay roles must reflect the needs of evolving institutions. There is often a lag between these various sets of changes. We suggest that there is a difference between change and transformation. Change may be spontaneous or unplanned and may be a response to external factors. Transformation requires intent and planning. Change can take place in a specific limited condition or set of conditions with or without intent; transformation requires a holistic approach with foresight and planning. While spontaneity at times leads to creativity, it can also produce chaotic conditions. Contemporary efforts to re-envision the synagogue must focus upon transforming the synagogue into the effective epicenter of Jewish life.

The following observations garnered from our study of synagogue transformation efforts have practical implications that must be considered as we try to re-envision the synagogue.

1. The synagogue is best viewed as *a multi-portal institution,* serving the various needs of Jewish life. While a synagogue cannot be all things to all people, it must encompass the diverse Jewish interests of its current and potential members. Effective synagogue change initiatives must address multiple aspects of congregational life. Congregations function at their optimum when conceived and structured as multi-storied "houses" of prayer, learning, and community

2. As noted previously, denominational structures started as support networks of like-minded congregations rallying around a philosophic consensus. Yet they often became a coalescence of opposition to a differing ideology. While those lines have hardened in many ways and inter-denominational cooperation is often limited to some shared non-synagogual Jewish concerns, many of the issues confronting the American synagogue transcend these divisions, which are more permeable than public organizational postures would lead us to believe. As noted above, denominational commitments are not a high priority for many congregants, yet the denominational structures do provide an excellent mechanism for reaching individual synagogues and providing a broad range of stimuli, even though they may be filtered through the denominational agenda and administrative process. Shared consultation and training in non-ideologically specific areas can benefit all synagogues. Cooperation across denominational lines on programs that are "non-threatening" could ultimately lead to greater understanding and cooperation in more sensitive areas.

3. Since early in the 20th century, federations of Jewish philanthropies have been the chief organizing factors of regional Jewish communities. Though the comprehensive

"Kehillah" experiment of 1909–22 was judged a failure, the idea of an umbrella communal organization was taken over by the growing fundraising and philanthropic bodies, which often included political and defense agencies as well—but they did not include the religious branches of the community, whose organizing principle continued to be fragmentation rather than unity. As the result, a schism developed between the religious and the sociopolitical life of the Jewish community, one that is only just now seeing some resolution. That resolution is coming in the form of Federation-sponsored synagogue renewal and the necessary cooperation between the formerly competing philanthropic and religious hierarchies. The desire to overcome historic tension between synagogues and communal federations often led to the creation of commissions on synagogue-federation relations in some large city federations. In some significant cases, these were not the product of a vision of a cohesive community, but flowed from a pragmatic understanding that the synagogue was the site where most Jews could be reached for fund-raising for local and oversees needs (most often under the banner of Israel or other areas of concern that would attract potential donors). Only later did the real issues of the role of the synagogue as a central institution of Jewish culture and education achieve greater prominence in some communities. That tension has only recently begun to dissipate, but many federations have not yet made this a focus of their communal agenda. Nevertheless, the minimal role assigned to the synagogue as represented by the denominations in the architecture of the new UJC (United Jewish Communities) indicates that whatever changes have taken place on the local level have not permeated the national level. Nevertheless, in recent years we have seen several communal initiatives that are new models of a partnership between federation and synagogue that could and should be replicated nationally. These federations have often become the catalysts for new programs in education on multiple generational tracks, encouraging new professional leadership training and employment and shared programs of community action and social justice that transcend denominations which they coordinate and often fund.

4. Synagogues and Jewish schools have often been viewed as distinct realms, one dealing primarily with adults and the other with children; one dealing with instruction and the other with practice. While this is really a false dichotomy, the integration and inter-relation of the synagogue and the school is a significant concern. The supposed tension between study and practice is not only an ancient philosophic debate, but reflects a significant contemporary institutional issue. The community must not only obviate issues of institutional "turf," must but also bridge the gap between the synagogue and the school and create a synthesis of their roles. This is especially an issue when one examines the relationships of synagogues and day schools. The recent development of "family education" is an innovation that holds promise of a more holistic approach. The synagogue and the school must partner in a coordinated multi-generational and multi-institutional educational initiative.

5. The Jewish Community Center is a 20th century innovation in American Jewish life. It often met needs that most synagogues did not confront or were not equipped to handle. At times, JCCs provided a Jewish venue for those who rejected the theological language and ritual practices of the synagogue. Paradoxically, the JCC sometimes became the venue where limited Judaic content programs, eventually became the path back to the synagogue for the children of the previous alienated generation. While the JCC is now attempting to create a "meaningful Jewish community," the American synagogue is once again expanding its parameters and attempting to be more inclusive. This is an appropriate time to reflect upon the relationship between synagogues and JCCs. How can a new relationship between the JCC and neighboring synagogues be enhanced and partnerships created for the benefit of both institutions and the larger Jewish community? Can the JCC be a common meeting ground for diverse congregations in a community? How can these roles be defined and relationships be delineated?

6. Synagogues have much to learn from each other and can benefit by sharing ideas, experiences, programs and perhaps even staff resources. The process of transformation and change to new modes is a difficult one. The best partners that synagogues have are other synagogues, whether

local neighbors or distant friends. The process of mutual support, whether within or across denominational lines is crucial to the advancement of this process. Networking is not only for a practical exchange of ideas, it is a source of support and reassurance that comes not from outside theoreticians, but from colleagues in the same struggle who share similar experiences. These inter-relationships must be created, nurtured and supported to strengthen the common denominators of Jewish identity and lower the barriers of divisiveness that threaten Jewish unity. We do not suggest a goal of Jewish homogeneity, we recognize the historic and contemporary validity of diversity, yet the value of such networking is in its ability to help the participants transcend their differences.

7. The new electronic technologies that just a few years ago were the province of the few have now become the common channel of communication for the majority in the Jewish community. There is a tendency to ascribe to the Internet all sorts of magical powers since that virtually instantaneous communication provides the opportunity to reach vast numbers of people with important news, both of communal and personal significance, as well as for the dissemination of educational material. There is, though, an inherent fallacy in confusing the valuable dissemination of information with personal human contact. One may be able to study text via this medium; it does not provide the opportunity for the teacher to become a personal role model. The virtual community provided by instant communication is not a substitute for the actual community of physical presence. Nevertheless, as technologies continue to evolve one must explore how they may be used in a manner that is more supportive of the human dimensions of community that the synagogue must represent.

8. With the growing participation and sophistication of lay people comes the question of reconfiguring the rabbinic role. Many rabbis explicitly supported the notion of the rabbi's position being decentralized in response to the increasing democratization of synagogue life. This is another delayed effect of the Havurah movement and its principle of "do-it-yourself" Judaism. As Jews become more knowledgeable and skilled at "doing Jewish," they become

less dependent on the expertise of religious professionals, especially rabbis. What then, is the role of the rabbi? Many rabbis complain about being overtaxed with roles that are not rabbinical. They are forced by circumstance to be administrators and not teachers, financial planners and fundraisers rather than arbiters of Jewish law or guides to the perplexed. There is no easy solution to this dilemma, but clearly careful thought needs to be paid to the issue in conjunction with planning for synagogue change and renewal.

9. Questions of synagogue governance and leadership are raised regularly by concerned leaders. How are leaders to be developed, what ought the committee structure look like, what are the best membership policies, what training is appropriate for lay leadership, how to draw peripheral members into the vortex of synagogue activity. Though many good lay leaders were "developed" by their successful hands on involvement and organizational skills brought from other arenas, no one, to our knowledge, has yet to undertake a serious study of these issues in the context of the American synagogue. Given the truism that "synagogue life is with people," such issues of political form and social structure are vital to the success of all content programming and spiritual substance. New models of leadership require new approaches to leadership training. Inasmuch as congregational life has become more complex in the past quarter century and the skills necessary for successful lay and professional leadership and administration have changed radically, it is necessary to adapt the pre-service professional skills training to these new realities and to provide new kinds of in-service programs for those already in the field. The often-stereotyped synagogue lay leader depicted as the dedicated benevolent autocrat is being replaced by a newer leadership model that must be equipped to deal with a new reality of the synagogue as a complex, democratic, voluntary association. The same leaders also need to be trained to deal with the new legal and financial realities and requirements of the not-for-profit/philanthropic world.

We view the Jewish community as an organic body where the range of Jewish communal institutions and agencies must relate to each other in a complementary manner. The synagogue as the central institution of Jewish engagement is also a microcosm of the Jewish community. Synagogues that are built upon the pillars of earlier historic institutions, but are resilient enough to accommodate to new circumstances, will strengthen Jewish life in North America and elsewhere. Such synagogues will be at the epicenter of Jewish communal life and will be the focal point of the lives of Jews only if they can articulate Jewish tradition and values meaningfully, educate competently and provide the social context for shared Jewish experience.

HISTORY: DESCRIPTIVE AND PRESCRIPTIVE

David Kaufman

David B. Starr

THE SYNAGOGUE AS A
MEDIATING INSTITUTION

David E. Kaufman

R ecent years have seen the emergence of a new movement of "synagogue transformation" in American Jewish life. In response to the rising assimilation indicated by the 1990 National Jewish Population Survey, communal concern was aroused and resources were directed toward the goal of group survival—or, in the catchphrase of the day, "Jewish continuity." Soon it became apparent that a central focus of the continuity campaign would be the individual congregation, and thus, combined with the fact that the American synagogue is always tending toward its own progress, a synagogue change movement has come into being. The movement, a range of spontaneously generated local initiatives and a handful of national projects, rests on the premise that the improvement of congregational life will help transform Jewish life overall. Change the synagogue for the better, the movement asserts (at least implicitly), and the spiritual health of American Jewry will be restored.

Yet the theory remains largely unproven. Despite the best intentions and some early encouraging signs, the results are not yet in—we have not as yet measured (using the quantitative research methods at our disposal) the effectiveness of synagogue change as a means to ensure Jewish continuity. Moreover, synagogues are notoriously difficult to change. As lay-led, "democratic" organizations, congregations often tend to be messy and even dysfunctional in their social and political dynamics. Though affiliated with nationally organized, ideologically defined movements, synagogues are stubbornly independent institutions, resistant to outside control and unresponsive to broad-based coordination.

3

Nevertheless, synagogue transformation is promoted as being critical to the American Jewish future.

Though I may sound somewhat skeptical, I do in fact agree
with this assessment—but for reasons that have yet to be fully elu-
cidated. Therefore, as we move into the next phases of the synagogue transformation trend, we would be wise to contemplate
some of the key questions underlying the enterprise: What is it in
the nature and function of the synagogue that makes it the best
option to effect broader cultural and deeper religious change? What
makes it so central to the historic Jewish tasks of religious transmission and communal preservation? Why the synagogue, after
all? I believe the answer to these questions can be summed up by
the phrase, "mediating institution." The American synagogue, as
this paper will demonstrate at length, is the Jewish mediating institution *par excellence*.

But what is meant by the term "mediating institution"? In sociological discourse, where it is most commonly applied, it refers to
those social agencies that are conduits between the individual and
society. Mediating institutions acquire a special importance in
American life insofar as individualism is so dominant in the culture. To bridge the ever-widening gap between individual preroga-
tives and greater social imperatives, therefore, institutions such as
political parties, religious organizations, the mass media, etc.,
enter the fray. The mediating institution thereby fulfills the need to
"mediate," or negotiate, the varied relationships an individual has
with aspects of the social structure, i.e. other people, other communities, authority structures, value systems, etc. Some commonly
cited examples of mediating institutions in contemporary society
are: television, web groups, voluntary associations, schools,
churches and synagogues—all providing the individual access to
the public sphere, and, at the same time, enabling the world at
large to reach the individual.

The local religious organization is especially pertinent here.
Larry McNeil, a proponent of congregational transformation,
recently stated: "The core of . . . renewed mission for churches and
synagogues should be an understanding of themselves as mediating institutions, institutions capable of connecting at the deepest
level with their members, assisting them in making sense of the
world, and equipping them with the power, strategies and skills to
intercede and negotiate with all other institutions that affect their
lives."[1] McNeil further defines the concept of a mediating institution

as follows: "First of all, they are a locus and setting for events that matter: celebrations, mournings, passages. They are built on relationships of affinity, not just economic necessity and utility. . . . They expand our relationships beyond family and clan. . . . They provide an instrument for engaging in sustained public life. When operating best, they are instigator, creator, defender, and protector. . . . Mediating institutions engage their members in the sharing of their stories, help them understand the meaning of their stories in the context of the larger world and of their own value tradition, and organize their members for action in the spirit of the Hebrew word, *tikkun*, to repair or heal the world."[2]

It's no coincidence that McNeil enlists religious categories to explain himself—the 'mediating institution' is a religious concept after all. What is religion if not the consummate mediator between the individual and the world, between the immanent self and the transcendent beyond? Hence a mediating institution may be defined in both sociological and religious terms. In the purview of sociology, it is an institution mediating between the individual and society; in the area of Religion, alternately, a mediating institution is a religious category that enacts and enables the relationship between Man and God. Serendipitously, the synagogue fits neatly into both these definitions. In the first case, the local synagogue institution serves as the connective link between individual Jews and the greater Jewish community, as well as with the larger American society. In the second case, the synagogue as a religious institution, also serves as the primary locus for the encounter between Jews and their God, principally through the mediating institutions of *Torah* (study) and *t'filah* (prayer). Since the performance of these essential *mitzvot* are the two central religious functions of synagogue life, the synagogue absorbs this quality of mediation and itself becomes the ultimate mediating institution.

The need for mediation suggests tension. Indeed, throughout its history, the synagogue has served to mediate the tensions and conflicts of Jewish life. Its very beginnings provide an illustration. Though its precise origins are hazy,[3] we do know that the ancient synagogue became a significant presence during the Second Temple period (c. 515 BCE-70 CE), the six centuries following the Babylonian exile, an era when the dispersion of Jews from their homeland proceeded apace. Consequently, the centrality and authority of the Jerusalem Temple began to recede for many in the growing "diaspora." The synagogue first emerged, in all likelihood, as a compromise solution for Diaspora Jews cut off from their traditional religious center—the new institution would not supplant the distant Holy Temple, but would provide a surrogate locus of religious service closer to home—hence, the creation of a *mikdash me'at* (lit. "mini-Temple"), the synagogue. From the start, therefore, the synagogue mediated one of the basic tensions of Jewish history—between Israel and Diaspora, *tzion* and *galut*.

The synagogue attained a new importance following the destruction of the Temple in the 1st century CE—again, as a means to mediate the tensions of Jewish life. As is well documented, 1st century Judean society was divided by Jewish sectarianism—Pharisees, Sadducees, Essenes, Zealots, and other lesser-known sects made up the Judaism of the time. But such social and religious schism was to be repaired at least in part by the advent of a new institutional resolution, the synagogue. As far as we know, the Pharisaic movement had utilized the incipient synagogue as its forum of public education, i.e., as a *bet midrash*, or 'house of study.' Based on archaeological evidence from the Zealot stronghold at Masada, we may surmise that during the Great Revolt against Rome (66–73 CE), Jewish insurrectionists resorted to the local synagogue as a place to gather the troops, a headquarters to meet and plot strategy, a *bet k'nesset*, or 'house of assembly'—it is quite possible that this was its original function, as evolved by ordinary Jews (hence, the word "synagogue" derives from the Greek for 'gathering place'). In the period following the destruction, the synagogue was again redefined by the emergent Rabbinic leadership as a *bet t'filah*, or 'house of prayer,' to provide a surrogate for the lost Temple rite. As it developed into the central institution of Jewish communal life, all three functions (study, assembly, prayer) were combined under one roof, and the synagogue came to embody the mediating quality of Rabbinic Judaism. "Which is greater," the Rabbis asked, "study or action?" In the multi-functional synagogue, such a choice (and its implied hierarchy of values) was moot, rendered unnecessary by the resolving effect of a mediating institution.

What has all this to do with the contemporary synagogue and its movement for transformation? Very simply, my hypothesis is that "mediation" (in the sense I have begun to elaborate) is **the** defining characteristic of the synagogue. As the discussion above suggests, the idea of mediation derives from the pragmatic perspectives of history and sociology. When tensions arise in Jewish life—as in the fractious early periods of Jewish history—the syna-gogue becomes the principal means of resolution, and this is no less true today than it was in the past. In fact, as I will argue below, the notion is especially applicable to the American experience, in which communal disunity and religious fragmentation have been pervasive and perhaps even defining features. The entire career of the American synagogue, therefore, represents an ongoing dialec-tic of tension and resolution. By tracing the mediating role of the American synagogue throughout its three-century-long history, we will come to better comprehend what has made it central to the American Jewish experience in the past, as well as the potential it has to ensure an American Jewish future. Further investigation of both historical/sociological and religious/theological modes of mediation will yield valuable insight into the process of synagogue transformation. We begin with the former.

I. The Synagogue as Mediating Institution in American Jewish History

Perhaps the most commonly cited characteristic of the American synagogue is its centrality; again and again, American Jewish his-torians note the central position of the institution within the life of the community. General statements to this effect are common-place, e.g., as historian Abraham Karp concludes: "Although the synagogue is experiencing some decline in membership and influ-ence, it continues to be the preeminent institution in American Jewish life and bids well to retain its centrality in the foreseeable future."[4] Likewise: "The core institution of the Jewish community is the synagogue. Though it . . . has changed throughout its devel-opment, it remains the focal point for communal Jewish life in the modern world."[5] And more recent still: "The Synagogue is the most prevalent and arguably the most important institution in American Jewish life."[6] Writing in the late 1950s, Moshe Davis similarly stressed the synagogue's key role in American Jewish his-tory: "The evolution of the Synagogue as the basic institution in Jewish group life is central to the history of the Jewish community in America. From the earliest settlements in Colonial days, when there were a handful of congregations all of one pattern, until our own day, when congregations are numbered in the thousands with diversified patterns of belief and practice, the Synagogue has been the cornerstone of the Jewish communal structure."[7] A generation later, Jonathan Sarna reiterated Davis's observation and noted that "in the interim, no major historian has seriously disputed this claim, yet at the same time none has adequately developed it, much less subjected it to close scrutiny."[8]

The contemporary movement to transform the quality of American Jewish life is premised on the notion that the synagogue is the central address of Jewish communal life, the one institution most American Jews tend to visit in their pursuit of Jewish meaning and identification. A recent accounting of synagogues in the United States notes that "one measure of its significance is that more Jews belong to a synagogue than to any other Jewish organization."[9] Isa Aron, a leading theorist of synagogue transformation, makes the point as well, describing the synagogue as "the Jewish organization they are most likely to join, and the one they are most likely to participate in regularly," and supports her contention with these basic statistics: "At any given time, forty percent of American Jews belong to a congregation; it is estimated that eighty percent have been members of a congregation at some point in their lives." But Aron goes further still, asserting as an "undeniable truth: *if there is one place that will preserve the Jewishness of the American Jew, that place is the synagogue.*"[10] The synagogue is the key to Jewish renewal precisely because it is central to the Jewish community and to the life of the American Jew. Indeed, this was Moshe Davis' purpose as well—to assert the pivotal interrelationship between changes in the life of the synagogue and changes in the life of the American Jew. But again, this common observation begs the question of why—what is it that accounts for the centrality of the American synagogue?

To start, the fact of synagogue centrality should not be taken as self-evident. As Joseph Blau reminds us: "In the perspective of history, this focus on the synagogue is a relatively recent and perhaps unfortunate innovation. The basic unit of Jewish organization throughout most of Diaspora history was not the synagogue but the community."[11] Though it certainly played an important role in the life of the pre-modern Jew, the synagogue was not the principal agency through which the individual connected to the greater sphere of Jewish communal life—only in the American experience has it become the norm to "affiliate" oneself with the Jewish community through membership in a synagogue "congregation." Yet even in America, this has been called into question. Toward the end of the immigrant era of 1880–1920, a healthy debate ensued in the American Jewish community as to what institution might best ensure the survival of Jewish life. According to educator Alexander Dushkin, three separate Jewish communal institutions were then in competition "to become the [primary] unit of organized Jewish life": the synagogue, the settlement, and the school.[12] Though Dushkin advocated the school as the "Jewish center," Mordecai Kaplan and others would bet on the synagogue instead— explaining that as a religious institution, only it could safely provide a setting for the "social autonomy which Jews should cultivate" in America. As Kaplan further opined, "that there shall not be the slightest reason to suspect [Jewish group life] of un-Americanism, it should center about the Synagogue. America rightly resents all social autonomy that is not lifted to the plane of religion."[13] The truth of Kaplan's observation is borne out by the subsequent triumph of the institution.

We have here a first explanation for the centrality of the synagogue—its role as an "ethnic church," a religious institution whose principal purpose is group survival. According to this view, the synagogue achieved its status due to a latent rather than manifest function, fulfilling a primarily social rather than religious need. Sociologists have repeated this observation many times over and I will offer my own take on it below. Others offer their own explanations of the synagogue's centrality, as when Jacob Neusner calls it "the most important religious institution of American Judaism," and attributes this to its high rate of affiliation, the depth and longevity of commitment, the symbolic leadership of the pulpit rabbi, and its being **the** setting for the practical expression of Judaism. Neusner furthermore asserts that the synagogue "is central to the life of the [entire] Jewish community," as it simultaneously serves as a general social center providing access to large numbers of Jews.[14] Along similar lines, Samuel Heilman attributes the primacy of the Orthodox synagogue—over and above other mandatory institutions of traditional Jewish life such as the yeshiva, kosher butcher, and *mikva*—to the fact that "none but the shul can count on the simultaneous involvement—albeit at very different levels of participation—of men, women, and children."[15] Such explanations add to our understanding of the appeal of the synagogue, but still do not get to the root cause of its preeminence. What, after all, is the source of its unquestioned centrality?

My answer, of course, is in the nature of the synagogue as a mediating institution; and it is in the history of the American synagogue where we find the most compelling evidence of its mediating qualities. In every phase of its development, the synagogue has played the role of mediating institution, repeatedly resorted to by Jews in the attempt to resolve the social and religious tensions they experience in the American context. To trace the historical development of the American synagogue, a useful model is the seven-stage model first offered by Abraham Karp in his 1987 article, "Overview: The Synagogue in America—A Historical Typology" (included in the collection, *The American Synagogue: A Sanctuary Transformed*, edited by Jack Wertheimer).[16] Karp charted the course of American synagogue history through seven successive stages, from the Colonial-era "synagogue community" to the contemporary service-oriented congregation, as follows:

1. Synagogue Community
2. Rite Congregations
3. The Reform Temple
4. The Orthodox *Shul*
5. The Synagogue-Center: In Its Urban Setting
6. The Synagogue-Center: In Suburbia
7. The Contemporary Synagogue: In Service of the Individual

As we shall see, each stage in this scheme may be understood as a form of mediation—and in each case, the mediating quality that first appeared in a particular historical era still holds important implications for the contemporary synagogue.

1. Synagogue Community

In 2004, American Jewry commemorated its 350th anniversary. The first group of Jewish settlers landed in New Amsterdam in 1654, and within a few decades had founded the first synagogue in North America.[17] But neither this original congregation, nor the several congregations founded in other colonies, followed traditional patterns of synagogue organization. For the first half of American Jewish history (from the late 17th to the early 19th centuries), synagogues were the only formal organizations of the community, having no institutional competition. Moreover, until the first congregational schisms of the 1820s, there was only one synagogue per community. As the solitary communal institution, therefore, the synagogue exercised a monopolistic sway over early American Jews and was understandably expected to provide for all the needs of Jewish life. The American synagogue thus became an all-encompassing Jewish institution and came to substitute for the pre-modern Jewish communal structure, or *Kehillah*. Since the colonial American synagogue literally *was* the formal community, this early iteration of the synagogue has been dubbed by historians the "synagogue community."[18] The concept was something of a novelty—never before in Jewish history had the synagogue been construed as an all-purpose, all-in-one institution.

So what accounts for the phenomenon? Karp's explanation, following the pioneering path of Jacob Rader Marcus, attributes the synagogue community to the model of the colonial church, e.g.: "What permitted the local synagogue to exert "monopolistic control" was the place and power of the church in colonial America. . . . The Jews, seeking acceptance, laboring at integration, took instruction and example from their Protestant neighbors, choosing the synagogue as the institution that would establish their community."[19] Early American Jews' reconstitution of Jewish community in the form of a synagogue is thus seen as the direct consequence of their environment. Colonial America was characterized by religious pluralism, the logical outcome of a heterogeneous society made up of diverse religious communities. For Jews to fit comfortably into this new social scheme, they quite naturally (and unconsciously) came to define their group identity in religious terms, and their synagogue became another "church" in the social order. As Karp put it, "the synagogue was becoming part of the religious landscape, its adherents clothed with an identity coherent and acceptable to the host community."[20] From the very beginning, therefore, the synagogue was the mediating institution between the individual Jew and the American environment.

Of course, the need to mediate between the general culture and Jewish particularism is not unique to the American experience. The same tension characterizes the modern history of European Jewry. In the eighteenth century, Enlightenment thinkers began to recommend that Jews adopt European culture as a prerequisite to their civil emancipation. This seemed a rather lofty goal at the time insofar as most Jews were still immersed in an insular culture of their own, living inside the organic Jewish communities of the European ghetto and shtetl. The first Jewish philosopher to suggest such social integration and cultural duality was Moses Mendelssohn, who recommended both the acquisition of modern culture—the thrust of the general Enlightenment—and simultaneously, the retention of Jewish culture. This dual message engendered and came to define a specifically Jewish movement of

enlightenment, the *Haskalah*. The *Haskalah* was a primarily intellectual response to the challenge of cultural dualism, ultimately
giving rise to a panoply of ideological movements of modern Jewish culture, religion and politics.

In America, the response was less ideological and more practical—its principal arena was the local synagogue. As in Europe, the
inherent tension between individual Jewish experience and the
larger environment would come to characterize a new "American-
Jewish" culture. The inherent tension between Jewish identity and
American acculturation is the central tension of the American Jewish experience.[21] When the colonial Jew felt the urge to remain
actively Jewish, while early America urged that he become American, then the synagogue alone of all available options provided the
resolution—the American Jew would preserve his Jewishness and
Americanize at the same time by building and attending synagogues. Both the building forms and the attendance patterns
would follow the American model of the Protestant church, while
preserving particularly Jewish practices in only the least obtrusive
and dissonant ways. According to most historians of American
Judaism, the most telling effect of the new environment was the
incorporation of a dignified orderliness, or "decorum," in the otherwise traditional religious service.[22] But this was only one of many
such changes. In sum, while retaining a modicum of traditional
Jewishness, the synagogue simultaneously absorbed American
symbols and values. A clear illustration of this is the Revolutionary
War-era practice of calling the synagogue lay leader "president"
and the set of synagogue regulations a "constitution."[23] The same
might be demonstrated by the church-like synagogue architecture
of the time, or the synagogue's propensity to celebrate and com-
memorate American political events, or the later custom of flank-
ing the sanctuary stage with both an American and an Israeli
flag—and numerous other examples might be cited, ranging from
seating patterns to musical styles to forms of governance. The synagogue thus became a seamless combination of Jewish and American elements, and remains so to this day.

Still mediating between the Jewish and American cultures, the
synagogue continues to serve a vital need of American Jews. That
need, as suggested by the principal American Jewish enlightenment thinker, Mordecai Kaplan, is to live fully in two civilizations at
once. The ideal is not so easy to achieve, however, as the experience

of "Jewish civilization" is difficult to create in the midst of a dominant American culture and society. As anthropologist Clifford
Geertz has taught us, we tend to operate within just one cultural
"web" at any given time; to add another is only possible to the extent
that its values and symbols are adapted to "fit" the majority culture.
But for a minority of American Jews, such a full-bodied sense of
Jewish culture is indeed familiar, those Jews who grew up in inten-
sively Jewish neighborhoods, those who have spent significant time
in Israel, those who attended Jewish day schools and/or summer
camps, all have an inkling of the possibility of Jewish civilization in
America. Applying this notion to the synagogue, we should highlight the critical goal of providing intensive Jewish experience. The
contemporary synagogue, among its other objectives, ought to be
giving its congregants a much greater sense of religious depth and
cultural breadth, that is, a taste of Jewish civilization.

The synagogue's accommodation to America, on the other
hand, is more of a given. While the cultural climate has certainly
changed over the past two centuries, and Jews are no longer the
insecure minority they were even a generation ago, they nevertheless continue to resonate to the American civilization of which they
are a part. In the current moment of cultural transformation, this
basic fact might be easily overlooked. The fashion of late has been
to lament the deleterious effects of American materialism, individualism, and religious iconoclasm upon synagogue life, while
eagerly looking for ways to reassert Jewish traditionalism and
"authenticity." Yet, while applauding the trend toward greater Jewish engagement, we ought not forget that it is the very ability of the
synagogue to combine American and Jewish religious styles that
accounts for its success, and there is no reason to believe this basic
fact will change anytime soon. The observation that "assimilation
is a blessing"[24] is counter-intuitive for many Jews. This view of Jewish survival is not easily grasped by those for whom conserving tradition means constant battle against the general culture. But
history teaches otherwise. Transformation of the synagogue must
necessarily acknowledge and then build on (rather than deny) this
first tenet: *the synagogue is central to the lives of American Jews insofar as it serves as a mediating institution between Judaism and Americanism*—together, the two co-existent religious value systems of the
American Jew.

2. Rite Congregations

Karp's second phase describes the typical synagogue of the first half of the 19th century, usually founded by Ashkenazic Jewish immigrants in contradistinction to the established Sephardic synagogues of the earlier period. Beginning in the 1820s, and accelerating through mid-century, the early American Jewish community first began to fragment. The formerly monolithic "synagogue community," in Jonathan Sarna's felicitous phrase, now began to break up into "a community of synagogues." Long before the American synagogue was differentiated by denominational affiliation, it divided along ethnic lines: German, Polish, Russian, Lithuanian, Rumanian, Hungarian, English, Dutch, etc. The principle of organization was now congregational rather than communal; and the mark of difference became liturgical custom, i.e., *minhag*, or "rite." Though history would brand them "German," the new wave of immigrants had brought a diversity of cultures and languages into the American Jewish community, and not surprisingly, the potential communal chaos was controlled—i.e., mediated—by the synagogue; that is, by the formation of multiple synagogues representing the disparate groups. Cultural and religious differences between them were both preserved and leveled out by the congregational solution. Hence the synagogue serves as a mediating institution between different kinds of Jews.

The pattern repeated itself with the next major immigration wave (from 1880–1920, principally of Jews from Eastern Europe), when the diversity of the much larger Jewish immigrant population expressed itself in a myriad of small synagogues. At the turn of the century, Jews from every individual *shtetl* (small town) of the old country tended to establish a *shtibl* (small synagogue) in its name—creating the synagogue type historians call the "*landsmanshaft shul*."[25] Though a one-generation phenomenon, it nevertheless had served a vital function—to allow the immigrant Jew to preserve for a time his former culture while undergoing the processes of Americanization, in particular, ethnicization—the transition from an entirely foreign orientation to a new hyphenated identity as an ethnic American. Again, synagogues played a pivotal role in this transformation, evolving, together with their constituents, from small *landsmanshaftn* to larger and more homogeneous American-style congregations. Once again, the synagogue provided the necessary mediation for a stratified, multi-cultural Jewish community.

Today, the synagogue continues to serve in this capacity. As Marshall Sklare demonstrated in his classic *Jewish Identity on the Suburban Frontier*, the suburban synagogue of the post-WWII period tended to differentiate according to religious, cultural, social, and economic factors distinguishing the sub-groups of the community—and the contemporary synagogue continues to play this role. Yet the American Jewish community of the 21st century is more diverse than ever, now including significant sub-communities from Israel, Russia, and the Near East; also being extremely diversified along religious/denominational lines; as well as comprising a population highly mobile within the United States. This potential 'tower of Babel' is yet again mediated by the synagogue. No matter their background, when Jews decide to join the American Jewish community they look to the synagogue, whose many varieties presents them an amicable way to express their sense of difference—and to be part of the collective at the same time. Hence, in Los Angeles for example, we see Israelis joining Reform temples and Persian Jews leading Conservative congregations (originally Ashkenazic)—all part of the process of Americanization. The synagogue has been, therefore, the unifying, mediating institution in a diverse and potentially fractious community.

In the contemporary transformation of the synagogue, the inherent diversity of American Jewish life is an advantage to be exploited. Our second tenet might be: *the synagogue is central to the lives of American Jews insofar as it serves as a mediating institution between separate elements of the Jewish community*. This evokes a pluralistic picture divided along religious, ethnic, class, generational, sexual orientation, (dis)ability, and ideological lines—which then suggests two possible futures for the American synagogue: one, in which mega-synagogues are comprised of sub-units catering to the diverse religious styles and social profiles of the congregation; and two, in which the community is comprised of diverse congregational choices. The first concept was pioneered in the 1970s by Rabbi Harold Schulweis (of Cong. Valley Beth Shalom in Encino, CA) and his congregational model of "synagogue *havurot*."[26] The individual *havurot* socialized and studied together, held family celebrations together, supported each other in times of distress, but otherwise joined the main congregation for communal religious services and other public affairs. More recently, a number of congregations around the country (mostly urban—e.g., Ansche Chesed in NY and Temple Beth Am in LA) have gone a step further, offering separate *minyanim*, essentially sub-congregations, for Sabbath and holiday services. While not a perfect system, the trend successfully mediates the tension between competing subgroups within a large congregation, and can be and should be emulated in creative ways.

The second case is far more common. Typical of both urban and suburban Jewish communities (and therefore applying to a wider demographic spread) is the scenario in which individual synagogues come to represent a particular segment of the community. As described above, this has its roots in the rite congregations and *landsmanshaft shuls* of the past. Both ethnic and religious diversity continue to be expressed through the synagogue; whereas the contemporary period has seen the rise of synagogues for special constituencies: New Age *havurot*, Gay synagogues, congregations for the Deaf, etc.—and who knows what else is to come? This process of differentiation is natural and normal, but does not by itself constitute mediation. Conflict is certainly diminished through differentiation, but how can tension be resolved further without continued contact and interaction? That is to say, once divided by interest and ideology, what remains to bond separate congregations into a community? It is here that the contemporary movement must take its stand. The change process fails if it concerns only the individual synagogue—we must instead treat the synagogue as part of an organic system, as integrally related to other congregations, to other Jewish organizations and frameworks, indeed to the community as a whole. How do we know this? From the history here reviewed of communal fragmentation (tension), synagogue formation (resolution), ongoing religious and social differentiation (renewed tension), and again, the current trend of synagogue transformation.

3. *The Reform Temple*

The third type of American synagogue is, according to Karp, the "Reform temple." The term is a bit misleading when referring to the American synagogue of the mid-19th century that was a pre-denominational institution undergoing a process of self-reforming. The "Reform temple" *per se* was only the end result of a historical process of religious Americanization. Between 1840 and 1880, the American synagogue found itself at the center of a sharp debate within the community as it addressed the question: what form of Judaism is appropriate to the new American context; and how might Jewish tradition be adjusted to suit the modern world? The debate took many forms, engendering heated discussions over synagogue honors, language, liturgy, music, seating arrangements, the place of women, and other questions of Jewish law. The common denominator was the ideological tension between tradition and modernity. A community that in 1840 was largely traditional in its religious orientation would become, by 1880, largely modern, i.e., "Reform." The Americanization of the synagogue[27] was the process by which this shift occurred. But that is not the end of the story. By the end of the century, two alternative forms of American Judaism had arisen to challenge Reform: "Conservative" and "Orthodox." Though each may trace its origins to historical factors other than religious observance *per se*, the balance of traditional and modern religious styles was nonetheless at the heart of the matter. And in each case, the process of denominational differentiation first occurred at the local level of the synagogue—only later would national organizations give formal definition to the denominations of American Judaism.

Synagogues thus mediate between Jewish tradition and Jewish modernity. Where competing interpretations of the tradition appear, the common result is the founding of a new congregation, split off from the old. If, on the other hand, neither competing faction within a synagogue chooses to leave, they must work out some form of compromise acceptable to the congregational community. In either case, the synagogue offers mediation of religious conflict. So too, with more recent innovations in American Judaism—Reconstructionist, Humanistic, Renewal, etc.—whose adherents consistently create new synagogues as expressions of their iconoclastic ideologies. Often, these latter-day synagogues begin as informal and intimate *havurot*, a form conducive to intensive discussion and deliberation regarding choice of religious style. Of course, the process is essentially democratic, in which the idiosyncrasies of individual preference are coalesced and subdivided into affinity groups—once again mediating between individual and group needs—so as to create a range of options. Yet it must be noted here that the course of Jewish denominationalism has not been nearly so fragmentary as that of American religion on the whole—a discrepancy accounted for, perhaps, by the principle of *klal yisrael* (Jewish unity). Nevertheless, religious differences persist, and it is the synagogue that mediates such varied religious preferences, especially between traditional and modern alternatives—synagogue transformation will have to take this basic function into account as well.

The third tenet, therefore, is: *the synagogue is central to the lives of American Jews insofar as it serves as a mediating institution between traditionalist and modernist tendencies in Judaism.* We will have much more to say on this subject in the final section of this paper, but suffice it to say here that whether the synagogue is Reform, Conservative, Orthodox, Reconstructionist, or "Other," it is subject both to the demands of traditional Judaism and to the dictates of modern thought, science, and culture. The balance may vary from denominational stream to stream, but the tension is always there. A celebrated recent example is the uproar that occurred after a prominent Conservative rabbi in Los Angeles suggested to his congregation that biblical archaeologists of late have called into question the historicity of key episodes of the Bible—in particular, the Exodus. The more traditional members of the congregation—especially those of Middle Eastern extraction—objected vehemently to what they perceived as blasphemy. The story was reported as a scandal at worst, a cautionary tale at best. But the same story could be spun far more positively. The disparate points of view are with us already—the modern perspective of the rabbi resonates with current university teaching and academic research; while the traditional cosmology is well represented in *yeshivot* and *haredi* communities from Los Angeles to Jerusalem. But note that it was only in the mediating space of the synagogue that the worldviews came into conflict, and ultimately arrived at peaceful dialogue. This was due largely to the diplomatic skill of the rabbi, but must also be seen as an opportunity provided by a uniquely situated public Jewish institution. The transformation movement ought to be encouraged, once again, to exploit the mediating quality of the synagogue—in this case to make it a place of active intellectual discourse and religious inquiry.

4. *The Orthodox* Shul

As described above, Orthodox synagogues appeared *en masse* during the immigrant wave of 1880–1920. The phenomenon may be related to a number of the mediated conflicts discussed earlier, but another communal tension now became paramount. As East European immigrants arrived, they created their own synagogue organizations, most often without the benefit of rabbinic leadership. Thus the *landsmanshaft shul*, like the earlier synagogue-community and rite congregation (as well as the later *havurah*), was most often a synagogue without a rabbi. Since Orthodoxy is premised on the authority of Jewish law, the traditional jurist, the rabbi, might well have been thought to be indispensable. But historical circumstances forestalled the availability of certified rabbis, and so the Orthodox *"shul"* began its American career as a folk institution bereft of elite leadership. When rabbis did enter the scene, they often encountered entrenched lay interests and experienced another characteristic tension of American Judaism—that between folk and elite, laity and rabbinate, membership and leadership.

It is a tension running throughout the history of the synagogue. From ancient times until today, synagogues are most often founded, built, and controlled by the laity. The rabbinate has a stake in the institution, of course, yet its more common and more natural operating base is the *yeshiva* (as well as the *bet din* and other institutions of rabbinic authority). Thus the synagogue has always been a site of nexus, and sometimes contention, between rabbinic and lay interests. As we've suggested, the tension continues and is heightened in the American experience. It reaches a crescendo of sorts during the immigrant period when both rabbinic authority and lay anti-clericalism reached new heights. For not only were "properly" Orthodox rabbis and cantors being imported from Europe during that time, it was also the formative era of American rabbinic seminaries. Hebrew Union College, America's oldest Jewish seminary, graduated its first class in 1883; the Jewish Theological Seminary was founded three years later and then reconstituted in 1902 under Solomon Schechter; and Yeshiva University has its origins in the 1897 establishment of the Rabbi Isaac Elchanan Theological Seminary. But little attention was paid in these institutions of higher learning to the thorny question of rabbinic-lay relations. That would have to be worked out in the field—in the mediating institution called a synagogue.

Today, the folk-elite tension persists, though the question of halachic authority has yielded to issues of leadership roles and functions. As has been the case throughout American Jewish history, the synagogue is a lay-sponsored and lay-led institution. Typically, the congregation hires a rabbi and other synagogues functionaries as contracted employees. Though the more charismatic figures manage to accrue some real authority, the power relationship between laity and rabbi is usually weighted in favor of the former. And yet, at the same time, the rabbi is expected to provide spiritual and symbolic leadership, and is looked up to by most congregants as an authoritative representative of the Jewish tradition—the very same congregants who balk at the notion of religious obeisance. Contained within the rabbi-lay relationship, therefore, is the modern conflict between religious authority and the autonomy of the individual. The tension is most often mediated, of course, within the sphere of the synagogue, but the issue is today more often couched in terms of leadership. What are the duties of the rabbi? What is the extent of his/her responsibility to the congregation? Where does their influence lie? How can they best motivate their congregants to be better Jews? And moreover, what is the most effective leadership structure for the contemporary synagogue? How can congregants lead as well? As the synagogue of today is further transformed into the ideal institution of tomorrow, such questions of rabbinic-lay relationships will be central.

Tenet number four: *the synagogue is central to the lives of American Jews insofar as it serves as a mediating institution between the rabbi and the laity,* that is, between elite and folk representations of Judaism. The culture of the synagogue is informed both by the religious professionals—rabbis, cantors, and educators; as well as by the lay leadership and membership. Mediation suggests treating each with equal seriousness, though such equanimity is not always in evidence. There are congregational settings today where the rabbi and professional staff are entirely relied upon for all decision making and implementation; at the other end of the spectrum there are *havurah*-style communities that eschew professional leadership altogether. Yet most synagogues occupy the broad center of the spectrum, and engage their professionals and laity in some sort of relationship, however dysfunctional it may become. What does this mean for synagogue transformation? Simply, it means that both the change "process" as well as the congregational "product" will require application of some form of collaboration. This entails a redefinition of leadership, moving away from the hierarchal models of the past to a collaborative process that both preserves the authority of the leadership and empowers the membership at the same time. A tall order, perhaps, but once again such mediation is suggested by historical experience. The synagogue has been and continues to be the primary nexus of the elite and folk of American Judaism; and thus, as always, the synagogue will continue to be the locus for mediation—between the often-competing concerns of the Jewish leadership and *"amcha."*

5. The Synagogue-Center: In Its Urban Setting

Admittedly, it is somewhat difficult for me to summarize the next phase in the history of the American synagogue, as it forms the subject of my book, *Shul with a Pool: The "Synagogue-Center" in American Jewish History* (UPNE, 1999). Briefly, then: the synagogue-center was the innovative combination of a synagogue and a [Jewish community] center, the latter an institutional type original to the American Jewish community. It represented an expansion of the traditional functions of the synagogue—religious worship, study, and assembly—into the modern realms of secular Jewish culture, social recreation, and ethnic community. An early version of the synagogue-center first appeared in the Reform movement toward the end of the 19th century, and then emerged more fully articulated in Orthodox and Conservative circles in the years following the First World War. A second-generation phenomenon, it was primarily intended to help revive, or 'reconstruct,' the more intensive religiosity and communality of the imagined past.

As explored more fully in *Shul with a Pool*, the synagogue-center movement emerged from a number of secular institutional sources, three in particular. In addition to the Reform temple, the synagogue-center concept also developed within the Young Men's/Women's Hebrew Association movement. The YM/WHA was an especially popular institution among the children of the immigrants (i.e., the "second generation") for its social and recreational offerings, but the "Y" also served as a setting for religious experimentation and youth congregations. A similar process occurred in the philanthropic movement of Jewish "settlement houses," which began as outposts of social welfare and developed into "department stores" of Jewish life, combining recreational, vocational, religious and educational programming under one roof. The movement's flagship institution was the famous Educational Alliance on the Lower East Side of New York. And third, the synagogue-center idea did not emerge from a modernizing Orthodox synagogue alone, but also from the contemporaneous movement to modernize Jewish education. Modern Jewish educators, under the influence of Samson Benderly, began to experiment with a new form of Jewish school, a "Jewish school center" that would include a full range of social and religious programs in addition to educational. From all of the above, one might already suspect what tension the synagogue-center was intended to resolve—the tension between social Jewishness and religious Judaism, the modern schism between secularizing Jews and spiritualizing Judaism. Where else but the synagogue might this key conflict find resolution?

Indeed, it is a conflict still central to the American Jewish experience. If only forty percent of identified American Jews belong to a synagogue, and thus see themselves as Jews in religious terms, then what do we make of the other sixty percent? Certainly, many of those within the ranks of synagogue members think of themselves as "cultural" (read: secular, or non-religious) rather than as religious Jews, and perhaps there are significant numbers of un-synagogued Jews who see themselves in religious terms. But the statistical divide is still telling, for the cultural schism between religious and secular Jews is with us nonetheless. The split is reflected as well in the Jewish communal structure, which similarly divides between religious and secular organizations and thus we have an ongoing *kulturkampf* in American Jewish life. Though the religious orientation is presently ascendant, the social-religious dialectic goes on, as demonstrated for example by Cohen and Eisen's recent study of American Jewish identity, *The Jew Within*.[28] As I argued in *Shul with a Pool*, both orientations should be seen as valid insofar as Judaism is inherently dual, a pre-modern integration of religion and peoplehood, still asserting itself as such in the modern age. Hence the mediating quality of the synagogue in this case is not simply an echo of the "ethnic church" concept, in which religious means serve social ends. Instead, the American synagogue mediates between two authentic expressions of modern Judaism, the religious and the secular. Secular Jewish concerns an intrinsic part of the religious synagogue? Though it may seem paradoxical, the movement to transform the synagogue must take cognizance of this notion if it is to be effective at all.

The synagogue is central to the lives of American Jews insofar as it serves as a mediating institution between the social/secular and religious aspects of Jewish life. What are the implications for synagogue transformation? Should secular Jews be wooed to the synagogue with secular programming? Is that not illogical and contrary to the religious mission of the synagogue? Or should contemporary synagogues recreate the synagogue-center experiment and simply increase their emphasis on social and educational programming in general? Understandably, this move tends to threaten the more explicitly defined social and educational institutions of the Jewish community. So what then? As in the preceding discussion of tradition vs. modernity, I believe the answer lies in being truthful—with ourselves and with each other. Let us acknowledge and honor the fact that many of our congregants are more culturally than religiously inclined; let us use language that will allow those alienated from the thick religiosity of synagogue life to be comfortable in a synagogue setting; and let us treat with sacredness those "secular" aspects of Jewish life such as politics (esp. progressivism/liberalism), philanthropy/social welfare, communal defense, Zionism, Holocaust commemoration, and modern Jewish culture in all its forms. At the same time, we need to find ways to counter the compartmentalization in the first place. That will require an understanding that the split between religious and social/secular readings of Judaism is a modern phenomenon, and the will to begin moving into a post-modern mode of integration. I hardly need add that the one institution of Jewish life suited to this historic task is the mediating synagogue.

6. The Synagogue-Center: In Suburbia

In the decades following World War II, third generation Jews transferred the synagogue-center concept to suburbia. As did their forebears, they founded synagogues in order to preserve Jewish life in the new milieu. A new set of motivations, however, refined the original center concept into something distinctive in its own right. Having moved away from their parents' urban neighborhoods, Jewish suburbanites unwittingly altered the relationship between their aging parents and themselves. Family visits would become less frequent, often taking place on holidays or other special occasions. When visiting the old neighborhood, the adult children might take pleasure in revisiting the familiar ambience of their parents' homes, at the annual Seder dinner for instance. But when the parents visited their children in their suburban retreats, they could not experience the same sense of familiarity, for nothing in the new environment resonated with their own experience and thereby reassured them that their children had not abandoned them completely. Enter the synagogue. Thus an additional motivation (beyond the conventional reasons) for the prodigious construction of suburban synagogues was the attempt to recreate some aspect of the old way of life, the fondly remembered Jewish milieu of "the city"—both gratifying the older generation and relieving the guilt of their suburbanized children.

Directly related to this attempt to placate their elders was the need to acculturate their own children into Jewish life. In the vacuous environment of suburbia, such Jewish acculturation would only take place with effort. Once again, the synagogue-center suggested itself as the best solution to this challenge, and the suburban synagogue was reconceived as a child-centered institution. But the results of this paradigm shift were not always fortuitous. All too often, synagogue sanctuaries went empty except when filled with bar/bat-mitzvah celebrants, synagogue schools became "bar-mitzvah factories," and synagogue social halls became the setting for lavish parties bordering on the gauche. Ironically, much of this activity was directed not just at the children but also at the grandparents, again attempting to assure them that Judaism had not died in suburbia. The suburban synagogue thus became a mediating institution between the generations, bringing together parents and children in a tenuously imperfect relationship.

Schulweis' "synagogue *havurah*" experiment of the 1970s may also be seen in this light, as the synagogue type that exemplified the mediating institution concept once again, by absorbing the counter-cultural *havurah* (to be discussed below) into the bosom of the established synagogue culture, and thus resolved differences between the older and younger generations. In like fashion, the contemporary movement of synagogue transformation must continue to address its constituents across generational lines, in the ongoing attempt to create intergenerational harmony, and hence, Jewish continuity. Perhaps the best contemporary illustration of this is the recent trend toward "family education" in which synagogue schooling unites rather then divides parents and their children. The American synagogue will continue to learn from the mistakes of the past as it continues to mediate between generations of Jews, adopting *"m'dor l'dor"* as its motto. #6: *The synagogue is central to the lives of American Jews insofar as it serves as a mediating institution between old and young.* This may sound self-evident, but ask: how much of our current synagogue transformation efforts make this a priority? How often are programs intentionally multi-generational? When was the last time you witnessed a synagogue service led by or a synagogue decision made by a grandparent and grandchild working together in unison? Geographic considerations aside, family togetherness and cross-generational activity ought to be considered an imperative in the contemporary synagogue.

7. The Contemporary Synagogue

In Abraham Karp's 1987 description, the contemporary synagogue was "in service of the individual"—in direct response to the over-sized, impersonal synagogue bureaucracies of the previous generation. Certainly, a new individualism came to be represented in the post-60s synagogue through the *havurah* movement and its "do-it-yourself" brand of Judaism. Synagogues became more intimate and participatory, and such responsiveness to individual needs continues today in the current emphasis on spirituality and community. But, to paraphrase John F. Kennedy, the real question is not what can the synagogue do for the individual, but rather, what can the individual do for the synagogue? The real contribution of the *havurah* and its ongoing legacy is an emphasis on increased participation of congregants in both the religious life and governance of the synagogue. As discussed above in the context of rabbinic-lay relations, the membership is a sleeping giant. They were put to sleep by decades of overemphasis on the rabbi's sermon, the cantor's performance, and the board's governance. In this outmoded model, the typical member of a congregation was expected to do no more than pay dues and show up at lengthy intervals. A new paradigm, suggested by Rabbi Sidney Schwarz among others, would have synagogues emulate the *havurah* by expecting far more of their members.[29] Judaism, like democracy, is a participatory enterprise, yet far too often, American individualism is expressed as an antipathy to group involvement. We have begun to enjoy "bowling alone" more than joining an organized league or group outing. The tension as it relates to the synagogue is not between being an outsider to the community and a participant insider; but rather between feeling "alone" within the synagogue and having a full sense of belonging and engagement. The challenge today is to engage every member of the synagogue—translating the full participation principle of the *havurah* to the contemporary congregation.

With the added perspective of the past fifteen years, we see another related tension being played out in the American synagogue: now the tension is between insiders and outsiders to the Jewish community. As more Jews assimilate out of the core community, and as more non-Jews find their way into Judaism through intermarriage and conversion, the boundaries between insider and outsider are contested as never before. While this has particular implications for the Reform movement, with its conscious policy of "outreach," the phenomenon is far more pervasive, in even the most varied religious settings (with the probable exception of Orthodoxy). In Conservative, Reconstructionist, Renewal, Humanistic, and Post-Denominational congregations alike (and we might add to this list some heavily Jewish Ethical Culture, Unitarian, and Buddhist houses of worship as well), more and more people are testing the boundaries of Jewish identity and synagogue participation. The underlying tension here derives from the open question of Jewish identity in modern society. Tradition ascribed Jewish identity to maternal lineage and/or proper conversion, but modernity has opened to the way to freer interpretation and individual choice in the matter. As the principal voluntary association of the community, the synagogue is most often the arbiter of this nettlesome problem. Thus questions of membership and participation for "non-Jews" are often hotly debated topics in contemporary congregations. The movement of synagogue change will have to come to terms with the "who is a Jew" question as well.

The final tenet therefore is: The synagogue is central to the lives of American Jews insofar as it serves as a mediating institution between insiders and outsiders, both within the individual congregation and within the changing Jewish community. The implication for transformation is the need for a much greater sensitivity and attention to questions of membership. Today, "who is a Jew?" often becomes "who's in or out in the synagogue?" While different denominations and different synagogues will certainly reach their own positions, the current movement can help by recognizing the problem and providing guidance for individual congregations in their process of deliberation. Like so much else in synagogue life, this issue is often experienced in isolation, without knowledge of other synagogues' decision-making processes and their results. A conscious movement of synagogue change can provide the means to conduct the discussion in a more rational, efficient, educational, and spiritual way.

Thus, we've offered several explanations for the phenomenon of synagogue centrality. Deriving our principles from the historical stages of American synagogue development, we found no less than seven forms of mediation characteristic of the synagogue as an institution:

1. between Jews and America
2. between Jews and other Jews

3. between tradition and modernity
4. between folk and elite
5. between social Jewishness and religious Judaism
6. between older and younger generations
7. between Jewish insiders and outsiders

Though culled from the historical record, each of these tensions is still observable and very much alive in the synagogue of today. Contemporary synagogues still allow for synthesis between Americanism and Judaism, and between Judaism and Jewishness; and contemporary synagogues still provide the setting for resolving conflicts between their varied constituents, native and foreign-born, old and young, born Jew and Jew by choice. For all these reasons and more, the synagogue can be said to be **the** mediating institution of Jewish life. Synagogue change processes will only succeed by strategizing with these principles in mind. "Transformation" should not be thought of as alchemy, as radical change—improving synagogue life only works when the original nature of the institution is acknowledged, preserved, observed, processed, and ultimately, progressed. In the future life of the American synagogue, that will mean honoring its past as a traditional Jewish religious institution led by a rabbi and made up of committed Jews. In the modern context of America, however, that older model will have to be negotiated by and merged within a dynamic new one—the synagogue as mediating institution, after all.

II. From Real to Ideal: Mediating Religious Value in the Synagogue

As suggested in the introduction, the notion of a "mediating institution" may be interpreted in theological terms as well. In this regard, let us think of the synagogue as the institutional embodiment of Judaism—its principal functions of prayer, study, and assembly correlating to the central theological values of God, Torah, and Israel. Not surprisingly, these are the very same values marking the theological dividing lines of American Judaism. To illustrate the point, we might well ask the following multi-part question: Ought Judaism in America be concerned primarily with ethical monotheism ("God"), as in the classical Reform conception?; ought it preoccupy itself with the study and observance of *halacha* ("Torah"), as in most varieties of Orthodoxy?; or ought it rest upon a foundation of Jewish peoplehood ("Israel") and folk culture, as in earlier forms of American Zionism, Conservatism, and Reconstructionism? Of course, many other theological disputes and divisions might be cited here; but the very fact that we can pose such a question indicates the general contentiousness of the competing Jewish belief systems of American Judaism.

Whereas Judaism in America is rife with tension, the American synagogue as always seeks resolution. When applied to the synagogue, the same line of questioning as above has a much clearer answer. If we ask, for instance, how best to characterize the synagogue—as a house of God, house of Torah, or house of Israel; then obviously, the answer is all three. A synagogue cannot isolate one element of the God/Torah/Israel triad, for the covenantal theology of Judaism construes the core elements of God, Torah, and Israel in symbiotic interrelation. Similarly, subcategories such as ethics, monotheism, study, observance, peoplehood, and culture are all essential components of the integrated system called Judaism. In this regard, we might conceive of the Covenant itself as the original mediating institution.

We now see from whence the mediating function of the synagogue derives; it is ultimately a manifestation of traditional religious values. It is worth noting, however, that the explicit observation of such a covenantal interrelationship in the synagogue is quite recent. As I have observed in another context: "Nowhere in rabbinic literature do we find a statement advocating the idea of the synagogue as an all-purpose institution; nowhere are all three terms [*bet t'filah, bet midrash, bet k'nesset*] found in unison. Yet in the contemporary era, they appear together with regularity."[30] It will surprise some to learn that the notion is, in fact, an American innovation. For the past century, the American synagogue has most often defined itself as a "house of prayer, house of study, and house of assembly," terms derived from the classical Hebrew names for the institution, though never before joined together as a prescriptive formula. The innovation takes place in the context of the American Jewish experience for a reason. American Judaism has been as conflicted in the theological sense as in the sociological, and similarly seeks resolution through its principal mediating institution, the synagogue. But the story doesn't end there.

Though the three synagogue functions are usually cited in unison, as if each were equally valent, the truth is that there is a hierarchy among them. The central one is unequivocally **prayer**, or *religious worship*. For nearly two thousand years, the prayer service has been the *sine qua non* of synagogue life. In America, prayer has attained an even greater position of priority, inasmuch as the synagogue resonates to the dominant culture. Inevitably, American Jews have come to perceive the synagogue as an analogue to the worship-based church, a religious sanctuary above all else. Secondary in importance is the function of **study**, or *religious education*. Though the traditional synagogue incorporated adult study (for males only) as a daily feature, the contemporary synagogue has, by and large, relegated study to children. Even where a more developed program of adult education exists, the educational function of the synagogue is still clearly subsidiary to its worship service. Judging by its schedule of services and activities, the contemporary synagogue also incorporates the function of **assembly**, or *religious community*, though this seems to reside at the bottom of its list of priorities. Stated priorities, however, do not necessarily conform to members' needs and expectations. As we know, many congregants join synagogues for purposes of communal identification and group sociability. As a manifest function of the synagogue program, social experience *per se* is devalued, but in a latent sense, it may be the key function after all. This suggests, at the very least, that the conventional ordering of synagogue priorities—prayer on top, study a distant second and assembly an afterthought—ought to be open to reassessment.

Such a reassessment would also include a reexamination of the broader objectives of each function. Currently, each of the three synagogue functions may be said to point toward the core Jewish values of God, Torah, and Israel. In this conventional scheme, Jews come to know "God" through prayer, understand "Torah" through study, and experience "Israel" (Jewish peoplehood) through assembly. Schematically, the synagogue functions something like this:

PRAYER	$\rightarrow$	GOD
STUDY	$\rightarrow$	TORAH
ASSEMBLY	$\rightarrow$	ISRAEL

Certainly, the ideal synagogue enables the fulfillment of these very aspirations. However, this conventional scheme is no longer adequate to the realities of American Jewish life. For one thing, we are somewhat limited by the terms themselves. The majority of American Jews today do not relate to the traditional conception of God as an immediately accessible presence in their lives. Similarly, that same majority is estranged from "Torah"; having little substantive knowledge of the Biblical text (the "Written Torah"), nor much familiarity with the Rabbinic deliberations of ritual and ethical law that follow from it (the "Oral Torah"). And lastly, the concept of Israel is becoming less and less meaningful to a generation of American Jews for whom Jewish peoplehood is a quaint notion more relevant to their immigrant grandparents and ethnic parents. So, it would seem, the familiar terms of Judaism require redefinition and reformulation in light of the realities of contemporary American Jewish culture.

The ideal synagogue will speak in the language of its time and appeal to the most vital needs of its constituency. Hence, the familiar scheme of classical Jewish values—God, Torah, and Israel—might well be reconceptualized as:

GOD	→	JEWISH SPIRITUALITY
TORAH	→	JEWISH LITERACY
ISRAEL	→	JEWISH CONTINUITY

The central Jewish value of "God"—creator of the universe, heavenly king of Israel, whom we are enjoined to love with all our heart, soul, and might—is today more often expressed in terms of individual religious experience, especially in the sense of seeking spirituality and attaining transcendence. *Spirituality*, a term made popular by the current "new age" religious culture, may be understood as a quality of experience distinct from, or a level of consciousness higher than, the mundane and material world of everyday life. A more traditional Jewish concept similar in meaning is *k'dusha*, holiness. Spirituality, like holiness, connotes a separate, higher reality, an apartness from the ordinary. *Transcendence* is perhaps even more relevant to the mission of the synagogue, insofar as it opposes the egoism and individualism characteristic of modern society and refers specifically to the negation of the self. The transcending path leads the individual away from a solitary focus on him/herself, and toward others: the group, the world at large, or, more "spiritually" speaking, the ultimate "other," God.

Besides updating our language, these redefinitions may also liberate us from a strictly linear relationship of value to function. In the old formulation of synagogue life, the God-value was actualized by the function of prayer alone—only in the worship service do we expect to encounter God. But once we expand the parameters of how and where one seeks or discovers "God" we begin to see that spirituality is also found in the study of the text, and that transcendence may be achieved in the act of communal assembly. God-as-spirituality is in Torah, and God-as-transcendence is in Israel, and all three are integrated in the ideal synagogue.

Similarly, a redefinition of "Torah" leads us to a new conception of synagogue education. It is a commonplace of Jewish studies to note that the term Torah has multiple meanings; it refers, alternately, to the Pentateuch (the five books of Moses), the entire Hebrew Bible, all of Jewish learning, and so on. In the context of the modern synagogue, however, it takes on still other connotations. Most Jews today are not only bereft of book learning in the classical Jewish sense of "Talmud Torah," they also lack the experience of Torah in the broader sense of culture. Beyond the actual text, Torah may also refer to the complex set of behaviors, experiences, values, and ideas that make up the Jewish culture based on the text. This expanded notion of Torah includes its study; it includes forms of Jewish practice that emerge from its study; and it includes the entire history of Jewish life based upon such religious study and practice. Jewish literacy entails familiarity with this cultural legacy, it entails broad and deep knowledge—a knowledge set that has so far eluded the majority of American Jews. Within the life of the synagogue, such literacy applies not only to Torah **study** *per se*, but also to a serious engagement with the Jewish liturgy **(prayer)** and with Jewish history and current affairs **(assembly)**. The attainment of such a complex culture cannot possibly be achieved on an elementary level alone. Education in the synagogue must not be restricted to the young, but ought to be a life-long pursuit, carried out at the highest level of intellectual sophistication. It must be seen as an essential and pivotal function of synagogue life. Only then will the synagogue become a "house of Torah" in the same sense that is a "house of God."

The ideal of "Israel" may be reevaluated as well. If the God-value is to be redefined as the seeking of *Jewish spirituality*, and the Torah-value as the goal of *Jewish literacy*, then the Israel-value can be nothing other than the desire for *Jewish continuity*, the third major objective of the ideal synagogue. Ensuring Jewish survival is premised upon the fostering of a strong sense of Jewish identification, in adults as well as in children. As discussed above, this is the most basic need of the Jewish community in America, and thus has always been the latent function of the synagogue—building a strong Jewish community for the sake of group survival. It follows that Jewish continuity can be abetted by the synagogue in three ways: first, communal prayer confers a sense of community; second, group study is a venerated Jewish tradition for good reason—it bonds Jews together, i.e., Torah study as social glue; and third, the very experience of joining and participating in the social life of a congregation is itself community and identity-building. It is this third function that requires the most affirmative action at the present moment. In this scenario, the kiddush following Sabbath prayers would become as important as any element at the heart of the service; family retreats as essential to the synagogue program as Bar/Bat Mitzvah celebrations; and the brotherhood/sisterhood (or other adult social/educational programs) as vital as the synagogue school. Once and for all, let us acknowledge that Jewish identity is shaped by positive and intensive social experience. We need no more survey research studies to tell us that Jewish youth groups, summer camps, and Israel trips are bulwarks against assimilation—it is self-evident. Less evident is the role such social activity ought to play in the synagogue.

In fact, too much social inwardness is to be avoided. The best antidote is another "assembly"related, Jewish value and synagogue function: the pursuit of social justice, or "social action." Such value-laden terms as *tikun olam* ("fixing" the world), *gemilut hasadim* (righteous acts), *tzedek* (justice), and *tzedakah* (obligatory charity) are commonplace in the vocabulary of today's synagogue. Historically, however, these socio-political attitudes and activities were less a function of the synagogue than of the Jewish community on the whole. In America, the philanthropic function of traditional Jewish life was largely taken over by secular agencies such as federations and fraternal orders. Yet, as the synagogue became the central institution of American Jewish life, more political content was added to its program. The synagogue-centers of the second generation were particularly oriented to Zionism. The *havurot* of the sixties were hotbeds of anti-war activism. The Reform movement has been especially attuned to the social justice aspect of synagogue life, sponsoring, for example, soup kitchens and homeless shelters. Today, more and more congregations are responding to the political commitments of their baby-boom members by adding various social action projects to their programs. One popular innovation is the so-called "mitzvah day," when every member of the congregation is called upon to donate their time to some worthy cause. We must point out, however, that such congregational projects serve not only to improve the outside community but also to build our own community. In the end, this is the other critical value reflected by social action/*tikun olam* activity—bringing Jewish community to life. It does not detract from the inherent "right"-ness of synagogue social action to note its additional contribution to the goal of Jewish continuity.

In the ideal synagogue, therefore, the classical functions of prayer, study, and assembly are all exploited fully and equitably to reach the contemporary objectives of spirituality, literacy, and continuity. In the ideal synagogue, each of the functions—all equal in importance—would relate to all three of the value/objectives. Schematically, such an organic and interrelated synagogue program would look something like the following:

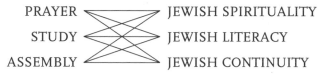

PRAYER   JEWISH SPIRITUALITY

STUDY   JEWISH LITERACY

ASSEMBLY   JEWISH CONTINUITY

Hence we've come full circle, back to the synagogue as mediating institution. The above diagram encapsulates the notion of an organic system in which the separate elements of an institutional program are fully integrated, and integration suggests mediation—the ideal synagogue would thus mediate between function and value, and between the different sets of function and value. If the synagogue is indeed an embodiment of the Jewish religion, just as it is a microcosm of Jewish life on the whole, then its mediating qualities may be understood as a response to tensions in American Judaism. Those tensions have only been hinted at here, and could certainly be explicated at greater length.[31] But the notion that the synagogue is the place where such tension can be worked out is by now familiar to us. If some synagogue participants (members as well as leaders) are intoxicated by "God," while others are more fascinated by "Torah," and still others are most energized by "Israel," then all may come together in the multi-theological setting of the synagogue. Having come to satisfy one interest or another, the individual may find his/her way to another realm of Jewish thought via the mediation of the synagogue. The synagogue furthermore serves as the setting for mediation between the religious worldviews of rabbi and laity, as in the Los Angeles example cited above. And finally, synagogue life provides the best opportunity for conflicting religious values and competing theological emphases to enter into dialogue and seek resolution. One might argue that only rabbinic thinkers and theologians are equipped for such a heady intellectual project; and yet, as implied by our discussion of synagogue **function** and theological **value**, abstract ideals are meaningless in Judaism without their practical correlates, and conversely, active religious behavior falls flat without being rooted in religious value and belief. Significantly, the realm of everyday religious experience has of late engaged the attention of both theologians and intellectual historians of Judaism.[32] And at the same time, more laypeople than ever are engaged in the search for meaning. But so far, these planes of inquiry are mostly disengaged from each other—where else but the synagogue might they be brought together?

In conclusion, therefore, let us reiterate one of the principal themes of the foregoing discussion. Synagogues don't work as well as we would like when they are characterized by imbalance and dysfunctional relationship(s)—between conflicting viewpoints, constituencies, levels of hierarchy, religious values, functional priorities, etc. All the various forms of mediation described herein have entailed some dialectical response to these inherent tensions. In each case, I have argued that the synagogue provides the means of resolution, that it is therefore the quintessential mediating institution of Jewish life. I have not as yet noted one of the key theoretical underpinnings of this approach. Social science of the recent past has been shaped largely by a thrust toward uncovering the hidden imbalances of power in modern society. This is especially true of contemporary feminist theory. The notion, for example, that synagogues are too often top-down institutions and ought to be more participatory is, in essence, a feminist critique. Similarly, the emphasis on communication and deliberation as the essential **process**es of synagogue change rather than an emphasis on programmatic **product** can be related to this underlying orientation. The foregoing paper is for the most part an historical and theoretical study of the synagogue as mediating institution, but we ought not conclude without some reference to the "feminist" basis of the current movement and methodologies.[33]

That the synagogue fulfills a mediating function is attributable both to its long development through Jewish history, and to its more recent manifestations in the American setting. As the most culturally integrated and socially successful Jewish community in history, American Jews and Judaism are beset by ever-mounting challenges to their survival. This is the great paradox of the American Jewish experience. For the past three centuries, the synagogue has been the principal means of meeting those challenges and resolving that paradox. As we now face the latest chapter in the saga of synagogue change and development, we cannot ignore this basic observation: only the synagogue can provide the necessary mediations to address the quandaries of modern Jewry. Only the synagogue, which has been and continues to be central to American Jewish life, can be the mediating institution of American Judaism; it is our Covenant!

Endnotes

1. From "Congregations for the New Millennium," by Larry McNeil, West Coast Director, Industrial Areas Foundation. http://www.nwje-suits.org /compan/cmpsu7/cmpsu706.htm

2. Ibid. For further discussion, see J. Philip Wogaman's chapter "The Church as Mediating Institution" in Michael Novak's *Democracy and Mediating Structures*; and similarly, Peter L. Berger & Richard John Neuhaus, *To Empower People: The Role of Mediating Structures in Public Policy*.

3. See: Lee Levine, *The Ancient Synagogue: The First Thousand Years* (Yale University Press, 2000) for a full survey of scholarly theories regarding the origins of the synagogue. Levine's own hypothesis is that the synagogue originated in the Hellenistic institution of the city-gate.

4. Abraham Karp, "Overview: The Synagogue in America A Historical Typology," 1-34 in *The American Synagogue: A Sanctuary Transformed*, ed. Jack Wertheimer (NY: Cambridge University Press, 1987).

5. Kerry Olitzky, Preface to *The American Synagogue: A Historical Dictionary and Sourcebook* (Westport, CT: Greewood Press, 1996), ix. In the same volume, Frances Weinman Schwartz adds: "The synagogue is the core institution in the Jewish community the heart of Jewish religion and the Jewish people."

6. Jim Schwartz, Jeffrey Scheckner, and Laurence Kotler-Berkowitz, "Census of U.S. Synagogues, 2001," *American Jewish Year Book* (2002), 112.

7. Moshe Davis, "The Synagogue in American Judaism," in *Two Generations in Perspective*, ed. Harry Schneiderman (NY: Monde Publishers, 1957), 210.

8. Jonathan Sarna, Introduction to *American Synagogue History: A Bibliography and State-of-the-Field Survey* (NY: Markus Wiener Publishing, 1988), 1.

9. Schwartz, Scheckner, and Kotler-Berkowitz, *op. cit.*

10. Isa Aron, *The Self-Renewing Congregation: Organizational Strategies for Revitalizing Congregational Life* (Woodstock, VT: Jewish Lights Publishing, 2002), 1 [emphasis mine].

11. Joseph Blau, *Judaism in America:From Curiosity to Third Faith* (Chicago: The University of Chicago Press, 1976), 91.

12. Alexander Dushkin, *Jewish Education in New York City* (NY: Bureau of Jewish Education, 1918), 366; as quoted in David Kaufman, *Shul with a Pool: The "Synagogue-Center" in American Jewish History* (Hanover, NH: University Press of New England, 1999), 127.

13. Mordecai M. Kaplan, "The Future of Judaism," *Menorah Journal* (June 1916); quoted in Kaufman, *Shul with a Pool*, 235. A similar observation was later expressed in greater detail by Will Herberg in his *Protestant, Catholic, Jew* (1955).

14. Jacob Neusner, *Understanding American Judaism: Toward the Description of a Modern Religion* (NY: Ktav Publishing House, 1975), 67.

15. Samuel Heilman, *Synagogue Life*, 5.

16. Abraham Karp, "Overview: The Synagogue in America A Historical Typology," *op cit.*

17. K"K Shearith Israel, also known as the Spanish and Portugese Synagogue. High holiday services were likely conducted soon after the refugees' arrival in the fall of 1654; though a formal synagogue was not established until sometime after 1664, when the British occupied the city (and renamed it New York).

18. The term was first coined by Jacob Rader Marcus, dean of American Jewish historians.

19. Karp, *op.cit.*, 3.

20. *Ibid.*

21. The relevant literature is voluminous, but see esp.: Charles Liebman, *The Ambivalent American Jew: Politics, Religion, and Family in American Jewish Life* (Philadelphia: Jewish Publication Society, 1973).

22. E.g.: Riv-Ellen Prell, *Prayer & Community: The Havurah in American Judaism* (Detroit: Wayne State University Press, 1989).

23. Jonathan Sarna, "The Impact of the American Revolution on American Jews," 20–30 in *The American Jewish Experience*, ed. Sarna (NY: Holmes & Meier, 1986).

24. Paraphrasing the classic article by Gerson Cohen, "The Blessing of Assimilation in Jewish History," reprinted in *Jewish History and Jewish Destiny* (NY: The Jewish Theological Seminary of America, 1997).

25. E.g.: Kaufman, *Shul with a Pool*, 166–74.

26. Bernard Reisman, *The Chavurah: A Contemporary Jewish Experience* (NY: Union of American Hebrew Congregations, 1977).

27. Leon Jick, *The Americanization of the Synagogue, 1820–1870* (Hanover, NH: University Press of New England, 1976).

28. Steven Cohen and Arnold Eisen, *The Jew Within: Self, Family, and Community in America* (Bloomington: Indiana University Press, 2000).
29. Sidney Schwarz, *Finding a Spiritual Home: How a New Generation of Jews Can Transform the American Synagogue* (San Francisco: Jossey-Bass, 2000).
30. Kaufman, *Shul with a Pool*, 6.
31. The best study of the current religious divisiveness of American Judaism is: Jack Wertheimer, *A People Divided: Judaism in Contemporary America* (NY: BasicBooks, 1993).
32. E.g.: Arnold Eisen, *Rethinking Modern Judaism: Ritual, Commandment, Community* (Chicago: The University of Chicago Press, 1998).
33. See, for example, our earlier *Report to STAR* (2000) in which two related issues were raised: 1) the benefits of the deliberative, process-oriented approach to synagogue change, as exemplified by Isa Aron's work in the ECE (Experiment in Congregational Education), and delineated in her recent book, *The Self-Renewing Congregation: Organizational Strategies for Revitalizing Congregational Life* (Woodstock, VT: Jewish Lights Publishing, 2002); and 2) the positive trend toward engaging outside consultants, most often someone trained as educator, social worker, or organizational consultant-the majority of whom are women.

A WORLD WITHIN A WORLD:
THE HISTORY OF THE MODERN SYNAGOGUE

David B. Starr

H istorians generally, and wisely, avoid blurring the lines between themselves and prophets, recognizing that dispassionate analysis of the past in context differs from passionate advocacy for the future. Yet a conference on the contemporary synagogue invites one to employ both scholarly methods and the search for the normative. I would like to try my hand at a bit of both, through the medium of historical study.

In that spirit I heartily endorse David Kaufman's call for historical study as a necessary element in a contemporary curriculum for Jewish knowledge and wisdom. History adds to, rather than detracts from, our search for that elusive elixir many term "meaning." It creates such significance by asserting in its own idiom that most ancient of Jewish notions, namely, that humans exist in God's shadow, created in His "image." By studying their thoughts and deeds, understanding how they sought to build their world, we take their human agency, and human dignity, seriously. So the study of one of the supreme Jewish institutions, the synagogue, bears within it the legacy of countless generations of Jews, for whom institution building represented a categorical imperative.

Dr. Kaufman's paper on the modern synagogue pointed to aspects of its structure, function, and underlying premises. He highlighted three tensions: cultural conflicts between American and Jewish modalities; the rabbinic/lay polarity; and the ambiguities of the synagogue as "ethnic church," i.e. the relationship of ethnicity and religion in Jewish life. I concur that these were and remain significant issues in synagogues, while at the same time they have and will always reflect deeper patterns of culture and community. My paper therefore probes Kaufman's categories while also trying to cast a different light on them by looking through the prism of the thought of one figure, Solomon Schechter. He occupied himself much more with matters of the spirit, the content and purposes of the synagogue, than of its phenomenology in actual terms. It reminds us that synagogues and synagogue makers always possess visions, as well as strategies and tactics, even if they pass unstated.

Any claims regarding the modern synagogue demand some attention to the pre-modern institution preceding it. A quick survey of Kaufman's concerns suggests that continuities as well as discontinuities existed connecting medieval Jewry with its successor.

The centrality of medieval typologies connecting and separating Jews and their chief neighbors, Muslims and Christians, suggests the importance of boundaries and content linking Jewish culture and external culture. Medieval Spain, at least in its so-called Golden Age, represented a certain kind of at least mythical ideal type of bi-culturalism, whereas medieval Ashkenaz, dominated by a more aggressive and less tolerant Christendom, produced a more blinkered Northern European Jewry, so the classical historiography posited.[1] I would only add that the entire subject of cultural boundaries involves a large assumption that we should be aware of; namely, that there is some essential Judaism that independently exists, that depending on historical circumstances may or may not come in contact with, and be affected by, external forces.

Kaufman understands the modern unfolding of this problem as stemming from the Enlightenment and its Jewish enthusiasts such as Moses Mendelssohn. The implications of the *Haskalah* remained contested in the minds of many. The common bromide called for Jews to live in two civilizations, such as Y.L. Gordon's famous dictum "to be a Jew in your tent and a man abroad." Many supposed that to mean possessing the capacity to live in two worlds, equally well. But in fact many *maskilim* thought more ambitiously; they wanted to create a kind of Jewish humanism that united the two in some glorious synthesis, so that universals enriched one's Jewishness, and one's Jewishness fructified the world, in seamless fashion.[2]

Of course, from our vantage point the evidence suggests the failure of such a vision. Antisemitism precluded full Jewish integration, often demanded Jewish self-annihilation, and Jewish cultural shallowness distorted the variables in the equation, preventing them from possessing equal value. Kaufman correctly notes that the decline of the Jewish family and of the Jewish neighborhood placed an intolerable burden on the synagogue, one that it could not possibly shoulder successfully.

And yet there is something profoundly ahistorical, or at least politically charged, lurking in this sort of declension thesis. Two important Zionist thinkers, Ahad Ha'am in the dawning of cultural Zionism, and much later the Zionist historian Jacob Katz, each in his own way contributed to this sense of modernity as spelling Jewish decline, and the synagogue as one of the primary exemplars of that alarming trend. Ahad Ha'am posited that the Diaspora lacked the means to withstand the homogenizing cultural power of the nation-state, hence the need for a spiritual center that would create and sustain organic Jewish culture. No accident then that the synagogue plays such a minimal role in Israel today, for secular and religious Jews alike. As a historian, Katz understood modernity in its intellectual dimension as the displacement of Jewish "values" via the adoption of Enlightenment and Emancipation.[3]

Yet these perspectives slight a more historically nuanced understanding of Jewish civilization building. Scholars such as Gerson Cohen and Ismar Schorsch, not coincidentally aligned with JTSA and Conservative Judaism, wrote seminal pieces that argued for Jewish agency and Jewish power as reflected in a whole variety of community building and culturally sustaining enterprises. Synagogues historically should be seen as such efforts at what Solomon Schechter called "Catholic Israel:" the dynamic whereby Jews throughout history created tradition, not merely passively received some sort of Platonic, essentialized set of books and practices.[4]

The implications of such a historical scheme resonate for contemporary views. Why consider Jewish history as a problem, a continual falling away from some imagined past utopian age. Why not see it progressively, if not Whiggishly, as the continual struggle of Jews to build culture and society. Why not see synagogue building in this light, paraphrasing Abba Eban's famous jibe at the Arabs for their inability to take yes for an answer. Just as we dwell excessively on modern Jewish lackings, so we omit the ample historical evidence of Jews falling short of Jewish norms like *mezuzah*, as the responsa of Rabbenu Tam record of twelfth-century Ashkenaz.[5]

No doubt one should avoid historical relativity that flattens out the landscape completely. The organic nature of semi-autonomous corporate Jewish communities that obtained in Ashkenaz broadly defined, and the medieval world in general, exist no more. That sea change affects synagogues, in content and purpose, to be sure. Yet it may also be that we recognize that we exist in the line of Jeremiah and the jeremiad. We feel most alive when we're on life support, clawing our way back to health.

Kaufman's final theme, that of the synagogue as housing and often failing to integrate the ethnic and religious dimensions of Jewish identity, surely stands as the most distinctively modern of the three themes. Much of at least European and American Jewish history of the last two hundred years comes down to the process whereby Jewish identity took the form of either of those categories as dominant, if not exclusive, markers of Jewishness. That often took on discrete geographical form, so that Eastern European Jewry, *ethnies* in a primordially ethno-cultural landscape, created distinctive ethnic ideological formulations like Jewish Socialism and Zionism; whereas emancipated western Jewries scrambled to re-present themselves as deracinated Jews of various religious denominational stripes. The synagogue, as a place where Jews came to talk either with God, or with each other, incorporated roughly both elements, indeed arguably remained the one place where that happened in an otherwise increasingly fragmented Jewish society.

Kaufman's second tension addresses the splitting of ethnicity and religion as desiderata of Jewish identity. This largely hits the mark—western religion expresses itself as "church" rather than as peoplehood, and that division seems to us as Jews as contrived in the context of Jewish history's yoking of the two.

While such a structuralist analysis works to a point, it also obscures the fluidity of historical change. The nation-state that spawned the modern denominations in Germany, certainly challenged Jews to make such explicit trade-offs—citizenship in return for integration as a religious "society" as German as any other such religious grouping. Yet such a quid pro quo means different things in a liberal state such as the United States. The nation-state viewed itself as serving the needs of a historical nation, however imagined, and made no room for separate nations to remain as such. The liberal state served the individuals, which theoretically allowed much greater space for all sorts of groups to experiment with their own group identities.

While cultural pluralism has not always been the norm on these shores, it has yielded the equation that Jewish + American may be as valid as Jewish or American. Synagogues embody this ever-shifting sense of what precisely is the admixture of people-hood and religion. If anything, one could argue that that most distinctive of American Jewish religious denominations, Conservatism, suffers from its emphasis on cultural and ethnic identity at the expense of a more coherent and explicit religious persuasion like that of Reform and Orthodoxy.

From the perspective of intellectual history Jewish life meant conversation, and arguably the perennial conversation consisted of debates about culture. What it was, who decided what it was, what education should be, and the like; all of those things affected synagogues, in terms of governance and content.[6] Zionism challenged this conversation, arguing for citizenship as the primary element in Jewish identity, not culture. The synagogue embodies this tension, since it embodies peoplehood, not just a church, yet it is not the same thing as a Jewish *civitas*, existing in the netherworld of a public yet voluntaristic social space. Tocqueville marveled at the American propensity for institution building, and ethnic communities built synagogues not just to further the process of integration but also to retain some degree of separation. Even today's synagogue lays claim to such a mixed legacy of purposes.

Finally we come to the historical tussles between rabbis and laity for power in the synagogue. This too will ring true to any student of medieval Jewry. Lay and rabbinic forces vied for power, in the realms of formal law as well as the elaboration of Jewish practice. Much recent work on early modern Jewry both in Poland and in France suggests the ways in which lay/rabbinic tensions existed, expressed in elite attempts to usurp rabbinic legal functions as well as in the realm of moral authority. The rise of new modes of spirituality and liturgical expressions such as the Lurianic Kabbalists of the 16th century, not to mention the better-known case of 18th century Hasidism came with ongoing tensions between these sorts of social groupings. [7]

Kaufman points out that this dynamic existed as a hardy perennial in Jewish life and he understands correctly that modernity involved changing currents of power allocation between the rabbi and the laity. But one could argue that the rabbis have not lost their authority, but rather the tradition, or the notion of tradition, has. That is the primary cultural move with which the entire modern western world struggles. If anything, in certain ways rabbis accrued more power. As the tradition declined people looked to rabbis to fill the void. Sometimes this took the form of symbolic exemplars, whose portraits took on the religious equivalence of a Honus Wagner baseball card.[8] The average rabbi today probably receives exponentially more questions from congregants about correct Jewish practice than Maimonides ever did, precisely because Jews lack knowledge of the tradition and remain unresolved about what authority it possesses for them. Solomon Schechter fulminated against the rabbi as priest, filling a sacerdotal function. But that was the point, the vacuum created by the de-centering of the tradition necessitated rabbis to play new, expanded roles in Jewish communal life.

The real problem with rabbis, and by extension synagogues, is that many fail to matter much in important areas of peoples' lives. Modernity values expertise and high standards of professionalization, and this holds true for rabbis too. Unfortunately they play lesser, different roles than do doctors and lawyers. How could it be otherwise in a worldview that fears cancer or bankruptcy more than it does hell? Rabbis lack cultural authority, or at least have less of it, because the definition of culture affords minority status to their sector of life, and so too with synagogues.

And that is the dirty little secret of synagogue life—most of them play in the minor leagues of peoples' lives. People expect little, demand little, pay little, and this demoralizes synagogue professionals and laity alike. Such dynamics appeal to highly motivated but often less talented figures, adding to the perception of the synagogue as second-rate. Rabbis now have more and more power over less and less.

Yet I protest too much. Synagogues of spiritual and intellectual depth are coming back, in part because people need them precisely at those moments when material concerns trigger spiritual reactions and needs. We want the doctor to heal our cancer, when we want treatment for our souls and not just for our bodies we call the rabbi. As long as we view ourselves as non-material creatures as well as physical beings, we will always make room for healers, counselors, teachers, and leaders, be they rabbis or some other form. Heaven and earth, high culture and pop culture, meet in synagogues. People connect with themselves, with one another, with their tradition, and with the transcendent. Historians make lousy prognosticators, but as long as synagogues fulfill these functions, they will matter to their creators and their inheritors, and in that way find their place in the annals of Jewish civilization.

I am suggesting that our concern with the synagogue sometimes reflects a degree of amnesia about its long history, or our freighting it with all of our baggage about the traumas inflicted on Jewry by modernity. That involved principally new concerns precisely because in our time the cultural consensus undergirding institutions like synagogues dissolved. Socio-economic modernization, population disruptions, political emancipation; all of these contributed to the breakdown of corporate Jewish life and the value system that supported it. People disagreed about core philosophical claims revolving around beliefs; who possessed authority, the sovereign self or the community or the tradition however understood, and the very notion of a common destiny and purpose seemed to vanish.

I want now to turn to a somewhat off-centered way of viewing the synagogue. This involves not dispensing with a contextual analysis of the synagogue, but rather broadening the framework of perception to include historical and contemporary considerations of normative aspects of what the synagogue is, and should be. For that the career of Solomon Schechter seems useful for us.

Schechter's world of the late 19th and early 20th century reminds us of how relatively recent the modern synagogue is, at least in this country. He thought and wrote a good deal about the synagogue and the rabbi and their place in Jewish life precisely because they were in transition, with various ideas bandied about concerning their content and scope in Jewish life.

The decline of traditional society gave way to new ideologies to fill the breach, namely Reform and Orthodoxy. Each involved new claims regarding the authority of tradition vis-à-vis the present, and that of the group vis-à-vis the individual. Schechter objected most strenuously to Reform claims that enlightened moderns stood in a uniquely privileged position to critically judge the weight of the Jewish past. He also disparaged Reform rabbinic attempts to constitute themselves as a new authority over the Jewish people and Jewish tradition, which he derided as "sacerdotalism" smacking of Christian ecclesiasticalism. Religion, he wrote, remained about matters of the heart and questioned the ability of any clique of leaders who claimed to represent others in religious affairs. He opined to one inquiring journalist "I hate and detest all priests, whether they breakfast on oysters or *shmurah matzah*."[9]

America and American Reform Judaism only intensified his opposition to such views of modern rabbinism and the modern synagogue. Rather than interpreter of the law, the modern rabbi saw himself as a lawgiver. The Jewish version of checks and balances had broken down in the West, since cultural illiteracy paved the way for rabbinic manipulation of the tradition and the helpless Jewish masses. He scorned synagogues where "loyalty to the Torah was largely replaced by devotion to the pet orator, where rabbis were actually "ordaining disciples" instead of examining pupils, where rabbis made invocation and imparted the priestly blessing with the most approved pontifical manner and mien, and where lastly, rabbis, lacking in all sense of humor and all sense of proportion, were talking of themselves as prophets and seers, only, of course, more advanced and more "evolutionized" than Isaiah and Micah." Such an inorganic culture must be resisted at every turn; to counter such invidious Jewish sectarianism only a needed healthy Jewish body politic could banish such views of rabbis and synagogue.[10]

At the same time he recognized that in its own way Orthodoxy too represented a deviation from tradition, increasingly defining Judaism and the Jewish people via formalistic notions of halakha, and granting new powers to rabbis to opine on all sorts of matters previously reserved for the community and its other mechanisms for governance.[11]

I mention these processes because it is important to recover the sense that basic areas of Jewish life, both implicit and explicit like the question of authority, affected perceptions of what role the synagogue should play. Schechter viewed the synagogue, mythically and juridically, as manifesting larger patterns that he either approved or disapproved of, like whether or not modern rabbis were attempting to arrogate to themselves power that should be reserved for the sovereign tradition and people. Synagogues, according to him, should not possess more or less power than the people/tradition itself possessed; the former existed as the institutional embodiment of the latter.

While still in England at the University of Cambridge, Schechter wrote as a public intellectual and scholar in 1896 an introduction to his published essays, *Studies in Judaism*. There he tried to articulate his view of the essence of Jewish culture. Assuming the centrality and difficulty of revelation and Scripture, he bore in mind a Judaism of text, of interpretation, of community, and of the locus of all three, the synagogue of history and of myth.

Since, then, the interpretation of Scripture or the Secondary Meaning is mainly a product of changing historical influences, it follows that the centre of authority is actually removed from the Bible and placed in some *living body*, which, by reason of its being in touch with the ideal aspirations and the religious needs of the age, is best able to determine the nature of the Secondary Meaning. This living body, however, is not represented by any section of the nation, or any corporate priesthood, or Rabbihood, but by the collective conscience of Catholic Israel as embodied in the Universal Synagogue. The Synagogue "with its long continuous cry after God for more than twenty-three centuries," with its unremittent activity in teaching and developing the word of God, with its uninterrupted succession of Prophets, Psalmists, Scribes, Assideans, Rabbis, Patriarchs, Interpreters, Elucidators, Eminences, and Teachers, with its glorious record of saints, martyrs, sages, philosophers, scholars and mystics; this Synagogue, the only true witness to the past, and forming in all ages the sublimest expression of Israel's religious life, must also retain its authority as the sole true guide for the present and the future.[12]

In this statement cited above, Schechter sought to place the synagogue within yet beyond its history. He recognized its centrality in functional terms as a crucial mediating institution, one that contained the polarities about which David Kaufman wrote: its bicultural nature, its ethnic church combination of *ethnie* and creed, and the lively rub of the rabbi-lay dynamic.

But anyone encountering Schechter in the above cannot help but notice his passion in the romantic quest for the transcendent resolution that sweeps all divisions and conflicts before it. For him, the actual record of the synagogue as physical place, as institution, pails before the real synagogue as the representation and reinforcement of the overarching unity of Jews and Judaism, past, present, and future, what he famously and mysteriously dubbed Catholic Israel. This also became important in his role as rabbinic educator at the newly reorganized Jewish Theological Seminary of America since its host country still possessed relatively few rabbis—giving him and his institution the chance to create a New World rabbinate that would re-create what he called the High Synagogue of traditional Judaism vis a vis his Reform antagonists.

Schechter defined his role in public Jewish life as defender of historical Judaism; the synagogue required definition as a key aspect of that process of definition. Here he contrasted two sorts of synagogues stemming from religion and geography, that of the east and the west, embodying different contexts and culture, radically different notions of the good, the true, the beautiful. He worried that the western synagogue had lost site not just of pietism but also of higher purposes—instead it focused overly on social work, philanthropy and all things practical rather than the religious and the intellectual. This reflected romantic style critiques of the Enlightenment as too mechanical and focused on parts rather than the organic whole. In such a worldview rabbis became managers rather than "saints."

Schechter affirmed the eastern synagogue because he viewed Judaism, however impractically, as constituting its own authority above that of either vox populi or rabbinic fiat. Only in an organic culture could such a cultural system actually function. The eastern synagogue manifested its greatness of mind in its production and nurturing of various types—producing pietists like the Ba'al Shem Tov, enlighteners like Nahman Krochmal, and scholars like the Vilna Gaon. This he termed the "High Synagogue"—the embodiment of Catholic Israel, the body of tradition and practice and belief that ran far deeper than disembodied exercises in theological formulations.

The historical synagogue, so ran Schechter's thinking, through its liturgical creativity, embodied the ever-renewing element of historical Judaism, with its emphasis on interpretation and the production of tradition over the more static view of culture as restricted to a written revealed Scripture.

This text revealed his in-between state of mind, actually trying to transcend contemporary divisions in Jewish life. His vision of Jewish history and Jewish authority wasn't orthodox—he recognized a shift when he invoked the idea of a "Secondary Meaning" emanating from history and the act of cultures interpreting texts in tension with a theology insisting on the primacy of a revealing God and the written text. He knew this placed him outside of his Orthodox contemporaries who insisted upon the divinity of *halakha* and not just its historicity as an aspect of Jewish civilization building.

Schechter's somewhat jaundiced take on the matter of what the modern synagogue should be, probably reflected his romantic unwillingness or inability to think of the synagogue as something to be built or managed. For him it existed in time yet above time, not as the object of strategies and engineering. Too, as a modern post-*maskil*, he recognized the impracticability of what he termed the "low synagogue" i.e. the *shtieblach* of his Hasidic Romanian and Polish youth. He missed their piety and authenticity, but he viewed them as not likely to garner much support among westernized

Jews. On the other hand, he viewed the already impressive record of liberal temple building as almost akin to the worship of the works of one's hands, bald evidence of the modern glorification of materialism.

By the time he arrived in America, the Progressive era proclaimed the virtues of organization and efficiency, and Schechter took it upon himself to tilt at these new values. No amount of engineering of the synagogue along lines of scientific management could take the place of the harder conversations concerning the purposes of the synagogue, its larger significance in Jewish life.

Yet as a rabbi of future rabbis and institution builders and leaders he had to, however reluctantly, validate the American gospel of institution building. The spectre of discontinuity failed to frighten him; he understood that the _shtiebel_ would never make it in America and welcomed the idea of a post-European English not Yiddish speaking American Jewry. But he also insisted, in what would become a pet peeve of his, that synagogues must reflect Jewish values and not just contain Jewish programs. They stood for a culture of Torah, of learning, and of _shalom_—communal harmony.[13]

Schechter recognized, even as he failed to solve, a central problem particular to Jewish life in a democracy. In a culture and a society enshrining individual freedoms and authority, how would a traditionally corporate culture like Judaism fare? As I mentioned regarding his antipathy for Reform synod schemes, he argued that, at one level, Judaism incorporated democratic notions, as in its rejection of papist sorts of ecclesiastical organization. Yet, in the end, authority in Judaism comes from Torah, not the sovereign people per se, which would later differentiate him from a more aggressive advocate of Jews over Judaism like Mordecai Kaplan. Any rabbi, in that sense, had to answer to two masters, the people Israel but above all the Torah of Israel. The notion of the "people," i.e. Catholic Israel, served as a check on the popular sovereignty implied in conventional understandings of synagogues, as places where the rabbis answered to the congregants. Schechter saw beyond the _shul_ audience to a mythic entity to which the rabbi must give heed. In that sense Schechter saw the synagogue as a profoundly authoritarian and conservative entity, organic in its reflection of its larger host culture (Jewish) and inevitably standing in opposition to liberal democratic notions of empowering of the individual in matters both political and cultural. The latter struck him as far too progressive in the literal sense, as future-oriented.

What does God want of us? Congregants and rabbis, then and now, struggle with what they want out of religion and its institutions: should the fashions of the day lead, or would people feel overwhelming anxiety about the lack of direction of liberal religion's validation of the individual's search for meaning cut away from an overarching tradition?

Schechter's Jewish world descended into loss and disintegration; a palpable decline of unity and harmony. He believed they were and would always be a "world within a world." We err if we expect too much of synagogues—they are only as strong as the larger culture of Catholic Israel.

The problem and opportunity of post-modernity stems from our loss of organic culture that is the set of assumptions about history and destiny and purposes. Once that broke down it became hard if not impossible to reconnect people, and institutions took on an intolerable burden, that of standing in for what only cultures can actually provide. That also explains the distinctive burdens of Conservative Judaism and Zionism, the only two movements within modern Jewish life that set the actualization of *Clal Yisrael* at the center of their agendas in a time of such fragmentation.

That seems to me the legacy of Schechter's contribution as a public intellectual, institution builder, and rabbinic educator. I think he would have nodded his head at Dr. Kaufman's analysis, agreeing that the synagogue is both enlivened and burdened by the tensions about which he wrote. But he would have said something to the effect that too much modern energy went into secondary questions: what functions the synagogue and rabbi should perform, how those things should be structured, rather than asking the philosophical question of how we justify Jewish life, what purposes does it serve. In the end, only the understanding and articulation of those claims will move people and breathe life - both into the people and their institutions. In his last commencement address, he cried out for the synagogue as a place teaching the characteristics of Torah and loving-kindness, not as just another organization embodying the merits of being well run.[14] Vision, not program, will rebuild the synagogue, by rebuilding the culture of the Jewish people. The synagogue will lead, but it will also follow, the larger trends within Jewish life.

Endnotes

1. The work of Ivan Marcus reexamines both sides of the coin; see *Rituals of Childhood: Jewish Acculturation in Medieval Europe*. (New Haven: Yale University Press, 1996).

2. Michael Stanislawski, *For Whom Do I Toil?: Judah Leib Gordon and the Crisis of Russian Jewry* (New York: Oxford University Press, 1988).

3. Jacob Katz, *Out of the Ghetto: The Social Background of Jewish Emancipation 1770–1870* (New York: Schocken Books, 1978).

4. Gerson D. Cohen, "The Blessing of Assimilation in Jewish History," *Jewish History and Jewish Destiny* (New York: Jewish Theological Seminary, 1997), pp. 145–156; Ismar Schorsch, "On the History of the Political Judgment of the Jew," *From Text to Context: The Turn to History in Modern Judaism* (Hanover: Brandeis University Press, 1994), pp. 118–132, and *passim*; Solomon Schechter, "Introduction," *Studies in Judaism; First Series* (Philadelphia: Jewish Publication Society, 1896), pp. xi–xxx.

5. R. Meir of Rothenburg cited this statement in his *Responsa* (Cremona, 1558) no. 108, and later by E. E. Urbach in *Ba'alei HaTosafot* (Jerusalem: Mossad Bialik, 1980), 1:82.

6. Moshe Halbertal, *People of the Book: Canon, Meaning, and Authority* (Cambridge: Harvard University Press, 1997).

7. On the struggles between laity and the Ashkenazic rabbinate, Western and Eastern Europe respectively, see Jay Berkovitz, *Rites and Passages: the Beginnings of Modern Jewish Culture in France, 1650–1869.* (Philadelphia: University of Pennsylvania Press, 2004); Edward Fram, *Ideals Face Reality: Jewish Law and Life in Poland 1550–1655.* (Cincinnati: Hebrew Union College Press, 1997).

8. On modern rabbinic iconography see Richard Cohen, *Jewish Icons: Art and Society in Modern Europe* (Berkeley: University of California Press, 1998), pp. 114–153.

9. Solomon Schechter to anonymous editor, December 26, 1898; private collection of Daniel Schechter, Glencoe, Ill.

10. "An American Jewish Synod: The Opinion of Dr. Schechter," *American Hebrew* 76 (1904–1905), p. 697.

11. In rabbinic parlance such expansion of rabbinic authority were termed "das Torah." See Jacob Katz, "*Da'at Torah*—The Unqualified Authority Claimed for Halakhists," *Jewish History* Vol. 11, No. 1 Spring 1997, pp. 41–50; Lawrence Kaplan, "Daas Torah: A Modern Conception of Rabbinic Authority," in Moshe Sokol (ed.), *Rabbinic Authority and Personal Autonomy* (Northvale, N.J.: Jason Aronson, 1992), pp. 1–60.

12. Solomon Schechter, *Studies in Judaism* First Series (Philadelphia: Jewish Publication Society, 1896), xvi–xvii.

13. Solomon Schechter, "Altar-Building in America," in *Seminary Addresses and Other Papers*. (Cincinnati: Ark Publishing, 1915), pp. 81–90.
14. Solomon Schechter, "Lovingkindness and Truth," in *Seminary Addresses and Other Papers*. (Cincinnati: Ark Publishing, 1915), pp. 245–253.

SYNAGOGUE DWELLERS AND SPIRITUAL SEEKERS

Hayim Herring

THE COMMANDING COMMUNITY AND THE SOVEREIGN SELF: INCREASING UNDERSTANDING BETWEEN SYNAGOGUE DWELLERS AND SPIRITUAL SEEKERS

Hayim Herring

Introduction

Several common trends are evident in the denominational world of the synagogue. All of the North American Jewish religious denominations—Conservative, Orthodox, Reconstructionist and Reform—are experiencing significant internal ferment. Issues relating to Jewish practice that have emerged within each movement are testing their respective boundaries. Additionally, several local and national efforts that fall under the rubric of "synagogue transformation" are underway to increase the feeling of satisfaction synagogue members feel about their synagogues. These initiatives are a reaction to recent studies that suggest that, while synagogues are meaningful institutions for a segment of the American Jewish population, the majority of American Jews find synagogues unresponsive to their spiritual needs. Finally, the proliferation of opportunities for Jewish spiritual expression outside of the denominations and the synagogue speak to the inadequacy of synagogue life.

Drawing upon the research of Ammerman (2000) and Caroll and Roof (2002), we hypothesize that the internal dynamics of boundary testing, the existence of external change initiatives and the availability of non-synagogue-based Jewish spiritual options are expressions of a tension between different approaches toward Jewish religious life. We call one approach the "commanding community" of the synagogue and the other the "sovereign self" orientation of many American Jews. The commanding community of the synagogue understands Judaism as providing a coherent narrative of Jewish life that members are expected to adopt, complete with values and behaviors. In contrast, the Jewish sovereign self expects synagogues to adapt to their spiritual quests on their terms. The threat of the commanding community is that it can lead to an inflexible expression of Judaism, while the danger of the sovereign self to synagogue life is that it undercuts the creation of communities of shared Jewish meaning. The challenge that synagogue leaders face is to navigate a path between these two extremes and create a coherent community that still allows for more individualized Jewish expression.

In good rabbinic tradition, we offer this paper as a "third way" between these two poles. We suggest a methodology—a way of thinking, speaking and acting—for bringing the worldviews of the commanding community and the sovereign self into dynamic, mutually enriching interaction. We wish to find a bridging framework that will enable the synagogue to hold on to those who value its efforts in creating a normative, bounded and binding religious community while still making room for the majority of individuals who reject *a priori* the authority of the synagogue. There is an urgent need for these two worldviews to coexist within the synagogue. We will not repeat the litany of serious concerns about the state of Jewish affairs in the United States. However, in trying to imagine the Jewish future in the United States several hundred years from now, we ask ourselves Hamlet's question: "To be, or not to be?"

All institutions—those that exist and those waiting to be born—will have to work collaboratively if we are to answer this question in the affirmative. As synagogues have a unique opportunity to reach Jews as no other institutions do, it is critical that they become more vital. Fostering both worldviews within the synagogue will contribute greatly to their vitality.

What is unique about synagogues? First, more synagogues exist than any other Jewish institution. They are the grassroots organization of the Jewish community and have endured for over two thousand years. Second, while synagogues are not the only institution that address the most basic human needs over the entire lifespan, they are the only institutions that can deeply touch people during the most critical times in someone's life—a birth, a wedding or wedding anniversary, a death, a bat or bar mitzvah, a "graduation" from the synagogue pre-school, a personal or family crisis. Through the interactions that people have during these profound moments, synagogues create relationships that can become the foundation for individual and communal Jewish growth. In building the Jewish identity of individuals, synagogues strengthen the fabric of the Jewish community.

Recent research on Jewish identity (Cohen and Eisen, 1998; Horowitz, 2000; Mayer, Kosmin and Keysar, 2001) confirms that many Jews are spiritually hungry but that synagogues are not able to feed their spiritual cravings. We stress this point because Jewish spiritual seekers are sometimes dismissed by synagogue leadership as "not serious" or blamed as being a part of "the problem." (By the way, have you ever been eager to join an entity that defines you as a problem?) We view the effort to make room for seekers in our synagogues to be authentically Jewish. We challenge those that negate the spiritual quests of individuals who may not fit a certain Jewish paradigm to rethink their position. Our genesis as a people begins with the seeker par excellence—Abraham—who takes both a physical and spiritual journey in pursuit of a new way of perceiving the world. Moses continues that tradition of great seekers when he pleads with God, "Show me Your presence" (Exodus 33:19). We could cite many more examples of great spiritual seekers, including Hasidic masters and modern Jewish philosophers. These examples are not tangential to our observations. Rather, they remind us of the value of making room for the spiritual seeker, for such individuals have changed the face of Judaism for the better.

Moreover, we might recall an earlier time when it was that very personal quest that led many of us into positions of leadership within the synagogue community. As Rabbi Arthur Green (1994) notes,

> The time has come for us to share our quest, including our unanswered questions, with some of the many thousands of young Jews who do not know that questing is possible within the Jewish tradition, and have come to see us as mere representatives of a closed and over-determined religious establishment.

Unfortunately, there are influential voices in the organized Jewish community who view spiritual seekers as self-indulgent or narcissistic. Their view, especially in the synagogue world, is that individuals need to be accepted on the synagogue's terms and remake themselves in the synagogue's image. Yet, this is also a form of narcissism, the kind that Dr. David Gordis has termed "communal narcissism."[1]

This kind of group-think claims that the institution of the synagogue has the correct prescription for being Jewish. Rabbi Michael Strassfeld refers to this phenomenon as "Jewtocracy," a community run by and for an all-knowing elite.[2] He further argues that, "The elitism of Jewtocracy has led to a new Choseness—the chosen few of the chosen people." Clearly, no one would suggest that a synagogue should meet every idiosyncratic Jewish need. But, synagogue leaders would enrich their community if they listen to what individuals desire for their spiritual growth and are not so hasty to dismiss these yearnings.

The same elite that labels seekers as self-indulgent often argues that Judaism must position itself as running "counter-culture" to the American experience. (Ironically, some of those who advocate a "counter-cultural" stance have themselves adopted values that are drawn from the prevailing majority culture, including feminism and full equality for gays and lesbians.) They suggest that Judaism's authenticity derives from its ability to offer counter-cultural positions on contemporary norms. For us, that is a distorted reading of Jewish history. Our strength and continuity derive equally from our ability to function as a sub-culture and adapt some of the values of each historical and intellectual era to a Jewish perspective, as well as from our tenacity to run counter-culture.

In the attempt to bridge two worldviews, we offer this paper. It begins with an analysis of the dynamics of these contemporary issues and concludes with a series of programmatic recommendations based upon our thesis.

One World, Two Worldviews

A clever person once said, "the world is divided into two kinds of people: those who divide the world into two and those do not." For much of this paper, we will be talking about two broad groups of people, within the context of the synagogue: those who place greater value on the responsibilities and meaning that community imposes and those who attach greater importance to open-ended, limitless choice that individual autonomy offer. We can think of Jewish life today as a spectrum, with one pole representing the community and the other the individual, and there are powerful forces presently at work that are causing people to coalesce around one of these endpoints.

What are some of these forces? Technological leaps in communications, global commerce and travel, genetics, neuroscience and medical technology and the hunger for increased forms of personal entertainment are among the more significant drivers of these fundamental changes in the way we live our lives. These forces leave the most basic assumptions about life open for revision. As Greenberg (1991) notes, "In the past, there was one thing you could depend upon. If you were born a man, you died a man. If you were born a woman, you died a woman. Now . . . you can switch!!" If biology is no longer destiny, then every assumption about life as we know it is up for grabs!

The ubiquity of satellite television and the Internet have abolished geographical distances and blurred cultural differences. This phenomenon has made for some very amusing cultural permutations, as Anderson (1995) notes:

> An American anthropologist visited Japan during the Christmas season and noticed that the retail merchants there had begun to take great interest in the symbolism of Christmas. When he wandered into a large department store in Tokyo, he saw a striking example of this: a Christmas display that prominently featured Santa Claus nailed to a cross.

Changes in social institutions have been equally profound, with classical social institutions dissolving or reconfiguring into new forms. Rabbi Jonathan Sacks poignantly summarizes the impact of these deep changes saying,

> (In the past) There were aspects of lives that did not change. Of these, the most important were a job for life, a marriage for life, and a place for life. Not everyone had them, but they were not rare. They gave people a sense of economic, personal and geographical continuity. They were the familiar that gave individuals strength to cope with the unfamiliar. Today, these things are becoming harder to find (Sacks, p. 71).

Given the profundity of these forces, some believe that we are on the way to or already in a new era, characterized by unlimited personal options in all arenas of life. For many people today, extreme choice and personal freedom allow them to customize multiple aspects of their lives, including their personalities, relationships and even their bodily appearance. Work, leisure, and relationships—those dimensions of our lives that gave us meaning and offered continuity of experience—are in continuous flux for many today. The impact of these changes has been so relatively swift and profound that it is easy to forget that life was qualitatively different not long ago. Cumulatively, because of the unrelenting onslaught of these changes, many are now experiencing a **difference in kind** in the way that they experience life and not merely a **difference in degree**.

These forces are creating conditions for a transition to a fundamentally new era. In fact, some argue that we are already in this new era! In the literature of philosophy, business, theology, sociology and psychology, these forces are labeled with a variety of terms, including modernity, high modernity, post-modernity, post-industrial, post-human and such similar rubrics. Regardless of the label, such terms are meant to capture the feeling that, ". . . something has ended, and there is no going back, even if we don't know what lies ahead, or even, exactly, what lies around us," (Anderson 1997, p. 261). We are creating new terrain, often without any clear notion of what it is that we consciously or unconsciously seek to create and with incomplete comprehension of what we might inadvertently and regrettably create.

Because of this, there has been a broad movement to limit the rule of the sovereign self, which admittedly contributes to a feeling of communal chaos. Without rejecting the value of personal freedom, some people are seeking to restrict some exercise of extreme individual choice for the sake of a greater societal good. These individuals prefer to live in a world in which there is a greater sense of shared clarity and agreement about roles, rules, boundaries, authority and correct beliefs. They are also reacting to the contemporary forces that we described earlier. While at one end of the spectrum we find people who want to expand individual meaning and choice, there are many who desire to enlarge the role of community.

Two Worldviews and their Impact on Religious Communities

These fundamental changes in society also affect communities of faith and are at the heart of many of the tensions that they are experiencing today. The particular expressions of these encounters between normative communities of faith and the sovereign religious self differ by faith community, but general trends are evident across all religions (Carroll and Roof, 2002). As we see with Christian denominations, Jewish denominations are attempting to create a coherent, normative religious community based on their denominational worldviews. On the other hand, the existence of a multiplicity of Jewish spiritual alternatives and the equally pervasive feeling of indifference to denominational demands is an expression of the sovereign self.

Why do these two different orientations toward religion cause misunderstanding and conflict? The way that many people understand religion today has undergone a revolution. In an earlier period (and not that long ago!), religion was viewed as a timeless, immutable body of truths given by a God that created and governed the universe. As such, it provided people with a metanarrative, or a story of mythic proportion that integrated philosophy, values, politics, art and wisdom and offered a comprehensive framework for individuals to understand and find meaning in their world. Religion gave individuals a correct way of representing reality (Anderson, 1995, p. 4).

Contrast this modern view of religion with the way that many other people understand religion today. Belief systems are often not viewed as divinely revealed but instead created by human beings who lived at a particular time and in a particular place. Religious truth, teachings, values and practices are not considered as absolutes because they have been socially constructed. Religious systems must therefore compete on a relative and equal footing with other socially constructed representations of the world. With the globalization of cultures, we can now construct an infinite number of belief systems. Ironically, whether in the realm of politics, academia or religion, every effort to identify a "core" or "true" set of beliefs is met with an alternative set of beliefs. The very act of attempting the identification of an absolute set of beliefs only underscores the impossibility of doing so! "In the collapse of (absolute) belief, a thousand subcultures bloom, and new belief systems arrive as regularly as the daily mail" (Anderson, 1990, p. 10).

Synagogue Dwellers and Jewish Spiritual Seekers

Current research on the state of the Jewish community in the United States suggests that these two parallel dynamics of the commanding community and the sovereign self are at work and will profoundly affect religious life for decades to come. On the one hand, we find that all of the denominational movements are articulating a clear message of what they expect of their adherents with regard to beliefs, attitudes and behaviors. Over the past decade, each religious denomination has been either redefining or clarifying its mission, message and leadership roles and energetically attempting to build a stronger denominational community around that message. While this kind of message crafting is occurring at the national level, it is at the local level, in the synagogue, where the message is being broadcasted and expressed. Some, if not the majority, of congregational rabbis are receptive to publicly defining the distinguishing features of their respective movements through sermons or *divrei torah*, synagogue bulletin articles and through classes. The strengthening of denominational rules and roles by synagogue professionals and involved volunteers is a sign of the commanding community orientation trying to reassert itself.

At the same time, while a segment of the American Jewish population finds synagogues spiritually satisfying, affiliation rates indicate that the majority do not. There is evidence that some of this disenchantment relates to the perceived inflexibility of synagogues in their presentation of the Jewish religious tradition. Synagogue change efforts, grassroots organizations that provide Jewish spiritual alternatives to the religion of the synagogue, and qualitative and quantitative interview and survey data on the synagogue together suggest a desire for change, innovation and different kinds of experiences in synagogues, or even different kinds of synagogues. The increase of individually customized expressions of Judaism is a rejection of the value of community in favor of a stronger voice for the sovereign self.

All Jewish denominations are charged, on some level, with preserving the values and norms of the Jewish tradition, or reinterpreting and mining the tradition to create new norms. On the local level, the synagogue is the repository and expression of these norms and values and the place where synagogue leadership tries to fashion a community that embodies them. While some synagogue members find this role of the synagogue to be personally enriching and communally valuable, others who attend or sporadically visit are only satisfied if the synagogue will accept them on their own terms. As Carroll and Roof (2002, p. 12) note,

> *The congregation is a crucial bearer of tradition. . . . As a bearer of tradition, a congregation is charged with passing it on to its members. . . . Biblical tradition and denominational heritage set normative standards for the gathered community. The vast and varied array of institutions and interpretations within Christianity, Judaism and other major religious traditions is evidence of the extent to which religious traditions, symbols, and meanings are contested and fractured in the modern world.*

Given that this is so, we can both better appreciate the effort of synagogue leadership to set standards and be equally empathetic to the frustrations that many Jewish individuals feel over these efforts. The synagogue is still anchored in the worldview of community and attempts to identify, articulate and transmit a set of norms to its members. This is a perfectly reasonable endeavor for synagogues, whose primary function is the transmission of the Jewish religious civilization. Additionally, in an age where values are perceived as relative, the synagogue assumes the important and lonely task of setting standards or, at a minimum, of offering guiding principles.

Yet, many Jewish seekers have adopted the worldview of the sovereign self, characterized by an unbounded, continually evolving, individualized, market-driven approach to religious practice and exploration. "Whereas only a small number of Jewish thinkers are actively exploring Judaism from a rigorously postmodern (in our words, sovereign self) viewpoint, the postmodern condition permeates contemporary Judaism and challenges individuals, institutions, and the tradition itself" (Margolis, 2001, p. 46). This personalist orientation often creates conflict when individuals come into contact with synagogues. Thus, as Anderson notes, "All the major-league belief systems are still around, but all of them are in some kind of postmodern trouble: internal civil wars. Believers moving in and out. Innovators creating strange new variations" (Anderson, p. 19).

The business of even attempting to establish norms is very complicated today. Even if the leadership of each denomination can agree upon a set of norms, will the well-intentioned drive to articulate them increase the number of positive connections that existing and potential members will have with synagogues? At the same time, if people continue to "make *shabbes* for themselves" (or more accurately, if they continue not to make *shabbat*!), how can we create a Jewish community that is essentially shaped by the religious dimensions of our past?

Turmoil in Every Temple: Encounters between the Two Worldviews

Often, in discussions about Jewish religious denominations, the issue of relationships across the denominational streams tends to make headlines. We read about sharp differences among the Conservative, Orthodox, Reconstructionist and Reform movements. For example, we are very familiar with the intense denominational border wars that have erupted over the past decade over the "who is a Jew" issue. The lines differentiating the movements have been clearly drawn by the religious leadership of the respective movements, although these differences are not always that clear among the popular adherents. Egalitarianism, patrilineal descent, homosexuality, interfaith marriages and the origins and binding nature of Jewish law are among the primary theological and legal issues that distinguish the movements from one another and that sometimes become points of cross-denominational dispute.

While these external border wars have received much media attention for well over a decade, lately, equally significant battles are actually occurring **within** the different movements that have little or nothing to do with the relationships across the movements. In other words, within each of the religious movements, there is a tremendous amount of internal pressure around their respective boundaries being generated by those who are committed to the synagogue. The denominational movements have been struggling to redefine or redraw their internal parameters and more clearly articulate the expectations they have of their members. As noted earlier by Anderson, these internal "border wars" are symptomatic of a meeting of the two worldviews that we described, the commanding community and the sovereign self. They are powerful testimony to the fact that the forces embodied in the sovereign self have affected even those that live within the synagogue universe. We now examine some of those effects by denomination.

Conservative Judaism. Previously, we analyzed how these differing worldviews have manifested themselves within the Conservative Movement (Herring, 2000). Despite a significant expenditure of much intellectual capital over the past fifteen years or so on making its ideological standards explicit, recent studies of dues paying members of Conservative synagogues (Wertheimer, 1996; Wertheimer, 1997) indicate that the laity is eclectic in its adherence to norms and standards. This erosion of authority between the leadership and individual members bears the fingerprints of a meeting between the commanding community and the sovereign self.

Most recently, as we predicated in our earlier analysis, the issue of homosexuality has resurfaced. Currently, the Conservative Movement officially prohibits the admission of openly gay and lesbian students into its rabbinical schools and does not permit its member rabbis to perform commitment ceremonies, although there are no sanctions for those who have begun to do so. The reopening of a discussion on this stance may be a reassertion of the sovereign self that seeks to broaden boundaries against the standards set by the commanding community.

Reform Judaism. While retaining its commitment to personal autonomy as an overriding value in decision-making, the Reform Movement has vigorously and unabashedly reintroduced the notion of commandment (*mitzvah*) in its religious lexicon and regularly invokes traditional categories of practice and values in its presentation to the public. This warm embrace of traditional practice is enshrined in the Statement of Principles for Reform Judaism that was adopted in May 1999. While this text is remarkable in many ways, for the purposes of this paper, a citation from the section on "Torah" that relates to the observance of *mitzvot* is instructive for understanding how the forces of autonomy and the drive for community are unfolding within the Reform Movement.

In 1885, the Reform rabbinate issued the following statement about *mitzvot* in its "Pittsburgh Platform."

> *We recognize in the Mosaic legislation a system of training the Jewish people for its mission during its national life in Palestine, and today we accept as binding only its moral laws, and maintain only such ceremonies as elevate and sanctify our lives, but reject all such as are not adapted to the views and habits of modern civilization. We hold that all such Mosaic and rabbinical laws as regulate diet, priestly purity, and dress originated in ages and under the influence of ideas entirely foreign to our present mental and spiritual state. They fail to impress the modern Jew with a spirit of priestly holiness; their observance in our days is apt rather to obstruct than to further modern spiritual elevation.*

In the same place, but over a century later, the Reform rabbinate spoke in a vastly different language and tone about "Mosaic" and rabbinical laws.

> *We are committed to the ongoing study of the whole array of mitzvot and to the fulfillment of those that address us as individuals and as a community. Some of these mitzvot, sacred obligations, have long been observed by Reform Jews; others, both ancient and modern, demand renewed attention as the result of the unique context of our own times."*

While the Reform Movement has adopted a more open stance toward traditional practice, we should remember that this is the same movement that has endorsed patrilineal descent, which represents a break of at least a two thousand year old precedent. This is also the same Reform Judaism that affirms the right of individuals to choose the content of their Jewish lives and that permits commitment ceremonies for gay and lesbian Jews. Thus, it is too simplistic to describe the Reform Movement's embrace of classical rituals as a "return to tradition." There is both a return to tradition and a departure from tradition happening simultaneously—a clear sign of turmoil as the sovereign self and the commanding community struggle to maintain their position. Not surprisingly, this revised Statement of Principles generated a fair amount of internal discussion and debate; some believing that it goes too far with others claiming that it does not go far enough.[3]

Reconstructionist Judaism. Unlike Reform, modern Orthodox and Conservative Judaism, whose European origins reside in a different set of historical, political and cultural circumstances, Reconstructionist Judaism had the benefit of being born in modern America. As the first native expression American Judaism, it highlights the value of democratic decision-making in building religious community. We might therefore think that Reconstructionist Judaism is more immune to the tensions created between the orientations of the commanding community and the sovereign self. Yet, this movement is also grappling with these tensions. For example, these tensions are reflected in the debate over the respective roles of rabbis and congregants. This issue is so critical that a joint commission of the three arms of the Reconstructionist Movement (the Reconstructionist Rabbinical Association, the Jewish Reconstructionist Federation and the Reconstructionist Rabbinical

College) recently completed a publication on this very topic (The Rabbi-Congregation Relationship, 2001).[4]

This focus on rabbi-congregant relations raises the question of where authority for decision-making lies, with the "specialist" or the "generalist." In an age where anyone can be an expert (see below), who is entitled to have the ultimate say about norms that will govern the community? Given the democratic decision-making process of Reconstructionist philosophy (read: we all have an equal vote) but a serious commitment to make decisions according to Jewish values and traditions (read: but shouldn't the rabbi's vote be more equal?), this report (p. ix) tries to recalibrate the balance in decision-making so that the rabbi's expertise is duly considered.

> There has been an evolution in the understanding of the role of the rabbi in Reconstructionist settings. Using a systems approach in which leadership is a valued and indispensable component of a congregational system, the report affirms that a rabbi can and should be a (not "the") leader, can and should be an (not "the") authority, and can and should play a leading role in congregational decision-making.

Orthodox Judaism. Even Orthodoxy[5] is not immune to these kinds of tensions. The sometimes-popular perception of a united Orthodoxy belies the reality of remarkable debates that have occurred within Orthodoxy over the past several years. A wide-range of issues have been aired publicly that show that Orthodoxy is also seriously struggling with boundary issues raised by the meeting of the sovereign self and the commanding community.

Most noticeably, Orthodox feminism has become a force advocating for such issues as expanded leadership roles within Jewish communal institutions, including the synagogue. In fact, the creation of the Jewish Orthodox Feminist Alliance (JOFA), and its ability to attract large numbers of Orthodox women and some men to its cause, is noteworthy.

We believe that this call for a greater level of participation for women in Jewish life is primarily driven by the forces that best fit within the rubric of the "sovereign self." In other words, individuals are asserting their right to import values from the broader culture, albeit in what they describe as an Orthodox legal (*halakhic*) framework.

With regard to the synagogue, calls for greater leadership roles are not limited to the "secular" roles of administering the affairs of the synagogue but also include expanded religious leadership roles. For example, based on a recent rabbinical responsum (Shapiro, 2001), several Orthodox *minyanim* have begun permitting women to read from the Torah in their main service, which includes both men and women. Other Orthodox congregations are experimenting with new roles for women as spiritual advisors on legal matters (sometimes called *yo'atzot halakha*) and as prominent teachers of Jewish classical texts. In fact, there are several well-respected schools whose mission is to advance women's study of classical Jewish texts.

This development within Orthodox Judaism suggests that no community can hermetically seal itself off from contemporary cultural forces and values. These forces are so powerful, and communities are so linked by technology and commerce, that there will always be some leakage of the sovereign self's yearnings into every community today. Indeed, we suggest that the wide range of choices that people have for identifying as Orthodox, from the extreme Edah Haredi to the moderate Edah, suggests that even within a binding legal framework, the sovereign self still has wide jurisdiction.

At the risk of oversimplification, it appears that in those communities where Jewish law carries greater weight and rabbis have played a more dominant role in setting the Jewish legal standards of the movement and synagogue (Conservative, Orthodox), the sovereign self as embodied in the lay leadership is pushing for greater determination in setting the movement agenda and advocating for greater diversity. In those movements where Jewish law has historically played a less significant role and rabbis have been less vocal about Jewish law (Reconstructionist, Reform), the commanding community as embodied by the rabbinate is asserting the need for more clear boundaries and norms. What is clear is that across the denominational spectrum, we can observe signs of the struggle between the sovereign self and the commanding community even among synagogue loyalists.

A Holy Alliance Between Social Scientists and Denominational Judaism

In each of the established liberal denominations (Conservative, Reconstructionist, Reform) there are efforts afoot to clarify role definitions and religious expectations for all those who would claim their identification with a particular denomination. What are the origins of those efforts? There are no signs of a groundswell among American Jews clamoring for the religious establishment of America to impose more demanding standards upon them. Rather, it appears that the religious leadership from all denominations is taking the initiative to increase the level of religious observance of its adherents. Those who identify most closely with the particular practices and values of the respective movements—primarily rabbis and sometimes synagogue lay leaders—are at the vanguard of this effort.

How can we account for this effort on the part of the religious elite to promote the norms of their respective movements? A scientific answer to this question would require a series of interviews with the denominational opinion leaders—something that is beyond the scope of this paper. If we conducted such a study, we would be likely to find several themes and not a single answer. However, we may conjecture that some social science research on American churches and social science research on the American Jewish community may have stimulated this effort.

We hypothesize that the religious elite may be reading some of the social science research on the Jewish community as well, or as least some of the headlines. For more than a decade, social science research has provided quantitative data about American Jews and their attitudes, behaviors and beliefs. Generally speaking, those data have been interpreted as a story of erosion and decline of the American Jewish community, with each successive generation possessing a lower level of Jewish identity as measured by the practice of traditional Jewish behaviors, like lighting Shabbat candles, attending synagogue and keeping kosher (Horowitz, 1999, pp. 22–23). In other words, these are the very behaviors that are especially valued in the synagogue world. Therefore, it may be that synagogue leadership has responded with a drive to promote these traditional behaviors in an effort to counteract what social scientists have described as corrosive trends. Yet, there are three serious limitations to this way of measuring the vitality of the American Jewish community when thinking about how synagogues can play an effective role in revitalizing Jewish life.

The First Limitation. A portrait of what a "normative" Jew is supposed to look like is embedded in quantitative survey research. In constructing scales of Jewish identity, a researcher typically develops a scale from "maximally involved" to "minimally involved" Jews to paint this portrait of Jewish identity. "Maximally involved" Jews perform more Jewish behaviors than "minimally involved" ones. It is against that portrait that individual Jews are viewed. To what extent do they approximate it? Extending the analogy of portrait painting, the palette from which the survey researcher paints the contours of the portrait contains a limited number of colors. As Horowitz notes,

> *One problem with the Generation in America approach to American Jewishness (that is, measuring Jewish behaviors in successive generations) is that it tracks only a narrow set of traditional Jewish ritual, religious and communal practices, without allowing for a wider range of variations in Jewish practice. In effect this accounting strategy gives higher marks to a more homogenous traditional Jewish population, and lower marks to a population characterized by a wider variety of less traditional Jewish behaviors (Horowitz, 1999, p. 23)*

When we look at the values suggested by those scales, we believe that we uncover a bias toward a coherent package of Jewish behaviors that is better suited to measuring an idealized picture that reflects the commanding community of the synagogue.

Yet, as we have learned from researchers like Horowitz (2000) and Cohen and Eisen (1998), the same eclectic religious belief and behavior that is so typical of Americans today is also characteristic of American Jewry. In a study of Jewish individuals between thirty and fifty years old, born between 1948 and 1968, Cohen and Eisen (1998, p. 36) note, ". . . we were struck . . . by the individuality and idiosyncrasy embedded in these (personal) narratives. . . . Choices and choosing are multiplied, cultural ferment is even more widespread, and geographic and social mobility make for less stability . . ."

The Second Limitation. Social science research on American Jews assumes that Jewish identity is a static category, something that does not change once it is acquired. However, Jewish identity is not a one-time goal to be achieved but an ongoing, fluid process (Arnow, 1994, p. 6). What social scientists have measured may be more accurately described as "Jewish identification," that is, acts of involvement with Jewish life and the organized Jewish community. In contrast, Jewish identity is,

the inner experience of the self in relationship to the religious, polit-
ical, ethnic and/or cultural elements of Judaism, the Jewish people,
and Israel; it is the reflection within an individual of this experi-
ence as expressed in thought, feeling and behavior (Arnow, p. 4).

Jewish identity, in prior generations, was something more easily conferred by family and community. In contrast, identity formation is a unique, individualized process in today's society. As
such, its expression will be idiosyncratic and evolutionary, contin-
gent upon specific needs and events in a person's life history. By
having static measures of Jewish identity, institutions are likely to
forget that Jewish experiences that speak to people at one time in
their life may be inadequate at other times in their lives, thus limiting the range of programmatic options that they offer to their constituents. They may also inadvertently dismiss those who are
struggling with one form of Jewish identity expression while seeking other alternatives.

Based on her research, Horowitz (2000, p. 7) suggests that,

To allow for a more pluralistic and perhaps more personalized view
of the possible ways that Jewishness may now be exemplified, it may
be more helpful conceptually to move away from thinking about
Jewish identity as a single quantity that can be scaled, and instead
to start conceptualizing Jewishness in terms of different types or
ways of being. We would then say that there are different ways of
connecting to Jewish life in America today, and what is needed is a
better understanding of the full range of connections.

Currently, the denominations on the national level, and many
synagogues on the local level, still seem to base their approach to
Jewish religious life on a conception of "maximally" and "minimally" involved Jews. In pushing for the adoption of greater religious behavioral norms, they begin with the assumption that there
is a "correct" form of Jewish religious life and gear their institutional resources toward that form. Given that denominations are
constituted to promote a particular understanding of what it means
to be Jewish, that is an appropriate focus. However, it is also important to find programmatic ways to incorporate into the synagogue
some more recent insights about the evolving nature of Jewish
identity and additional ways of conceptualizing Jewish identity. As
Horowitz (2000, p. vii) notes about her subjects,

For Jewish institutions, it is crucial to learn that 60% of the people in the study experienced changes in their relationship to being Jewish over time, suggesting that Jewish identity is not a fixed factor in one's life but rather a matter that parallels personal growth and development. There are critical periods and moments in people's lives that offer potential opportunities for Jewish institutions to play a role, if only these institutions can be open and available to individuals in a way that meets their changing needs and concerns.

The Third Limitation. Conceiving of Jewish identification (a person's Jewish behaviors) as a coherent, prescribed package makes it difficult for us to locate and imagine emerging and new ways of identification with the Jewish community and its institutions (Blanchard, 2002, pp. 39–40). As we each see the world through our own prisms of understanding and experiences, the act of identifying different ways in which people express their Jewishness becomes virtually impossible unless we have alternative maps of the Jewish community at our disposal (Herring, 2001, pp. 4–5). Equally true, synagogue leaders unconsciously may not want to imagine new ways of people expressing their Jewish identity (their evolving feelings) and identification (their current behaviors) because such alternative expressions may challenge their own patterns of living Jewishly in which they are spiritually, emotionally, intellectually and financially invested.

There is value in religious leaders holding passionate commitments to a religious ideology and practice. Nonetheless, as the denominations continue to promote their brand of Jewish living, synagogue leaders should also question whether their approach of increasing standards, norms and expectations will enhance or diminish the involvement of existing and potential synagogue members and constructively address the disenchantment that many feel with the synagogue. This approach will certainly appeal to some, but synagogues must also be laboratories for experimenting with additional forms of Jewish expression. Israel (2001) summarizes the challenges confronting synagogues today. "As for individual synagogues, with the exception of a few congregations in the largest cities with easily identifiable heavily young adult areas, in this respect most are still living in the 1950s." While she made this observation with reference to vastly changed demographic realities, we believe that it is also true with regard to grasping the challenges and possibilities of functioning in an age of extreme personal choice.

Proponents of increasing Jewish norms and standards will often point to the growth of demanding, conservative evangelical churches and the decline of liberal, mainline churches. Taking a cue from this phenomenon, the religious elite will claim that ratcheting up the demands for observance will have the same salutary effects on their institutions. However, Hoffman cautions against this kind of simplistic analysis. While Hoffman (2002, p. 25) acknowledges that demanding churches have had success, he believes that, "The sociological research (on conservative churches) is, therefore, somewhat ambiguous, but nonetheless, it does seem now that doctrinal strictness *per se* is not the sole influence." Rather, he hypothesizes that these conservative churches embody the "cultural ethos" of the times because they emphasize religious authenticity while also building their ministries around the need for transcendent, personal and joyous meaning (pp. 25–28). Thus, it is no mere return to old-fashion conservatism and doctrinal demands that account for the success of these churches but the crafting of a distinctively new kind of church that blends the authority with room for autonomy.

Jewish Spiritual and Cultural Alternatives

As noted earlier, there is a significant amount of evidence from within each movement to suggest that the commanding community and the sovereign self sometimes exist uneasily on the part of those who are committed to synagogue life. It is outside of the denominational movements that we really witness the full power of the sovereign self. There has been a veritable growth industry of religious and cultural expressions of Judaism that are bypassing existing denominational structures. Some of these alternatives are tried and true while others break new ground.

Among the more institutionalized expressions of the sovereign self-orientation, some *havurot* are laboratories for a more individualized approach toward Jewish worship. There are also many novel illustrations of Jewish spiritual expression occurring outside of denominational synagogues. The Jewish Renewal Movement, with its emphasis on personal spirituality, can actually be viewed as a critique of existing denominational synagogues that are perceived as paying insufficient attention to the inner, spiritual dimensions of ritual and worship. A number of Jewish meditation and healing centers have been opened around the country in places like New York, California and Texas. An Internet search under "Jewish spirituality" will reveal an eye-opening sample of Jewish spiritual resources that are not denominationally based. Internet searches list numerous virtual sites for locating Jewish spiritual texts, physical addresses for meditation and Kabbalah group meetings, virtual spiritual communities, Torah and yoga groups, opportunities to enroll in real-time Jewish spiritual retreat programs and listings of organizations devoted to promoting Jewish spirituality.

The realm of Jewish culture also provides evidence of creative, individualistic energy finding expression outside of the synagogue (Siegel, 2002; Tobin, 2002). There has been a tremendous growth in the Jewish music industry that encompasses both popular and liturgical music. Additionally, there has been an explosion of Jewish museums, with sixty professionally staffed museums and more than one hundred Holocaust centers in existence (Decter, 2001). Jewish cultural expression also encompasses film, literature and Jewish scholarship. In fact, approximately sixty Jewish film festivals are held annually in the United States, which attract individuals and families that are not likely to feel at home in the synagogue (Berkofsky, 2003). Taken together, these examples suggest that there is an impressive array of options for Jews wishing to construct their Jewish spiritual lives outside of synagogues instead of through them. These options are consistent with the findings of those researchers who have studied the personalist, idiosyncratic journeys of Jews today (Cohen and Eisen, 1998; Horowitz, 2000). As we shall see below, the younger the generation, the more idiosyncratic is the journey.

Recent Studies About Generations in American and Contemporary Religious Life

With advances in medicine, we have the unprecedented phenomenon of having significant numbers of four generations of people alive. These four generations are described as the "Veteran/Silent Generation," "Baby Boomers," "Gen X'ers" and "Millenials." While researchers demarcate these generations somewhat differently, Veterans are defined as those born from 1922–1943, Baby Boomers from 1943–1960, Gen X'ers from 1960–1980 and Millenials from 1980–2000. Different historical forces influence each generation. As a result, "It is further assumed that the cultural definitions of reality forged by a generation in its formative years are carried, to a greater or lesser degree, throughout the lives of its members"

(Carroll and Roof, 2002, p. 6). There is a range of tremendously significant implications in this assumption. For our purposes, the primary importance of understanding the impact of generational experience is that it helps us appreciate that each generation brings different values, attitudes and expectations to all facets of life including work, education, family, relationships and civic and religious involvement, and the institutions that they inhabit.

While conventional wisdom holds that there is always a "generation gap" as one generation experiences its children come of age, generational differences are more pronounced in periods of social and cultural instability.

> In a stable period of history, generations come and go and are not marked by a huge cleavage between them; children live pretty much by the values and standards taught to them by their parents and in time pass those values and standards on to their own children. But in a period of social discontinuity or rapid technological and cultural change, people's life worlds are likely to be reshaped—especially if, as has come to be the case for young people, they are differentially exposed to the sources of social innovation (Carroll and Roof, p. 8).

When reflecting on the vast differences in life today as experienced by an eighteen year old and an eighty year old, we can immediately grasp the rapidity of fundamental change that has occurred in this relatively brief period of sixty-two years. Technology, communications, transportation, education, family structures, government, individual freedom, medicine—so much has changed in such a brief period of time that it is easy to understand why one generation experiences the world so differently from another!

Not surprisingly, the religious identity characteristics of each generation also vary. Attitudes toward organized religion on the part of the Veteran Generation are very different from those of Millenials. While some of these differences are likely related to psychosocial developmental differences, others are clearly related to generational differences. In this section, we review some fundamental characteristics of Baby Boomers, Gen X'ers and Millenials as they relate to synagogues. We will not review attitudes of the Veteran Generation as unfortunately, to the best of our knowledge, no similar research has been conducted on them within the Jewish community. However, we will make recommendations about them in the concluding section of this paper.

Baby Boomers and Religious Institutions

The questioning of inherited religious belief systems and structures and the exploration of spiritual alternatives outside of the denominational movements is no longer considered a surprising phenomenon. While Veterans often bring automatic loyalty to religious institutions[6], Boomers offer automatic skepticism, questioning everything from organizational structures to traditional beliefs. Roof (1999, pp. 41–42) observes that,

> . . . at this juncture in history, inherited religious traditions face severe challenges. Tradition as memory and authority, or as a means of organizing the past in relation to the present, is eroded in a secular world; religious scripts that once communicated deep meanings, symbolic frames of reference, and defined modes of action must now compete with other stories in a pluralistic and media-saturated society that encourages a mixing of religious themes. Religious truths that were once closely linked to place and context are undermined by high levels of geographic and social mobility, rapid social and technological changes, and by a mass culture made up increasingly of images and symbols that often retain very little to locate and anchor them in a particular place and time. The result is a proliferation of religious scripts, greater selectivity of practices from a variety of sources, the possibility of multilayered religious worlds, and often a softening of personal commitment resulting from what has been described as a shift 'from a world in which beliefs held believers to one in which believers hold beliefs.'

These changes on the part of Boomer believers create a significant challenge for established religious institutions. How can they create lasting relationships with individuals who are spiritually questing? Many Boomers today, who carry little if any institutional loyalty, approach religious institutions with a desire to bring their open-ended search for spiritual meaning into a church or synagogue that have fairly structured and non-negotiable religious scripts. This interaction then pits what sociologists have coined the "sovereign self" (Roof, p. 130) against an authoritative religious community. The result of the interaction is that, "Organized religion can be experienced as distant and out-of-date; spiritually it can be dry" (Roof, p. 37).

The shortcomings that Boomers from other faith communities perceive with their religious institutions also have echoes within the

Jewish community, and the effort of denominational religious leadership to articulate norms is not likely to satisfy the spiritual cravings of many American Jews. There is a growing recognition that synagogue leadership is not speaking the same language as many American Jews. We can find evidence for dissatisfaction from multiple sources, some of which we examine for illustrative purposes.

First, we can observe the number of synagogue transformation efforts currently in existence on a variety of levels. Some are national, like STAR (Synagogues: Transformation and Renewal), Synagogue 2000 and ECE—Experiment in Congregational Education; some are regional, like the Koret Synagogue Initiative; and, some are local, like the efforts in Boston, Hartford, Bergen County, New York and Philadelphia. Additionally, some individual synagogues have made fundamental changes without the support of any external efforts.

A succinct summary of major issues that face synagogues today once appeared on the web site of Synagogue 2000, a national synagogue change initiative. While written as a rationale for the creation of this particular change effort, it would probably be acknowledged as true by all those working to make synagogues more vibrant and compelling institutions. Some of the findings that led to the creation of Synagogue 2000 included:

- A phenomenon frequently described as a "search for meaning" characterizes most other Jews, who often flirt with non-Jewish religious alternatives when synagogues do not address the "big questions" of life.
- Rabbis and laity are often as wary of each other's agendas as they are positive about each other's roles. Rabbis tend to suffer from "burnout," brought on by their perception that they are working alone, rather than as a team with their congregants.
- Laypeople describe synagogues as necessary and doing some things well, but (except for the highly involved synagogue leaders) they find religious services banal and baffling.
- Unaffiliated Jews find the ambiance of synagogues cold and unwelcoming.

An important qualitative study on synagogues that have succeeded in reaching Baby Boomers (Schwarz, 2000) offers abundant and rich information on the challenges that synagogue leaders face in attempting to engage this generation. Writing generally on the interest of younger Americans in spirituality, Schwarz (p. 28) notes that,

> *Some religious institutions have been adept at tapping into this inter-est in spirituality and have incorporated the most popular elements of spiritual exploration into their synagogues and churches. This is not always easy, as more conservative members of these institutions will invoke tradition, branding such experiments as beyond the pale. Clergy, who often serve as gatekeepers and arbiters of what is and is not acceptable, face a choice between attracting new, younger congre-gants who want change and satisfying existing members, the loyalists who are already part of the leadership of the institution. Unless a reli-gious institution starts from scratch with a mission to address the baby boom age cohort, existing synagogues and churches are destined to wrestle over each and every innovation that pits religious conven-tion against the interests of a younger generation.*

Schwarz (pp. 28–29) continues,

> *Within the synagogue orbit, individuals who have a substantial investment in Judaism understand why such innovations must be carefully deliberated. But to many baby boomers, often raised with but a token commitment to the Jewish community and to Jewish tradition, there is little understanding of or patience for synagogues that agonize over changes that appear so obvious. Since there are so many spiritual options available in American society today, most pass on joining synagogues and come to satisfy their spiritual needs elsewhere.*

Indeed, it is frequently younger generations who contribute to Jewish cultural, educational and spiritual innovations noted earlier and who bypass the institutions of the organized Jewish community.

Gen X'ers and Millenials

Looking to the future of synagogue involvement, it appears that even greater challenges lie ahead. The tendencies of the sovereign self that often make connections with synagogues problematic are already evident in the Baby Boom Generation and many of the cur-rent synagogue transformation efforts are led by Boomers seeking to satisfy their spiritual needs. However, there are two generations that are quickly maturing, displaying even greater tendencies toward personalizing and customizing their identity. They will only take their place in synagogues if we can determine how to make room for them. These two generations, Gen X'ers and Millenials, have grown up in a world that is different from their Boomer parents and, not surprisingly, have a different value set that they bring to all aspects of their lives, including synagogues.

What do we really know about these upcoming generations? There is a significant body of literature on the Millenial and Gen X generations from outside of the Jewish community. Within the Jewish community, there is some scientific research, primarily on Jewish Millenials and even less on Jewish Gen X'ers (Sales, 1994; Leffert and Herring, 1997; Cohen, 1998; Kadushin, Kelner and Saxe, 2000; Kosmin, 2000; Sax, 2002). Nonetheless, within the past decade, the few studies that have been conducted on these generations paint a fairly consistent picture. What follows is a composite summary of that research.

While most Millenials express pride in being Jewish, the way that they express their Judaism is different (and some might say inferior) than prior generations. They are generally unsatisfied with the Jewish education they received and therefore find serious study of Judaism appealing. It is not clear if spirituality, an interest of Boomers, is a category of experience that resonates with them. Those from unaffiliated and interfaith families are especially interested in cultural and artistic expressions of Judaism. Typically, young women are more active in organized Jewish activities than are their male counterparts. These same studies indicate that Jews of these generations value academic achievement and attach a high priority to financial well-being. It is therefore not surprising that we find that they spend a considerable amount of time working for pay already as teenagers, often at jobs that they do not find meaningful.

Millenials are generally interested in learning about Israel and the Holocaust and desire raising their children as Jews. While celebrating holidays with their families is enjoyable to them, formal affiliation with Jewish institutions is unimportant, as is the practice of ritual behavior and attendance at synagogue services. Millenials are universalist in their worldview, value cultural diversity and are unconcerned about dating non-Jews. They do not like labeling other groups and, in a related vein, dislike barriers that separate people from one another, both within and outside of the Jewish community. Interest in volunteerism and making the world a better place is of great importance to them. Research from outside of the Jewish community on Gen X'ers and Millenials also has important implications for synagogues.

What implications for future synagogue life can we tease out of research findings from within and outside of the Jewish community? They suggest that:

- Although their Jewish behaviors may be different from ours, upcoming generations are proud of being Jewish;
- These generations have fewer memories of Jewish family celebrations and fewer experiences of being in the synagogue with their families;
- They are less interested in Jewish rituals;
- They are accustomed to self-directing their life choices;
- They celebrate religious, cultural and ethnic diversity and having weaker feelings of Jewish ethnic solidarity;
- They value subjective experiences as a way of knowing the world over traditional propositional truths;
- While they value education they also value entertainment, especially if it has an edge to it;
- They need to be reached through multiple media channels;
- They need to have their loyalty earned and maintained on a regular basis, especially Jewish males, who already tend to be less involved in Jewish communal life;
- They value a community that provides them physical and emotional safety;
- They expect to see a diversity of people within their midst;
- They want to be respected as individuals capable of contributing to their community.

Today, synagogues are structured as venues for community building through expressing ritual behavior and sharing the wisdom of the Jewish tradition, with rabbis often serving as the authorities in both areas. While many teachings in our tradition are timeless, we have to learn how to translate them into meaningful categories for younger generations if we want them to remain timely. Synagogue change efforts have been focused on reaching the Baby Boom generation. Synagogues now have the challenge of adapting to two other generations, Gen X'ers and Millenials, unless they also want to risk alienating them.

Another contemporary challenge synagogues face is the demographic realities of the American Jewish community. Our community is comprised of diverse family structures. Today, there are significant numbers of people for whom being single is a not a temporary state but a voluntarily permanent status, or one that they will retain for long periods of time. In addition to large numbers of singles, we have in our community single parents, empty nesters, interfaith families, gay and lesbian families, bi-racial families, adoptive families and other kinds of as-yet-unimagined families. While we often act as if these phenomena are tomorrow's realities they are already today's facts! Synagogues have the daunting dual challenge of serving multiple generations and of engaging a very diverse community with regard to family structures.

Rabbinical Training: An Unintended Factor in Promoting Tensions?

Rabbinical training may actually have the unintended effect of exacerbating some problems that surface around the issue of authority and decision-making in the congregation. First, consider that rabbinical programs average between four and six years in length. During that time, the typical model of learning to which students are exposed is hierarchical.[7] A knowledgeable professor/rabbi fills eager students with vast amounts of information and skills in an array of Jewish subjects. Certainly, students question their teachers, but the system of rabbinic education anoints teachers as authorities and students as novices.

There is nothing new about this model. Indeed, its roots are deep in the Jewish tradition. "Make your home a regular meeting place for the scholars. Sit eagerly at their feet and drink their words with gusto" (Avot 1:4). Rabbinic literature is replete with stories in which disciples demonstrate great respect for their teachers. In fact, Jewish law prohibits a student from teaching in the presence of his teacher (*shulkhan arukh, yoreh de'ah 242: 4*), a law that reinforces the authority of the master teacher.

Fast-forward now to a newly minted rabbi who has been socialized into this model of learning for a lengthy amount of time. In this setting, it is the rabbi who now functions as the expert authority and the congregants who are supposed to play the role of respectful "students." However, rabbis learn quickly that congregants do not automatically display respect toward their authority by virtue of their title and their learning. Indeed, in an age when the sovereign self rules supreme, everyone can be an "authority." Because of their access to Jewish knowledge, there has been a shift in the center of gravity from the rabbi to the individual Jewish seeker when it comes to learning and authority (Margolis, p. 41). A generation ago, Baby Boomers developed the reputation of being skeptical of authority. Today, a new phenomenon is occurring, namely that everyone can be their own authority!

A few examples will easily make this point. Movie-making is not limited to Hollywood anymore, but to one's video camera and personal computer. Anyone can publish his or her thoughts on the Internet, presenting that individual with a patina of expertise. Patients come armed to their doctors with medical research and drug requests. Anyone can be a trader on the stock market—and the list of possibilities for the average person to know and do what only experts used to is expanding.

Is it any wonder that many individual Jews, regardless of their formal Judaic training, want to be their own authorities on how to live their Jewish lives? Jewish learning, which was democratized by the classical rabbis following the destruction of the Second Temple, has undergone an even more powerful revolution because of the Internet. Information on virtually any Jewish topic is now available in English and in Hebrew. Additionally, many younger Jewish individuals have either had a college-level course in Jewish studies, a day school education or attended a Jewish camp for a period of years. These congregants can just as easily come in armed with questions and answers about Judaism that may feel threatening to rabbis trained in a hierarchical model.

While this topic deserves greater treatment, we introduce it briefly because it is so critical to understanding many of the underlying causes for lay-rabbinic misunderstanding. Some of the movements, especially the Reconstructionist Movement, are examining rabbinic roles today. But in broad strokes, what will be needed is a less hierarchical, more collaborative partnership between rabbis and synagogue volunteers.

> *The move from hierarchical to collaborative leadership is especially difficult in the rabbinate. For centuries, rabbis have been viewed as the ultimate religious authorities, and the rabbinate tends to attract people who expect to function as hierarchical leaders. Congregants, for their part, look to their clergy for definitive answers to questions of religion, morality and even social and psychological concerns (Aron, 2002, p. 23).*

Training on how to develop a more collaborative rabbinate will need to take place at the local and national levels: in rabbinical school programs, rabbinical and congregational organizations and independent foundations interested in this issue.

Wanted: A Third Way

Ammerman (2000, p. 367), in an essay entitled, "Conservative Jews within the Landscape of American Religion," offers a hypothesis about the need for a "third way" between the commanding community and the sovereign self.

> *Neither an intolerant fundamentalism nor an accommodated and tolerant liberalism seems to promise a way forward. More promising are proposals that postmodernity will be inhabited by people who are (at least culturally) bilingual, speaking a native, parochial language while also speaking a common language shared with people they do not know.*

"Parochial," she explains (p. 367), is

> *to have a community, to go beyond one's presumed autonomy as an individual. The presumption of autonomy is neither so unquestioned today nor so welcomed as it once was. While choice and volunteerism are still celebrated as the hallmark of democracy and a key source of religious vitality, both constraints on choice and the commitments implied by choice are entering the vocabulary of social observers. The picture that is slowly emerging emphasizes the complexities of the relationship between individual and community over time, space, and function. We are neither as free and disconnected as the modernity paradigm would have had it nor as utterly embedded in ascribed communities as our traditionalist forbears. In the nexus of choice and community new understandings of person and commitment are emerging.*

Ammerman (p. 367) posits that Orthodoxy represents the "modernist" paradigm (the commanding community) and Reform the "postmodernist" paradigm (the sovereign self). For her, Conservative Judaism is that "third way," joining these two orientations into a new synthesis. Her hypothesis misses the mark on several counts but still has some general merit for our consideration. First, as previously noted, all of the denominations are feeling the impact of contemporary cultural trends and are struggling to find the balance between communal norms and individual needs. This balancing act expresses itself differently within each movement, but the existence of this kind of encounter with these forces of Jewish personalism across all of the denominations is irrefutable. Additionally, does Reconstructionist Judaism have a place in her schema or does she exclude this fourth denomination of Judaism? Finally, just how widespread the disenchantment with radical autonomy is really remains an untested assertion. The emergence of so many spiritual alternatives outside of established faith denominations suggests that the "sovereign self" continues to rule in the realm of religion as it increasingly does in every other aspect of life.

Nonetheless, when applied to all of the denominations, her observation about "a third way" that bridges the orientation toward the self at one end of the spectrum with the orientation toward community at the other, bears serious consideration for those who care about the complex enterprise of maintaining and expanding the Jewish community today. Sometime in the late 1980s, while attending a meeting of rabbis, I heard a colleague proclaim that the role of the religion is to do the dirty work of society and uphold standards. I would not phrase it as he did, but I believe that he was correct in grasping the cultural forces in contemporary America that treat all values as relative propositions and that turn ethics into personal opinions. The question is how Judaism can remain relevant, allowing space for individual Jewish expression, while still articulating a clear religious message that does not alienate those who are open to guidance from the Jewish past.

We hypothesize that a space for a middle ground between the sovereign self and the commanding community can be created for the elite synagogue leadership (rabbis, committed volunteers) and the many more Jewish individuals and their families who do not participate in synagogue life or do so only sporadically. Why do we believe so? Because the gap between these two orientations may not be as large as it is often portrayed. Conservative, Reconstructionist, Reform, and to a lesser degree, some liberal Orthodox rabbis, are exposed to constructivist interpretations of the Jewish religious tradition in their training and bring those interpretations to their congregations. For example, Conservative, Reconstructionist and Reform Torah commentaries and prayer books reflect the belief that Torah and Jewish religious practice are humanly constructed. These prayer books also consciously offer variety and options, reflecting the idea that there is not a single, authoritative way to pray.

What differentiates these rabbis is their behaviors but not their beliefs. They and their volunteer leaders have chosen to accept a more coherent, consistent pattern of behavior, rooted in traditional Jewish practice and belief, that allows for the creation of a community of shared values and practice. But they are clearly not without contemporary cultural sensibilities. As we have seen from the internal debates within each movement and the way that they publicly present their liturgies and interpretation of the Jewish tradition, they also selectively assert the values of the sovereign self.

On the other hand, many American Jews, while autonomous in their behaviors, are more open to constructing a belief system that respects the desire for community. They have no qualms about customizing their Jewish practices to suit their individual needs and tastes. But, as Ammerman suggests, they may also be open to guidance from the voice of tradition. Miles (1997) offers some proof for this openness based on many conversations that he had while promoting one of his books. He encountered a widespread acceptance of the proposition that doubt and religious faith are compatible, a proposition that was new for many people that he interviewed. Interviewees expressed a willingness to doubt fundamental beliefs but within the context of a faith community. In speculating on the origins of the willingness to doubt religion, Miles asks, "Are the doubts mainly doubts about God? Or is society in question and religion one of the proposed answers, notwithstanding the difficulty of belief?" He concludes that it is the failed promise of secular alternatives to religion that is stimulating a cautious, critical openness toward religious belief.

In a similar vein, Ammerman (p. 366) observes,

> To invoke the postmodernist paradigm is to suggest that the realities of the modern situation are still with us, but their limits are recognized and overcome. Reason, specialization, and pluralism are not likely to go away, but we are beginning to recognize that what looked solidly modern has all sorts of cracks and crevices in which new forms of life are emerging, and old, unnoticed ones have been thriving all along.

The well-documented openness to "spirituality" is a partial reflection of the willingness to listen anew to more traditional sources of wisdom.

In summary, it is our hypothesis that many American Jews, both those heavily involved in Jewish life and those episodically involved, have absorbed the ethic of the sovereign self. What distinguishes the religious elite from other Jews is that they have voluntarily chosen to accept some measure of the authority of the religious tradition in the name of community, as opposed to the non-elite, who reject authority *a priori*, but may be open to learning from the tradition. While unwilling to adopt wholesale a pattern of pre-defined behavior, they are willing to experiment both with innovative and traditional Jewish practice. They are even willing to become a part of a community that has articulated norms and values provided that it first affirms "where they are."

If synagogue leaders better understand the temperament of most American Jews, and can convey information and create institutions that reflect this understanding, they may find a more receptive audience than they expect. The gap between the pulpit and the pew may therefore not be as great as it first appears. Each denomination will need to carve out a "third way" that has internal integrity, but the idea of creating a "third way" at least offers an option of bridging the differences between the commanding community and the sovereign self.

Conclusion: Creating a "Third Way" Congregation"

Carroll and Roof (2002), based on their study of twenty congregations (including several synagogues) and two campus ministries, have created a typology of congregations that is helpful in thinking about creating a "third way" for the synagogue world. They speak of three different kinds of congregations: the inherited congregation, the generation specific congregation and the blended congregation. The inherited congregation adapts little to contemporary culture and instead seeks, ". . . .to conserve that which they have inherited from their denominational tradition, their own congregation's experience, and their respective ethnic heritage" (Carroll and Roof, p. 137). In our terms, it is a fairly pure example of the commanding community orientation. The generation specific congregation stands at the opposite pole of the spectrum. It is consciously designed to appeal to the needs of a particular generation, typically those that are younger, and is "posttraditional" in that it minimizes the influence of inherited tradition (Carroll and Roof, p. 173) and maximizes its engagement with contemporary culture. We would describe this as a collection of sovereign selves.

Yet, these researchers (Carroll and Roof, p. 168) have also identified what they describe as "blended congregations."

A blended congregation is not easily pulled off in any way that is totally satisfactory to all participants. It involves a precarious stance that both values the inherited traditions of faith while seeking to adapt traditional practices and programs in sensitivity to contemporary culture. The result is a negotiated and often fragile normative order. It is not surprising that a blended congregation is likely to experience tension and conflict over these efforts to be generationally and culturally sensitive while at the same time giving expression to the traditions of the faith community.

The blended congregation is best suited to our era, where community and individualism and obligation and autonomy, need strategies for coexistence. It is a dynamic model, with ongoing negotiation between a religion that values tradition and a contemporary society that prizes innovation. The synagogue that consciously strives to be a "blended" or "third way" congregation understands that we are living in a transitional era that requires both the ability to experiment and the capacity to maintain traditions.

Aron (2002, pp. 9–10) uses different terminology to describe these kinds of congregations, calling them "self-renewing" congregations. She suggests that there are four characteristics of "self-renewing" congregations that require paradoxical thinking and action. They are:

- Thinking back and thinking ahead: being both reflective and proactive
- Enabling leaders to follow, and followers to lead; practicing collaborative leadership
- Seeing both the forest and the trees; creating community among diverse individuals
- Honoring the past while anticipating the future; balancing tradition and change.

It is this kind of paradoxical thinking that is required for enabling congregations to live in a period of *bein ha-sh'mashot*, between the twilight of one era and the beginning of another. This approach allows for a "both-and" approach to Jewish life instead of an "either-or" orientation, which is often characteristic of discussions about strategies for enhancing Jewish life. And, the Jewish tradition often allows for the retention of paradoxical beliefs. (For example, while classical Jewish liturgy and theology imagine a transcendent God, they are also permeated with images and language that reflect a belief in God's immanence.) Holding onto two concepts at opposite ends of a spectrum of belief is an authentically Jewish way of thinking.

The thesis of this paper has been that there is a tension between the commanding community worldview of the synagogue and the sovereign self worldview of many American Jews. The former can lead to a rigid expression of Judaism, while the risk of the latter is that it undercuts the creation of communities of shared Jewish meaning. The primary challenge that synagogues face today is to navigate a path between these two extremes and create a "third way" that allows for the existence of a coherent community that also cherishes individual expression.

Toward an Action Agenda: Assumptions for a "Third Way" Congregation

As is often the case, the description of a situation is significantly easier than the prescription of it. This is especially true of synagogues because they are very local institutions that also operate within a denominational context. Congregational history and tradition, professional and volunteer leadership and denominational needs all express themselves in a unique way within each congregation. Therefore, there is no single plan available to synagogues to guide them through becoming a "third way" congregation. However, we can lay out some assumptions that they may use in constructing a congregation that inhabits the space between the commanding community and the sovereign self. These assumptions must inform all aspects of congregational life, from staffing patterns to organizational models. They directly or indirectly rest on the research cited in the paper. However, they require further discussion, application and refinement. It is hoped that this paper will stimulate this process.

These assumptions for creating a "third way" congregation fall into the following categories: Community Building, Governance, Networking and Collaboration, Organizational Learning and Renewal and Innovation in Prayer and Ritual. Following this section, the reader will find comments on the challenges of innovating in congregations and a suggested policy study agenda based on the issues raised in the paper.

Community Building

- **While synagogues should clearly articulate the religious expectations of their members, they should also explain with equal clarity the values underlying these expectations.** Tightly framed behavioral norms or expectations allow scant room for individual negotiation. The risk in articulating them is that they convey a "take it or leave it" perception. We are not suggesting that synagogues should function without boundaries. However, they should recognize that as a starting point, individuals can more easily embrace value statements even if they are not at the moment able to commit to particular boundary-defining practices as envisioned by the congregation. This approach allows synagogues to maintain their religious institutional integrity, makes room for individuals to enter the synagogue in terms of their current beliefs and also enables them to grow spiritually in terms of their practice.

- **Synagogues should consciously think of themselves as multigenerational institutions.** People undergo spiritual, emotional, cognitive and physical developmental changes throughout their lives. What suits them at one stage of life will not necessarily appeal to them at another stage, as is apparent in a multigenerational institution like a synagogue. This awareness should be reflected in all aspects of the congregation, including programs, dues structures and the ability of staff to relate to members regardless of age or stage of life. This does not mean that synagogues should try to be "all things to all people." Rather, it means that through creative partnerships with other institutions and multigenerational representation at all levels of synagogue leadership, synagogues can fashion and serve a multigenerational community.

- **In a related vein, synagogues should embrace diversity.** In addition to being diverse from a generational perspective, synagogues are comprised of singles, interfaith families, gays and lesbians, single parents, empty nesters, bi-racial families—as well as two-parent families. This diversity should be reflected in the life of the congregation and should be evident in the kinds of programming made available to members, the marketing of these programs and the composition of the board and committees.

- **Synagogues should recognize that for many people today, the decision to become a member is a process.** Clearly, there are still some people who will automatically become synagogue members and will remain members throughout their lives. However, there are many others who view synagogue membership as any other commodity. They will buy it only when they need it. This is a reality that needs to be institutionalized instead of lamented. What kind of membership model is needed in this kind of environment?

  For starters, synagogues would abolish the terms "affiliated" and "unaffiliated" from their vocabulary. These terms send the wrong message about the values prized by a synagogue. What does "affiliation" really mean? It means that someone pays dues to a synagogue, suggesting that synagogues measure their "bottom line" in the way that corporations do—by how much money they accrue. The word affiliation says nothing about the level of involvement of those who pay synagogue dues. Instead of maintaining a uniform category like "affiliation," synagogues might offer different categories of involvement or participation, with different fee structures. Thus, synagogues could educate people into the idea of joining a participatory community, whose message is that while we need money to run our institutions, what we ultimately value is membership involvement.

- **Synagogues need to create more small group experiences.** Jewish community today is not built in cathedral-type experiences. Rather, it is developed in small groups, in which participants have the opportunity to explore the subjective dimensions of their Jewish identity. This is not to suggest that large-scale experiences have no place anymore in a congregation. To the contrary, they can be very powerful (consider the community feeling around the time of *yom kippur neilah*). However, the success of *havurot*, journey and spiritual biography groups, "library" *minyanim* and other intimate group experiences attests to the appeal and desirability of small group experiences.

- **Synagogues should develop more effective ways of communicating and marketing to members and to non-members that may be potentially interested in them.** There are several implications in this recommendation. Meaningful communication is a two-way street, a process that involves both getting information to people and listening and responding to their reactions. Yet, for many, trying to communicate with a synagogue is more like driving down a dead-end road. Often, calls to synagogues are not returned in a timely fashion, information about programs and services is not available, follow-up is limited—there is no appreciation for the concept of "customer service" and that is frustrating for sophisticated congregants who expect better because they must deliver high quality services in their own professional lives. Moreover, synagogues typically do not evaluate their professionals or programs and thereby deprive themselves of feedback that could help them improve their staff and increase the relevance of programs and services.

Additionally, this recommendation means that synagogues need to learn how to use different media for communicating to differentiated target audiences. Advertising, which relates to how synagogues get information to people, is equally important. Ask yourself, how many hours a year does the average synagogue member spend inside of the synagogue? That number is probably somewhere between fifteen and twenty hours annually. Therefore, synagogues must do a much better job at getting information to its dues-paying constituents, who often do not read the synagogue mail on a regular basis. Use of the Internet, public interest stories and advertisements in the secular press, billboards, public access television and radio commercials, targeted marketing in health clubs, bookstores and other venues visited by Jewish people, one-on-one personal outreach—all of these venues need to be pursued. Doing so provides a way to reach those who pay dues and also creates awareness on the part of potential seekers and joiners.

- **Synagogues need to think creatively about how to reach their members where they spend the majority of their time and not only expect to reach them in the limited time that they spend in synagogue.** People who care about synagogues are often frustrated that lively, engaging programs that take much effort to implement are not well attended. However, we also need to look at this reality from the perspective of the individual. How hard do synagogues try to reach members when and where it is convenient for them?

As noted previously, most American Jews do not spend much time within the synagogue, nor do they spend all that much time within Jewish institutional space. Therefore, if synagogues want to reach them, they will have to get better at connecting with them in their homes and neighborhoods, in cyberspace and retail space, and at entertainment, sports and cultural venues. Through creative collaborations, they can better accomplish this goal.

Governance

- **Synagogue business models require reexamination.** Others have made this observation (Marker, 1999; Tobin, 1991) and it bears repetition. More specifically, I am suggesting that there is something dramatically wrong with a business model that invests huge amounts of capital in a facility whose worship space, which consumes a significant amount of square footage of most synagogues, is vastly underutilized except for several days each year. Large, underutilized facilities are a drag on already stressed synagogue budgets.

  Surely, we are creative enough to think of alternatives. In fact, Chabad seems to have identified a very successful model that requires much lower overhead. By moving into strip malls, they can keep their general and administrative costs at a minimum and pour capital into staff and programs. Could congregations downsize their buildings and work with Jewish Community Centers or other local facilities to meet extra-capacity services and events on the few occasions a year when they are needed? Would that enable them to pour more resources into staff and programming? These are questions that increasingly require a serious examination that may lead to fundamentally new synagogue business models.

- **Synagogue governance and staffing models also require reexamination and change.** Currently, it often seems to take an eternity to institute a new idea or program within a synagogue and synagogues often do not give enough latitude to volunteers to take responsibility for their own Jewish needs. Both of these issues need to be addressed if synagogues are to be taken more seriously by those who are Boomers and younger. In a related vein, staff needs and roles would also be ripe for congregational examination. How would the expertise of rabbis and cantors be redeployed in blended, "third way" congregations? Could executive directors function differently, allowing them to concentrate more on the day-to-day management of congregations, so that the religious and educational staff have more time to focus on existing and emerging spiritual needs of congregants? What roles could volunteers play that they typically do not at the present moment? What staff positions that do not exist need to come into being and what positions need to be eliminated? A congregation that actively and consciously seeks to be relevant to contemporary Jews while remaining faithful to its denominational and congregational past will ask these and many additional questions.

To imagine what a restructuring of roles would look like, let us examine rabbis and executive directors. Rabbis spend five or six years of study in attempting to master key aspects of the Jewish civilization. Most rabbis lack training and expertise in organizational and management skills. Yet, they are expected to function like the chief executive officer of the congregation, knowing about budgeting and fundraising, board governance and leading a complex non-profit organization. Even in the best-case scenario, rabbinical programs will be limited in the amount of time they can devote to the leadership and managerial aspects of running a congregation. Alternatively, executive directors often have skills in non-profit management, including an understanding of information technology, fiscal administration and human resource management.

Accepting these realities, perhaps the role of synagogue executive director can be enhanced to include more of the managerial functions of a synagogue so that rabbis can concentrate on the areas in which they are knowledgeable: teaching, spiritual guidance, pastoral counseling, program development and liturgical and ritual direction. A shared professional leadership model, in which the rabbi functioned as C.R.O. (Chief Religious Officer) and the executive director functioned more like the C.O.O. (Chief Operating Officer) could help congregations use their staff more effectively.[8] Clearly, rabbis will have to be involved in some of the managerial aspects of a congregation. However, their time will be better utilized (and they will find more satisfaction) if they spend less time on management and more time using their unique skill set.

While we have illustrated this suggestion by referencing the roles of rabbi and executive director, we are suggesting that every role be similarly reexamined. In this reexamination, we should remember an immutable law of successfully staffing any position: it is much more effective to play to an individual's areas of strength and expertise than to try and build up areas of deficiencies.

- **In a related vein, synagogues should seek to increase the leadership roles of volunteers within their congregations.** There are several conditions that make this a necessity. The primary reason for doing so is that synagogues are charged with helping people grow Jewishly and greater involvement is the best means toward that end.

There are very compelling secondary reasons as well. We are reaching the stage where we can begin to harvest the fruits of Jewish experiences like day schools and adult Jewish learning programs, like the Wexner Heritage Program, Me'ah and the Florence Melton Mini-School for Adults. Many adults have often taken some Jewish studies courses on an undergraduate level or have even majored in Jewish studies. Some of the graduates of these programs, with guidance and additional training, can be used creatively within the congregation to share their Jewish knowledge and passion with their peers. Additionally, the Jewish community is rich in cultural and artistic resources that can be brought into the congregation. When it comes to technology and communications, many volunteers are willing to help their congregations use their state-of-the-art knowledge to more effectively reach and teach their members.

These are just a few illustrations of how synagogues can utilize volunteers in ways that enrich the individual and the institution. By tapping into a highly sophisticated volunteer talent pool, synagogues can expand their range of programs and services. American Jews enter Jewish life through many Jewish portals: study, social action, culture, prayer, spirituality, *tzedakah*, and peoplehood. Therefore, synagogues must press more volunteers into leadership roles so that they can expand the entry points into a congregation.

Networking and Collaboration

- **Synagogues need to develop organizational partnerships with institutions within and outside of the Jewish community in order to serve successfully a diverse, multi-generational community.** I have written elsewhere about the need for synagogues to network with other institutions, allowing them to expand their ability to offer services to members through collaborations with other institutions and, at the same time, focus on areas of program and service that they are uniquely situated to provide. Given the diverse, multi-generational composition of the Jewish community today, no one synagogue can be self-sufficient so synagogues must create these partnerships. Even if it were theoretically possible for a synagogue to offer "birth to the end of life" service, there would still be a need for synagogues to network with other institutions because synagogue members use additional organizations to fulfill their Jewish needs. Collaboration is a necessity for a host of reasons.

- **Synagogues need to engage with the broader community.** Many synagogues already are part of an interfaith network, in which they practice acts of *hesed* for the community-at-large with people of other faith communities. Younger generations in particular do not like boundaries erected between their Jewish lives and other dimensions of their lives. Therefore, experiences that express a particular Jewish message but that happen in more universal settings will have special appeal to Baby Boomers and those that are younger.

Organizational Learning and Renewal

- **Synagogues should intentionally create in-house laboratories for experimentation with new forms of ritual, liturgy, and spiritual and cultural expression.** That laboratory would be a safe vehicle for determining which innovative forms of expression fit within the culture of the congregation. In a sense, there is ancient precedent for this concept (Mishneh Berakhot 5:3). In the classical rabbinic period, liturgy was more fluid. The prayer leader *(shaliah tzibbur)* had the latitude to use his creativity while leading the congregation— but within limits. If he overstepped his bounds, the congregation would silence him. The community, in this laboratory setting, would serve as the filter for accepting or rejecting innovations. Again, it would be important to involve multiple generations in this laboratory, especially younger generations. The mere presence of such an experimental venue would make an important statement about the effort to carve out this "third way."

The concept of synagogue laboratory could easily be combined with the concept of networking. A synagogue could network with a local dance company to create representations of Jewish prayer or a theater company to explore new ways to present the Torah reading or Jewish rituals. Networking would also allow a congregation that does not have the resources to dedicate to its own laboratory to collaborate with other congregations and create a community laboratory. Whatever form it may take, this concept is very important as synagogues are risk averse. Understandably, synagogue staff members are reluctant to unveil an experiment for the first time in a public setting. The synagogue laboratory for creativity creates a safe vehicle for experimentation.

- **Synagogue professional and volunteer leadership should participate in ongoing continuing education programs that help them better understand the contemporary realities of American Jewry.** For example, businesses are very concerned about how to appeal to Gen X'ers and retain them in the workplace. There are many books,[9] courses and organizations that offer excellent ideas about how to engage this generation and the synagogue community can learn much from them. While some of these continuing education programs can be offered at the national level, rabbinical schools and denominational organizations are often slow to recognize these changes. Therefore, it is important that learning about these issues occurs at the local level.

Innovation in Prayer and Ritual

- **More synagogues should undergo a serious revamping of their religious services.** Very often, based on the feeling in religious services, many synagogues could be called the Temple of Gloom. The litany of complaints about services is well known: too long, too boring, too stiff, too joyless, etc. On a positive note, there are many exciting efforts underway to change that feeling, from Carlebach-style *minyanim* to the formation of synagogue orchestras that play more vibrant compositions of Jewish liturgy. Our sages noted (Shabbat 30b), "God's spirit does not rest upon an atmosphere of gloom . . . but through the joy of the performance of a *mitzvah*" and we can take our cue from them. The challenge is to provide enough diversity of prayer services to appeal to different spiritual needs. With the help of talented volunteers, that challenge can be met.

- **Synagogues should be willing to work with the trend to privatize and customize life cycle events, including bar and bat mitzvah celebrations.** Life cycle events are places where the worldviews of the commanding community and the sovereign self often conflict. Classically speaking, there is no such thing as a private life cycle celebration. In Judaism, we celebrate as a community, with fixed liturgical scripts, or at least with certain elements that are non-negotiable. Yet, the desire to privatize and customize life cycle celebrations is one of the hallmarks of contemporary society. People often believe that a personal celebration is "their celebration" and that they should be able to invite or exclude whomever they wish and tailor it to their tastes. Ask congregational rabbis about the number of conversations they have had with b'nai mitzvah parents or with couples about to be married as to why they must include certain parts of a service or why they cannot add to them in the way they wish. These are very difficult and frustrating conversations for each side, as each side brings different assumptions and values about the meaning of a life cycle event to the celebratory table.

Specifically, this values clash is a problem with congregations that have a large number of *b'nai mitzvah* each year. The group of "regulars" often feels that there is too much attention on the bar or bat mitzvah, while the bar or bat mitzvah family feels that there is not enough focus on its child and not enough places in the service for family members and friends. (This situation does not arise when the bar or bat mitzvah family is a part of the regular crowd.) Often, what happens is a compromise, where both sides feel that their spiritual needs are unmet. The regulars really do not want to hear another bar or bat mitzvah speech about how unique a child's athletic prowess is and the family does not want to give up an *aliyah* for a regular attendee or to have to feed so many people that are not their invited guests.

Why create compromises that leave everyone dissatisfied and have no lasting effect on promoting the values for which the synagogue stands? Advocate, argue and try to persuade families celebrating life cycle events to do so in the ongoing flow of the congregation. However, in cases of serious conflicting values, it might be preferable to have a separate bar or bat mitzvah celebration and also to offer services for the regulars in a different space. Indeed, some Reform congregations are increasingly working their way into this paradigm by trying to cultivate a regular Shabbat morning group that studies Torah and prays and is not connected to the bar or bat mitzvah service. Working with individuals and families in this way to accommodate people's choices around life cycle events can be good for them and for the congregation.

Carroll and Roof (p. 171) offer some insights on blended congregations that are sobering yet hopeful. On their analysis of three blended congregations, they write,

> these . . . congregations show that efforts to blend traditional practice and con temporary culture are neither impossible nor easy. It is difficult to maintain the integrity of the traditions and ensure, at the same time, that they are culturally current. Such living traditions . . . always involve continuing argument about what it means to live by them. They are always in the process of negotiation and renegotiation. The blended congregation requires hard work on the part of both leaders and followers to maintain its often-precarious normative order.

By transforming traditions in a sensitive, conscious and continuous manner, congregations may find that "third way" through the worldviews of the commanding community and the sovereign self.

The Complexities of Innovation for Synagogues

Innovation, whether in the for-profit or the non-profit sector, is always a challenge. In the religious sector, this challenge is exponentially greater. Religious institutions are the guardians of traditions that have withstood the test of time and are therefore understandably resistant to innovations. When they adopt them, they typically do so after a lengthy process. After all, why should a religion that has been in "business" for about four thousand years (in the case of Judaism) bow to the latest fad? This is a very legitimate question and those who argue for innovation must bear the burden of answering it.

Gary Hamel, internationally renowned strategist on helping companies renew their core businesses, makes the case for continuous innovation in business, especially in downward economic times. We summarize some of his observations because they merit our consideration when thinking about synagogues. Of course, it is necessary to make the leap from a business to a synagogue when considering his words. Hamel (2002) argues that:

1. Things that cannot go on forever do not go on forever. The example that he uses is that the positive and negative forces that fueled the economic boom of the 1990s have ended. We can enjoy a long run of a trend, but should prepare for the time when we can no longer ride that wave. **Application:** the trend of high percentages of individuals automatically joining a synagogue is over for most American Jews and while we may lament it we also need to work proactively with this reality.

2. Going back to the basics alone is not enough to spark renewed growth. Rather, businesses have to bring something new and exciting to their customers. A radical rethinking of the "basics" is necessary in today's environment. **Application:** focusing on the "basics" of prayer, celebration and learning as they have typically been offered will not in themselves create a Jewish spiritual renaissance. By analogy, Starbucks did not invent coffee. But, while ensuring a high-quality product, it reinvented the experience of drinking coffee.

3. Most organizations are built for perpetuation and not innovation. The virtues of control, hierarchy, efficiency, quality and replication brought much economic good in a stable world. "In a discontinuous world, we need to turn down the dial a bit on perpetuation and turn up the dial a bit on innovation." This statement requires no commentary for the synagogue!

4. Variety is positive for an organization. An obsession with "alignment" will drive innovative ideas and people out of an

organization. **Application:** synagogues should honor the diversity of their members by utilizing it as an asset.

5. New people bring in new ideas. An organization that relies upon new ideas only coming from the "top" will not innovate. Synagogues need to examine why they often fail to find ways to capture the interests of exceptionally talented volunteers who make time for volunteer commitments outside of the synagogue but shun synagogue involvement.

6. Companies should think of themselves as a portfolio of tangible and intangible assets and competencies and not as a business. How a company organizes and concentrates its assets will determine its ability to grow by adopting new business models. **Application:** synagogues should think about the portfolio of skills found within their professional staff and volunteer leadership and deploy them to a fuller extent through collaborative teamwork and ongoing professional training.

7. The large industrial organization deserves respect because of the prosperity and efficiency that it created. As it took time to create that business model, it will take time and measured steps to develop innovative business models. This is especially true for synagogues which are conservative by nature.

As we see, we may draw the analogy between Judaism and a business, keeping in mind that our "bottom line" is different. Our business is to provide the Jewish community with a vision of perfecting the world through a program of values, reflecting our understanding of God's will, that find action through commandments (*mitzvot*). Others will formulate our business differently, but regardless of how they do so, like a business, we have a mission; we have a vision of what we would like the world to look like and we have a series of tactics (*mitzvot*) that we pursue in attempting to attain this vision. How has our business been doing lately? Not very well by all accounts! A large percentage of people who identify as "secular,"[10] report that our institutions lack meaning and are increasingly seeking spiritual meaning outside of synagogues. These observations are rightfully disconcerting to those who care about synagogues, because of our belief that the religious core of the Jewish civilization, currently embodied in and symbolized by the synagogue, has contributed greatly to the welfare of the Jewish people and to all of humanity.

As Hamel notes, when businesses are threatened, some leaders want to return to the basics and adopt a "circle the wagons" mentality. We are witnessing the same reaction in many corners of the synagogue. Exacerbated by economic woes and statistics that paint a picture of erosion, new voices and ideas often find a tenuous place inside synagogues. While the temptation to keep doing essentially more of the same of old thing with greater vigor is understandable, it is a guaranteed recipe for continued decline. Without discarding our "core businesses," we need a radical rethinking of how to increase the relevance and meaning of Judaism through the synagogue. The rethinking must be "radical" in the sense of getting at the root structures, processes and programs of the synagogue. Contemporary society, with its many blessings and problems, has thrust this challenge upon us. Fundamental changes have been happening in society and synagogues need to start paying closer attention to them. There is abundant expertise available to manage a change process that can help us better adapt to the powerful currents of individualism. What we seem to lack is an understanding of the critical need to innovate and genuinely embrace experimentation while still honoring our heritage.

Some will be intimidated by the word "radical" in thinking of transforming the Judaism of the synagogue. Here is what Hamel (2002) says about those who fear it in the business world.

> "Does the word 'radical' still make you uncomfortable? Get over it. Today's world is a tough place. It's going to remain a tough place for the foreseeable future. You can wallow in timidity, or you can realize that the case for radical innovation is stronger than it has ever been, because there are fewer options than there have ever been. My question to anybody who's still skeptical is this: What other choice do you have? What's your Plan B?"

While the tone of these comments may be harsh, the substance is hard to ignore. We have a choice either to maintain commanding synagogue communities, knowing that the results will be further decline, or to make more room for the many sovereign selves who feel disenfranchised with the synagogue world, and enrich their lives and ours.

Personal Postscript

At the end of his book on synagogues, Schwarz (2000) addresses a common misperception about "unaffiliated Jews." Often, Jewish leaders assume that those who do not join or participate in Jewish religious life lack interest in Judaism. Schwarz's research leads him to a different conclusion.

> *For every one of the people whose spiritual journeys we have chroni-*
> *cled in this book, there are thousands of Jews whose journeys do not*
> *end up in a synagogue. This is not because they do not find syna-*
> *gogues on their journeys; they do. But most synagogues are deaf to the*
> *needs of this generation. Synagogues want the new American Jew to*
> *join their membership rolls on the synagogues' terms. Increasing*
> *numbers are not interested . . . The tragedy is that the unaffiliated,*
> *whom the sociologists might dismiss as "dropouts," are in fact seekers*
> *. . . Most synagogues have failed to engage these Jews (pp. 260–261).*

Perhaps an even greater sorrow is that some of these Jews will become involved with other religions, either through intermarriage or through formal conversion (Wertheimer, 1996; Mayer, Kosmin and Keysar, 2001). While most Jews do not undergo formal conversion, many quietly fade out of the organized Jewish community, abandon Jewish behaviors and relinquish Jewish sensitivities. I wrote this paper because I am a believer in the power of synagogues to make the lives of Jews, and the many individual and family forms that they come in today, better. I want to see synagogues have greater success in helping individual Jews experience the beauty of belonging to a community that endows them with transcendent meaning. More vibrant synagogues will mean a more dynamic Jewish community.

For several decades, two parallel discussions about synagogues have occurred with frequency. One discussion relates to the disappointments that synagogue leaders have about the participation levels of their congregants and frustrations over the number of people who no longer see the value even in paying dues to a congregation. The other discussion is about the dissatisfaction that synagogue members and non-members often feel about the religion of the synagogue. In order to maintain a vibrant Jewish religious community, these two discussions need to intersect with and enrich one another. Open, direct and empathetic dialogue around them is critical if synagogues are to achieve better success rates in shaping the attitudes, values and ideas of contemporary American Jews and their families. At this moment in Jewish history, defining categories of Jewish authenticity too tightly is as equally risky as not defining them at all.

Needed: A Policy Research Study

Whether there is merit to my thesis of using the conceptual lenses of the commanding community and the sovereign self to understand some of the challenges that synagogues face and my preliminary suggestions about a "third way" as an option to meet these challenges, ideally requires a systematic, scientifically sound policy study. A proposed policy research agenda would examine questions including:

1. Do rabbis and synagogue volunteer leaders operate within different frameworks for decision-making (that is, rabbis representing the commanding community and volunteer leaders representing the sovereign self)?
2. How does this difference in orientation influence issues related to change and innovation within congregations?
3. Do synagogue professional and volunteer leaders operate within different frameworks for authority and decision-making from Jews that are uninvolved in synagogue life?
4. What approaches are likely to increase participation in synagogue life with regard to Boomers, Gen X'ers and Millenials?
5. What recommendations for a congregational setting can be made to increase understanding and communications among rabbis, congregants and potential members around change-related issues and how can change-related processes be maximized within congregations?
6. What recommendations can be made to maximize synagogue change efforts at the national level?
7. What recommendations can be made with regard to rabbinic training and professional development to help facilitate change efforts?
8. What recommendations can be made with regard to volunteer training and development to help facilitate change efforts?

To date, no such study using the conceptual lenses of the commanding community and the sovereign self has been conducted. The goal of such a study would be to further stimulate the creation of this "third way" between these differing orientations, to create a common space between these two frameworks in which rabbis and congregants can respectfully dialogue and work through issues of change and innovation, while retaining their different perspectives. With such a study in the fundamental differences in orientation to the synagogue, synagogue change efforts will be much more fruitful because they will identify root issues and differing perspectives and offer solutions to use these differences creatively and constructively with the support of empirical findings.

Endnotes

* When the original version of this paper was presented at the Re-envisioning the Synagogue Conference in November 2003, Rabbis Saul Berman and Gordon Tucker were the discussants whose insightful critiques were the basis for important revisions that appear in this version of the paper. While their specific comments are not reproduced in this volume, some of their ideas find resonance here and we are most grateful to them.

** Rabbi David Gordis and Rabbi Zachary Heller, Director and Associate Director respectively of the National Center for Jewish Policy Studies (successor to the Wilstein Institute), have again provided an outstanding discussion forum for critical issues in contemporary Jewish life. David Gordis critiqued several earlier versions of this paper and I thank him for his customary insightful improvements. Zachary Heller is a patient, tireless editor whose broad knowledge of Jewish life and skillful pen greatly enhanced each of the many iterations of this paper. I have learned much from both of these teachers and have acquired friends in the process. My heartfelt appreciation to others who read parts of many drafts or entire manuscripts, and to Terri, Avi and Tamar Krivosha-Herring for their patience in listening to my ceaseless discussion.]

1. Gordis used this phrase in a conference on "Re-envisioning the Synagogue" sponsored by the Wilstein Institute for Jewish Policy Studies and STAR (Synagogues: Transformation and Renewal), on November 24, 2003, in Boston.

2. My thanks to Rabbi Strassfeld for sharing his Rosh ha-Shanah sermon delivered in 5764, in which he used this phrase.

3. See, for example, *Reform Judaism*, Spring 1999, 27 (3) and the *CCAR Journal*, Winter 2000.

4. We do not mean to imply that the Reconstructionist Movement is the only one to experience rabbi-lay tensions. In fact, we credit them for directly dealing with this issue. We use this example merely to illustrate that all religious movements are experiencing the challenges of navigating the differing orientations of the commanding community and the sovereign self.

5. We restrict our observations on Orthodoxy to American Orthodox Judaism, although similar comments could be made about Israeli Orthodox Judaism.

6. Note: we are not suggesting that all members of the Veteran generation were automatically loyal toward existing Jewish institutions and syna-gogues. Those who opted out often did so with a vengeance, creating "Yom Kippur Balls" as a sign of their disdain for synagogue Judaism and rabbinic authority. Some of their offspring appear ready to resume a spiritual search that their ancestors had discarded, reminding us to be careful about excluding people from the community.

7. Students in most programs must now take required field internships and often study in *hevruta* in preparation for class, but the hierarchi-cal classroom model is still influential in rabbinical school programs.

8. The author would like to thank Sandy Cardin, Executive Director of the Charles and Lynn Schusterman Family Foundation, for this idea.

9. See, for example, Karen Ritchie's *Marketing to Generation X*, Lynn C. Lancaster and David Stillman's *When Generations Collide*.

10. As noted by Mayer, Kosmin and Keysar (2001), "secular" Jews often report that they believe in God, miracles, pray and join synagogues, so synagogues should not quickly dismiss them. They may reject the label of "religious" because of the negative connotations it has for them.

References

Arnow, D. (1994). Jewish identity: A psychologist's view. *Agenda. Jewish Education*, (4), 4–6.

Aron, I. (2002). *The self-renewing organization: how ideas from the field of organizational development can revitalize Jewish institutions*. [Report]. Jerusalem: Department of Jewish-Zionist Education of the Jewish Agency.

Aron, I.(2002). *The self-renewing congregation. Organizational strategies for revitalizing congregational life*. Woodstock, VT: Jewish Lights Pub-lishing.

Ammerman, Nancy (2000), "Conservative Jews within the Landscape of American Religion," in *Jews in the center. Conservative synagogues and their members*, Jack Wertheimer (Ed.), Rutgers University Press, New Brunswick, N.J.

Anderson, W. (1990). *Reality isn't what it used to be: theatrical politics, ready-to-wear religion, global myths, prmitive chic, and other wonders of the postmodern world*. San Francisco, Harper.

Anderson, W. (1995). *The truth about the truth. De-confusing and re-con-structing the postmodern world*. New York, Tarcher/Putnam.

Anderson, W. (1997). *The future of the self. Exploring the post-identity soci-ety*. New York, Tarcher/Putnam.

Bellah, R. (1985). *Habits of the heart. Individualism and commitment in American life*.

Berkofsky, J. (2002, December 24). From celluloid to synagogue: do film fests build Jewish identity [online]? *Jewish Telegraphic Agency*. Available: http://www.jta.org/page_view_story.asp?intarticleid=12230 &intcategoryid=5. (January 2003).

Blanchard, T. (2002). How to think about being Jewish in the 21st century: a new model of Jewish identity construction. *Journal of Jewish communal service, 79*(1), 37–45.

Carroll, J. and Roof, W. (2002). *Bridging divided worlds. Generational cultures in congregations.* San Francisco, John Wiley.

Cohen, S.(1998). *Religious stability and ethnic decline: emerging patterns of Jewish identity in the United States* (Report). New York: The Jewish Community Centers Association.

Cohen, S. and Eisen, A. (1998). *The Jew within. Self, community and commitment among the variety of moderately affiliated.* Boston, MA: The Susan and David Wilstein Institute of Jewish Policy Studies.

Ephross, P. (2002, November 21). Film about gay Orthodox Jews makes waves as it makes rounds [online]. *Jewish Telegraphic Agency*. Available: http://www.jta.org/page_view_story.asp?intarticleid=10569 &intcategoryid=5. (December 2002).

Decter, A. (2001, June). New Vistas on Jewish History and Culture. Sh'ma: A Journal of Jewish Responsibility [online]. Available: *http://www.shma.com/jun01/decter.htm.* (January 2003).

Green, A. (1994, December). Judaism for the Post-Modern Era. The Samuel H. Goldenson Lecture. Delivered at the Hebrew Union College-Jewish Institute of Religion, Cincinnati, Ohio.

Greenberg, Y. (1991, June). Freedom, Power, Affluence. The Hilary Pryer and Charles Berg Memorial Lecture. Delivered at the B'nai Brith Center in Sydney, Australia.

Hamel, G. (2002, December). Innovation now [online]. FastCompany. Available: *http://www.fastcompany.com/online/65/innovation.html.* (January 2003).

Herring, H. and Shrage, B. (2001). *Jewish networking. Linking people, institutions, community.* Boston, MA: The Susan and David Wilstein Institute of Jewish Policy Studies.

Herring, H. (2000). The Conservative movement: whither or wither? *Conservative* Judaism, 52(3), 3–21.

Hoffman, L. (2002). *BJ: a model for a revitalized synagogue life.* [Report]. New York: Congregation B'nai Jeshurun and Synagogue2000.

Horowitz, Bethamie (1999). "Indicators of Jewish identity. Developing a conceptual framework for understanding American Jewry." [Paper] Delivered to the Mandel Foundation, New York City.

Horowitz, B. (2000). *Connections and journeys: assessing critical opportunities for enhancing Jewish identity.* [Report]. New York: UJA-Federation of New York.

Israel, S. (2001, September 16). American Jewish public activity—identity, demography, and the institutional challenge [online]. Available: *http://www.jcpa.org/jl/vp462.htm*. (November 2003).

Kadushin, Kelner and Saxe (2000). *Being a Jewish teenager in America: trying to make it*. December 2000. [Report]. Boston: Cohen Center for Modern Jewish Studies/Brandeis University.

Kosmin, Barry, (2000), "Coming of Age in the Conservative Synagogue: The Bar/Bat Mitzvah Class of 5755" in *Jews in the center. Conservative synagogues and their members*, Jack Wertheimer (Ed.), Rutgers University Press: New Brunswick, New Jersey.

Leffert, N. and Herring, H. (1998). *Shema: listening to Jewish youth* (Report). Search Institute: Minneapolis, MN.

Mayer, E., Kosmin, B. and Keysar, A. (2001). *American Jewish Identity Survey 2001. The religious and the secular*. [Report]. New York: Center for Jewish Studies, the Graduate Center for the City University of New York.

Marker, R. (1999). Beyond Renewal: A Call for Transformation. *Sh'ma*, 30 (564), 1–3.

Margolis, P. (2001). Postmodern American Judaism: origins and symptoms. *CCAR Journal*, 47(2), 35–50.

Miles, J. (1997, December 7). Faith is an option. Religion makes a comeback. (Belief to follow) [online]. The New York Times Magazine. Available: http://query.nytimes.com/search/restricted/article?res= F50911F73D590C748CDDAB0994. (March 2003).

The rabbi-congregation relationship: a vision for the 21st century (2001). Philadelphia: The Reconstructionist Commission on the Role of the Rabbi.

Roof, W. (1999). *Spiritual marketplace. Baby boomers and the remaking of American religion*. Princeton, New Jersey: Princeton University Press.

Sacks, J. (2003) *The dignity of difference. How to avoid the clash of civilizations* (revised). New York: Continuum.

Sales, A. (1996). *Jewish youth databook. Research on adolescence and its implications for Jewish teen programs*. (Report). Boston: Cohen Center for Modern Jewish Studies/Brandeis University.

Sarna, J. (1995). *A great awakening. The transformation that shaped twentieth century American Judaism and its implications for today*. New York: Council for Initiatives in Jewish Education.

Sax, L. (2002). *America's Jewish freshman. Current characteristics and recent trends among students entering college*. (Report). Los Angeles: Higher Education Research Institute/University of California.

Schwarz, S. (2000). *Finding a spiritual home. How a generation of Jews can transform the American synagogue*. San Francisco, CA: Jossey-Bass.

Shapiro, M. (2001, June). Qeri'at ha-Torah by Women: a halakhic analysis [online]. The Edah Journal. Available: *http://www.edah.org/backend/JournalArticle/1_2_shapiro.pdf*. (January 2003).

Siegel, R. (2002). *Report on the future of Jewish culture in America*. (Report). New York: The National Foundation for Jewish Culture.

Synagogue2000. The research behind synagogue 2000. Available: *http://www.synagogue2000.org/Information.html*. (February 17, 2002)

Tobin, G. (1991, August). Will the synagogue survive? *Moment Magazine*, volume #15, 44–49.

Tobin, G. (2002). *A study of Jewish culture in the Bay area* (Report). San Francisco: The Institute for Jewish and Community Research.

Wertheimer, J. (1996). *Conservative synagogues and their members. Highlights of the North American survey of 1995–96.* (Report). New York: The Jewish Theological Seminary.

Wertheimer, J. (1997). *Jewish identity and religious commitment. The North American Study of Conservative synagogues and their members, 1995–96.* (Report). New York: The Jewish Theological Seminary.

Zemke, R., Raines, C. and Filipczak, B. (2000). *Generations at work. Managing the clash of veterans, boomers, xers and nexters in your workplace.* New York: Amacon.

RE-ENVISIONING THE
AMERICAN SYNAGOGUE

Richard A. Marker

Riv-Ellen Prell

Michael Hammer

Morris Allen

THE CHALLENGE OF RENAISSANCE

Richard A. Marker

I t was a remarkable meeting of "world religious leaders" in Seville, Spain. We were Buddhist, Hindu, Moslem, Christian and Jewish—gathered in a relatively intimate setting to discuss and understand our respective traditions' views of "Hostility and Hospitality—The View of the Other."

It wasn't initially clear why one of the Buddhists and one of the Moslems seemed so drawn to the Jewish caucus. Then we learned that the head of one of the leading Zen Centers in the United States was born Jewish and, amid her mid-life searching, discovered meaning in the Buddhist Traditions. Her curiosity, though, stemmed not from any apparent ambivalence about the religion of her adulthood but from the choices of her sons. Living in Tokyo as young adults, perhaps feeling the sense of disconnect so typical of ex-pats, they entered a synagogue and found meaning. Now they are fully observant Orthodox Jews living in the States. Their born-Jewish Buddhist mother was trying to understand the alien tradition her own children have chosen.

The Imam's story had its own twist. Born in Paris to a North African Jewish family, as an adolescent he was seeking answers to life's mysteries. His first stop was his synagogue. The answers—or perhaps lack of them—so turned him off that he went next to a mosque. There, a welcoming and patient Imam engaged him sufficiently that he converted to Islam and has now become one of Europe's leading Imams. His world-view and politics are sympathetic to those of the Jewish community, but one must ask what might have happened had his first stop been more satisfactory.

I have spoken and written about synagogue change for some years. I have been both a commentator on and advocate for a rethinking of the role of the synagogue in the 21st Century. Yet these two closely connected anecdotes underscored for me the historic centrality of the synagogue as the primary gateway to Jewish life. For most, it is an open door through which one passes freely—if infrequently—as one needs its services during a lifetime of passages and holidays. For some, these portals open to a wonderful world of satisfaction, fulfillment, and inclusion. But for far too many Jews, those gates seem impenetrable or entrapping, and those inside inscrutable and judgmental, making the visitor feel as an outsider even after daring to enter. The synagogue is filled with symbol and represents the institutionalization of Jewish memory and meaning. And as with all symbols, it can be filled with positive and negative connotation.

It is important, of course, to remember that the synagogue as an institution has changed profoundly and regularly over time. Its role and style was surely different in Babylonia of the first exile, in the Hellenistic and Roman diasporas, in the far flung reaches of the Islamic hegemony and the "Golden Age of Spain," in the Franco-German centers of Ashkenazic culture, the Austria-Hungarian Empire, the East European shtetls, the post Emancipation West, and post World War II America. While many of the words and traditions of the synagogues may be recognizable across borders and over the ages, the aesthetic, the style, the leadership, the power and governance structures, and the role within the communities varied greatly. Often forgotten in the discussion of the contemporary synagogue is that in its post World War II form, the suburban destination full-service institution, is in its way a radical departure from the synagogues of much of history. In re-examining the synagogue's role, functions, and styles, we are only continuing a 2500-year process.

This historic apologia is very relevant to our challenge. The chorus of those advocating a renaissance or transformation of the American synagogue has grown quite loud. And the number of alternatives—post denominational, multi-denominational, independent, invitational synagogues and services—are staggering. Some of these emphasize spirituality; some community building and intimacy; some challenge the boundaries of *halachah*—while struggling to remain within; some are committed to inclusiveness with *halachah* being quite irrelevant. Surely these innovations tell us that the post World War II model has run its course. People want something different because the circumstances that yielded the model of the second half of the 20th century synagogue are no longer sufficient to inspire and engage generations that have a different ethos and aesthetic.

While I have analyzed these changes in more detail in other settings, suffice it to say here that the all-encompassing "birth to death" full service institution has too often resulted in mediocrity in most things rather than an exciting and caring Jewish community. A synagogue that is perceived to be a holy place for special occasions becomes an institution too easily ignored during the everyday. As synagogues are perceived as places of refuge and solace, places for rites of passage or for transmission of token knowledge to the next generation, they lose their power to speak to the normal mysticism of Jewish life and the integrative power of the Jewish tradition to bridge the sacred and the secular.

Yet every one of us who has addressed the subject of synagogue transformation has discovered a deep resistance to change. There are, too be sure, some excellent reasons for that resistance: After all, some synagogues really are doing many things well, and some are truly innovators. Moreover, there are many congregants who are happy and like the way things are. Very often the response to my analysis has been: "what you say is absolutely correct, but not here. We like it here." Those who do like their synagogue are much more likely to attend and to, legitimately, protect their turf. Those of us who advocate change must honor and respect those whose spiritual, emotional, educational, or communal needs are being met by the synagogues they attend. Change must not disenfranchise the satisfied to engage the dissatisfied.

But in reality, the satisfied, in most places, are the minority and the growing number of those who don't even make any pretense of affiliation underscores the trend. There are profound changes in demographics and in the relationship to institutions in general. There is the pervasive self-authentication of post-modernity, the access to information and knowledge in new and more diverse places, and the emerging and controversial new concepts of community [virtual or otherwise]. Those who are cavalier about these radical changes, as some are, only serves to isolate the synagogue as an institution out of touch with its populace.

That resistance is more than a shame; it is a potential tragedy. There is no other institution that can be perceived as the primary entry point. Synagogues are local; they are everywhere; they are visible; they are [at least in theory] accessible. And except for High Holidays, the cost of entry is non-existent, [that is a big "except"!— more about it below.]

The North American synagogue model, a freestanding membership organization, is counter-cultural in the current milieu. For those above a certain age, membership represents "commitment"; the details of how much one uses the services of the institution or club matter less than one's formal membership. To those below a certain age, membership is typically simply a fee-for-service relationship; it is rarely based on loyalty or commitment but rather an efficient way to fulfill certain needs through purchase. And, if it is rare for the boomers and younger to feel institutional loyalty to a particular synagogue, it is even more rare for that loyalty to percolate up to a "stream" or "denomination."

Ideology may play a key role for those on the edges [on the left and right], but for the majority, synagogue participation and/or affiliation is more likely to reflect issues of convenience, style, friendship patterns, and the like. The internal structure of most synagogues continues to reflect a very different understanding of how people work and spend their disposable time and money. Do the classic sisterhoods and brotherhoods really speak to dual income families who are juggling soccer, piano, supplementary school, and a shamefully increased number of work hours? Do they ring true to the growing number of single parent families, or singles, or other "non-traditional" family structures? Do they anticipate the needs that arise from the sense of alone-ness that even many nuclear families feel around holidays and special occasions?

There was a time, some 15 years ago, when I first started speaking about synagogues, that I advocated that synagogues become surrogate families and surrogate communities. I now believe that I didn't have it quite right. A synagogue is NOT a family or community—it is an institution. What a synagogue can do is to foster family or family type experiences or communality of feeling. The question isn't "how do we bring these people inside our doors?" It IS, what we can do to make sure that their Jewish needs are being met—even if it means serving them outside the gates.

It is constructive to examine the successful models in Jewish life of the last decade: most are independent in style if not in governance [e.g., alternative services in or outside of established synagogues]; many are "location friendly" [e.g., study groups in homes and offices]; some emphasize exuberance or spirituality; others appeal because they are large, anonymous, and non-demanding [e.g., film festivals, BJ in NY]; most speak to the essential loneliness of American experience without making *a priori* institutional demands; an emerging trend is for affinity connections which are not geographically bound [e.g., Wexner Heritage; virtual communities for teens].

A close look at these characteristics will reveal that they are, in some cases, mutually contradictory. But what they have in common is that they are not the typical ways in which most people would describe their synagogue experience. Fortunately, we are seeing more and more synagogues [and JCCs and Hillels and federations] begin to apply these approaches, but these are still considered the exceptions and not yet defining norms.

Many of us have addressed the structural dilemmas which limit the agility of most synagogues: a huge investment in infrastructure and the programs necessary to fund them; an assumption that a synagogue should be self contained, financially and programmatically, and responsive to all constituencies; the denominational limitations which are superimposed on a population which is post or non denominational; the tension about what are the proper and most effective roles of synagogue professional staff and lay membership; etc. Most synagogues are really not very well equipped to expand the way they do things.

Change, if it is to come, must reflect a real commitment to see things differently. Rabbis have to leave their comfort zones—whether that means their offices or their *bimah* or their traditional roles; lay people have to adjust and expand their thinking about how to maximize both the effectiveness and excellence of what their synagogues do; synagogues need to be wiling to surrender their autonomy if certain things might be done better by collaboration or by others [e.g., teen programming; education]. There needs to be a rethinking of the meaning of "membership" given the pervasive change in the meaning of loyalty and affiliation referred to above.

All of these recommendations deserve greater analysis than is appropriate here. I will limit some further comments to two key areas: Financing and rabbinic roles.

Cost and financing: As an advisor on the grant making side of philanthropy, I have been struck by the number of synagogues which request outside funding to do what they want to do from philanthropists and foundations beyond their own community. It is clear to me that there is a fundamental problem if synagogues, as membership organizations, cannot fund their own needs. If so, it means that there is a structural dilemma. Is it because synagogues have the requisite funds but choose to use them ineffectively—perhaps for facilities that are only needed a few times a year? Is it because their members simply don't value their offerings sufficiently to support them at the level necessary to provide what they want? Is it, perhaps, because synagogues are in fact providing community services that should be under the auspices of other organizations or agencies? Whatever the explanation, there is an inherent conflict: one cannot remain a self-contained membership governed institution and still believe that others should be providing ongoing core financial support.

A related question is how to serve those who don't choose to affiliate with a single institution because they wish to pick and choose based on who does what well. I know of many people who like Shabbat services at one place, high holidays at another, educate their children at a third, and participate in educational offerings at an altogether different place. Should these people pay four memberships? Should they pay separately for each and affiliate at none? Perhaps they should pay a *kehillah* fee that gives them access or at least reduced fees everywhere. And this does not even include the absolute majority who, at any one time, affiliate nowhere. If the synagogue is indeed the most widely used portal to Jewish life, community needs require that communal policy address this group as well. Some communities are beginning to think this through. It needs to be higher on the communal agenda.

Rabbis bear the brunt of the pressures on synagogues. For the most part they are "victims" of rapidly changing expectations. Rabbis from all sides of the ideological divides articulate these pressures—in addition to all of the recent expectations of the mid-twentieth century, to be an educator, a scholar, an orator, a counselor, a teen worker, a therapist, an authority, a representative to the outside world, and a role model, have been added the institutional expectations of the twenty-first. Now they must be a CEO, a supervisor, a planner, a fund-raiser, and a web expert. No one, in any profession, can do all of those things well.

Ironically, the instincts of so many of the synagogue change approaches is to superimpose a new management training stratum on the rabbi. Yet, the expectation that all rabbis will be managers simply adds to the scope of responsibilities that cannot be done well. Instead of building on and enhancing the rabbis' strengths, such approaches simply build on weakness. Put another way, by making the rabbis' job more undoable, it simply reinforces that what is done is inadequate. It is the wrong way to solve a genuine problem. We should be asking what needs to be done and what resources are necessary to get it done—not what additional portfolios can we give the rabbi.

Rabbis can help to address this challenge by spending more time away from their own inner sancta. Given the autonomy of synagogues, it is all too easy for their worlds to become self-reinforcing and limiting. There is always work to be done, but it is psychologically too easy for any professional to assume that all needs are being met well because one is busy. It is the experience of being outside of the safety of one's office that one sees the world as it really is, not as it presents itself within the office. This is not an issue only for rabbis, but because rabbis are senior executives of self contained institutions, the burden is on them to exercise the discipline to expand their understanding of how others are doing the work and what expertise still needs to be honed.

One common response from many rabbis is that they are overworked. It may be true, but it is equally true of most of the congregants. Rabbis may have the problem of an overabundance of roles and expectations; that is a different problem to solve than having too little time. And, in fairness, rabbis are indeed more masters of their own schedules—most of the time—than most other professionals. What other professional can refuse to meet before midmorning because they don't want to have to travel in rush hour? I have heard too many of my rabbinic colleagues make just such a case. In a world where even senior executives are not fully in control of their schedules, it appears self-indulgent and out of touch. It is important for my rabbinic colleagues to help formulate the dilemma in a constructive manner respecting the perspectives of those whose voluntary money and time allow the synagogue to function at all.

Thus, I am a strong advocate for a serious revision in job descriptions and renewed clarity about how to use congregational resources more effectively—to build on real strengths and to compensate for honest weakness. It is valid to identify staff needs and specialties that are not being met at the standard one should expect. And it is also valid to understand what work expectations are—or should be in a much too busy world.

∾

Institutions of this century will look and feel different than those which came before, and the synagogue is no exception. We do live in a time of transformation and inconsistencies. Synagogues face many challenges: The tension between authentic innovation vs. syncretism is not new, but it is very real today. The struggle between the values and rewards of an open society, which most American Jews cherish, and a three thousand year tradition which makes more exclusivist demands, are palpable; the unprecedented anarchy of knowledge vs. an established authoritative system create dilemmas for Orthodoxy as well as for the more liberal streams; the absence of any real consensus on what defines community has as much impact as the more public debate on who is a Jew. We have only begun to come to grips with an emerging consensus in some circles that we should be a more proselytizing people. Just as medical research allows genetic engineering and the potential ability to design human beings, we must confront the most profound question of all—what is a human being and who will [or should] decide.

All of these battles move from the theoretical to the real in the synagogue. To return to where we started our discussion: we should take comfort from the history which shows the agility of the synagogue as an institution, and trust that what will emerge is but the latest variation of the 2500 year tradition of the most widespread and diverse Jewish institution. Let us hope that those who enter the doors of this latest re-engineered synagogue find a place that honors, respects, and engages our ever more diverse and demanding population. The transformed and revitalized synagogue of the 21st century: The Jewish people want it; Judaism deserves it; the Jewish future requires it.

THE SYNAGOGUE AS A COUNTER-CULTURE: A LONG RANGE VIEW

Riv-Ellen Prell

To think about the future of the synagogue is to think about the future of American Jewish life, about American Jewish culture, about American Jewish families and about American Jews. It is to ask the toughest of questions, about boundaries between "us" and "them," and "us" and "us." It is to ask about how to envision a future and a past and above all, how to shape ourselves as men and women, as a culture, and as a people. It is not only to ask who we are, but who we should be, and how to think about that question in the institutions that will not only define us, but through which we will transmit what is most important to future generations. The stakes are high. The questions are critical.

I respond to these questions as someone who thinks about Jews in particular historical moments in the United States, and how what they do becomes defined and experienced as Jewish by them. To that end I have spent years doing research in synagogues and alternatives to synagogues listening to Jews talk about who they are and what they want. I also come to these questions through the world of scholars who are interested in religion, culture, and ethnicity.

I believe that there is one crucial platform on which any discussion of Jews in the United States in the present and the future rests and should shape these discussions. To be a Jew is to engage in a counter-culture, literally to stand apart in varying degrees and various ways from the larger society and social worlds in which one operates. Without understanding oneself as different, without creating institutions that acknowledge that difference, without engaging in the world with a sense of that difference, there cannot be either Jews or Judaism.

What that difference might be, what its relationship is to traditional Jewish authority, what the process of expressing and transmitting that difference cannot and will not be determined in a uniform or widely shared way in the 21st century. That is as it must be and should be in the context in which American Judaism has taken root. American Judaism developed in a pluralist, Protestant nation in which Judaism functioned as a religion or "faith community," not something that it was intended to be. But there is no question that the process of differentiation will be worked out in the world of the self, in the family, but most assuredly in synagogues as well. How to think about that process is related to thinking about its future and that is what I would like to discuss.

If we live in what scholars variously call high modernity or post modernity, what does it mean to see oneself in a counter culture and what are its implications for synagogues? There are, given the brevity of time, two critical features of modernity and high modernity on which I will focus. **First and foremost, the move from the pre- modern to the modern world changed the way we experience the nature of authority and how we know the world around us.** The supreme authority of the modern world was and remains rational knowledge and science. Though Jews, among others, attempted to integrate the rational world with that of traditional authority, that rational knowledge and the world it opened has shaped Jews' experience of the world for centuries.

Ironically, rational knowledge does not guarantee certainty and the modern world created anything but certainty. Hence, modernity introduced science and with it the right to question all ways of knowing. The hypothesis is nothing else if it is not the demand to have something proven. Rather than certainty, we live with an abundance of choices, and finding a way to negotiate those choices with some sense of coherence becomes the requirement of our time. As people of high modernity we are beset by doubt, or confusion, or an ever-growing array of authorities among whom one must choose with ever-lessening confidence. It is that very surplus of options that explains what is so peculiar about the world we negotiate. For example, in a period in which Western medicine has solved a vast number of medical problems, its authority is constantly challenged. Self-prescribed herbal supplements, alternative healing, belief in angels, and skepticism about medicine are ubiquitous in our culture. Indeed, in the twenty blocks I walk to work each day this year in Philadelphia, I have not one, but four opportunities to have my palm read and my future predicted in stores that occupy the fashionable Walnut Street in which the young urban professional class traverses daily. The doubt of rationality has given rise to the claims of, in many cases, the self-evidently irrational.

A study cited in the *Chronicle of Higher Education* (October, 2003) learned that well over half of the students surveyed at UCLA were interested in spirituality and faculty was admonished to be certain to integrate those concerns in the curriculum. We do not have to dwell on the differences between spirituality and religion here to make the simple point that modernity did not solve the problems of meaning. To some extent, this period created them. Late or high modernity has only created more choices and is simply different in degree to the rise of modernity.

If the synagogue is a setting for creating a counter culture in the middle of the twenty-first century, then Judaism must respond to this lack of confidence, uncertainty about authority, and the need for people to find some coherence to their own stories about their lives. Clearly one approach of our time is fundamentalism, but that is not synonymous with Judaism. What synagogues must do however, is to focus above all on what it means to live Jewishly. If the synagogue cannot be a setting for shaping one's own story in relationship to the demands and pleasures of living life as a Jew, then there is little point to attend.

In my research in a Conservative synagogue in the 1990s, a woman I interviewed taught me something about how this might work. Most of her life she was beset by major illnesses, and traumatized by rabbis who came to hospitals who patronized her and offered banalities. She had found in her current synagogue a more satisfying Jewish life. When I interviewed her she recounted an experience that she had had earlier in the year. After another major surgery, her rabbi suggested that she visit the mikvah to mark this passage in her life and health. She hesitated, and told me that in the end she went because it was important to him. But to her astonishment, what happened at the *mikvah* for her was entirely unexpected. The rabbi placed her own illness, surgery, and recovery within the story of the exodus from Egypt. It was the season of Pesah. He talked with her about illness as a narrow place, the meaning of *Mitzraim*, and he then offered her the image of the *mikvah* as part of the crossing of the sea. Her life, her personal experience, and her body became part of a collective story that in turn changed the way she understood Pesah, exodus, and health. The private and the collective were brought together for her through ritual.

The conditions of high modernity require just such experiences, not as exceptional moments of passage, but as the foundation for life. These fusions and formulation are not only the work of rabbinic leadership, but can be made and lived with groups within the synagogue, by educators, or in a more intimate setting with friends.

Membership in a synagogue should be grounded in knowing that however one defines Judaism, whether in prayer, rites of passage or study, the work of Judaism is to offer Jews as many ways as possible to understand that Judaism is a system of knowledge and meaning in which one is situated as an actor. The fragmentation of high modernity is answered by Judaism not as a set of rational prescriptions, but as a way to live.

This suggests that synagogues must make themselves, to use Isa Aron's felicitous phrase, congregations of learners. One cannot draw on Judaism to negotiate life without living in it. Different Jews will do that differently, but if Judaism is a counter culture, it must first be a culture in which education is at the core of the experience.

This task is a hard one, unquestionably made harder by the options that may serve as an alternative, and by the fact that fewer Jews have either the memory of a vibrant Jewish life or the skills to create one. But that does not make the task less transparent; it only asks that we think clearly about the requirements of the task.

The second issue of high modernity, related of course to authority, is the notion of **community**. Literally thousands of scholars and pundits have written about this issue. It is here that the internet has radically intervened in making the world both smaller and more atomized. We have access to the global world, but we can do it in individualist ways. Synagogues can have web sites and must make use of technologies. But to understand Judaism as a counter culture is above all to acknowledge that Jews live in community and that it is only in community one can be a Jew.

Can Jews feel Jewish without community? There is no question about that. Can going to film festivals or playing klezmer or purchasing art express ones identity? A number of scholars have ably demonstrated that that is the case. But feeling Jewish is only

one component of what it means to be a Jew, and one that is notoriously unsuccessful at making Jews actors within Jewish life. Feeling passionately about being a Jew, even being proud of being a Jew
is not the same as living as a Jew. Its most serious limitation is
quite simply that the world of feeling or encountering the arts have
no system in place to transmit Judaism. These experiences cannot
do the basic work of any culture in the world. They will not repro-
duce Judaism through other generations. Let the Jewish arts
bloom, but let's not pretend that they can do what synagogues do
or what a counter cultural Judaism must do. They do not yet, as far
as I know, create community, mutual responsibility, or a vision for
the future.

Synagogues must do more than make Jews feel Jewish. They
must foster community because without community Jews cannot
experience Judaism as a living and shared reality. The project of
community building is exceptionally difficult in our time. The
world is smaller because of globalization, and yet people are more
radically cut off from one another and will continue to be so according to virtually all speculation about the future. The nature of community is changing, but it has been changing for Jews for many
decades. Indeed, since suburbanization, which swept American
Jewish life after World War II, the model of Jewish community as
neighborhood-based disappeared.

What is challenging about the future is the central role of
media and the network which individualizes experience and takes
people out of not only neighborhoods, but out of a shared work
place and shared public spaces. And yet, we know that the condition of high modernity is often one of loneliness, yearning for connection, and confusion about how to create it. The so-called
tribalism of Generation Xers claims to offer an alternative form of
connection.

How can synagogues do the work of community building in
the face of these challenges? It is important to keep in mind that
in contrast to virtually every other organization and institution of
Jewish life, the synagogue is best prepared to serve as a source of
community. It is grounded in a liturgical cycle, a holiday cycle, and
the human life cycle that bring people in connection to one
another. Its symbolic structure depends on notions of community
and collectivity. It is crucial to guard and maintain Judaism's
dependence on community. Judaism is about community because
it is about obligation, responsibility, and a vision for the future.

And it is no accident that what most often draws Jews to synagogue, for better and for worst, is children to whom they want to transmit some version of that Jewish counter culture.

Synagogue leadership, professional and lay, needs to understand that community is a component of every aspect of synagogue life. Education, prayer, life cycle events, social justice work and more, are occasions to foster connections and obligations between and among congregants.

One very small example makes this point effectively. When I was once teaching Wexner fellows, an Orthodox student shared the following story. In the first weeks of the semester at Teacher's College, one of their colleagues' wives became very ill during her pregnancy. The seminar wanted to do something and could not figure out what to do. Should they send a card, buy a plant or a gift? They were literally paralyzed. He suggested that they take turns making meals for the couple and deliver them. The suggestion astounded them and rapidly built a deep sense of connection. Throughout the semester they pointed to this suggestion as one that had been crucial to forging a sense of deep connection. They marveled at the idea. Here is a wonderful example of the impoverishment of the culture in which we live and the cultural vocabulary that Judaism as a counter culture made available to a group of young men and women.

Nevertheless, One of the great challenges for American Jewry in the next fifty years is the fact that we live in a time when of the concept of peoplehood is waning, and Judaism is becoming more of a "faith community," and less a collective culture. As discouraging as this fact is, the synagogue continues to offer a local level community and one of the hallmarks of high modernity is an extreme polarization between local and global. Localism may serve us well as we think about the synagogue of the future. Hopefully, we can shape synagogues to be local enclaves even as we must struggle to keep notions of peoplehood alive.

Of course, synagogues have been local level organizations for many generations. Small synagogues in Europe and immigrant America were organized around trades and then around geographic locales. My own research on the history of the American synagogue convinced me of the extent to which generations gravitated to their own vision of a synagogue that they believed was the final and most beautiful articulation of American Jewish experience, only to be replaced by a competing vision by the next generation.

We foster community best in our time by encouraging diversity within the synagogue, the synoplex or big tent version. It encourages different generations, or groups with different views of prayer to gather and take responsibility for services of study. Community is rarely created in the aggregate and more often around smaller groupings. A synagogue that encourages this diversity is encouraging leadership, responsibility and living Jewishly.

When I advocate for Judaism as a counter culture I am saying we live within time, but we can never be solely bound by that time and its imperatives. I do not offer a vision for American Judaism that will attract the most people. I am calling for a Judaism whose goal is to transform and reformulate the world in which we live and will continue to live. My focus on meaning and community is, I believe, essential to a Jewish life. We live in a highly polarized time. Differences between and among Jews in the United States are enormous and will continue to grow. The more our communities are willing to assert what Judaism is and what it is not, the more creative we can be about making the synagogue a place to create Judaism. That process depends on strong rabbinic and lay leadership and great attention to building community within the context of a Jewish culture that can, does, and will always change in response to the cultures in which it is lived.

I am not advocating for what form Judaism should take. What I am suggesting is that this will always be the work of synagogues and that in doing that work in education, prayer, the festival and life cycle, in educating children and adults, that work will succeed when it challenges the world in which we live. After spending a year studying two very successful Conservative synagogues, what I learned was that almost all of what drew Jews to synagogues in the 1950s, what many think of as a golden era of Jewish life, has disappeared. Jews no longer needed to socialize only with Jews. They didn't need to create bonds of ethnic solidarity against a hostile gentile community. They didn't even need to hold onto the memory of European Judaism and to Americanize worship. They probably didn't need dances, or Friday night socializing. Many were there to give Judaism to their children, but surprisingly, and a survey bore this out, most came to services and joined the synagogue so they could find in their Judaism a way to live their lives.

That is the task now and I believe it will be in the future as well.

RE-ENVISIONING THE SYNAGOGUE: GETTING THERE FROM HERE

Michael Hammer

T he basic question for our consideration in this discussion can be phrased quite simply: Is the synagogue in the United States in good shape or is it in bad shape? I would suggest that the answer is an unequivocal "yes."

Any generalization of such a disparate and diverse phenomenon like the synagogue fails from the outset. Certainly, many synagogues today are thriving and many are experiencing grave difficulties. However, in thinking about the institution of the synagogue as a whole, I start with a point of view that comes from my study of many kinds of organizations over many years. Any organization is a system that was designed and built to solve certain problems at a certain point in time. It is inevitable that as circumstances change and the problems for which the institution was fashioned give way to new problems, that the institution itself must adapt and undergo fundamental change.

The problem is that organizations are burdened with great inertia. They are self-reinforcing and self-perpetuating entities, which continue in the mold in which they were formed long after the world around them has changed. It is only with great strain and travail that human organizations can jettison their received structures and adapt themselves to new realities. In the business world, most corporations were configured for the post-World War II environment of free-spending customers, genteel competition, and modest rates of change. Starting in the 1980s, these conditions changed beyond recognition, but corporations continued to operate as they had for decades. Even today, for instance, the major airlines continue to employ hub-and-spoke systems and to follow human resource policies that were conceived thirty years ago and that have been rendered obsolete by deregulation and the rise of the discount carriers.

A similar situation applies to the synagogue. The canonical model of the American synagogue, across all denominations, is one that was designed for an era now long gone, to solve problems that American Jews were facing at the time. Today, American Jews face very different problems, but the synagogue still lumbers along in the way in which it was conceived. Going forward, we need to re-envision and redesign the synagogue to address the problems that American Jews now confront.

Since there is no solution without a problem, I would venture to suggest that the defining issue that confronts Americans, including American Jews, today is what sociologists call anomie: a loss of connection and a loss of identity in a fragmented society. (The late novelist Walker Percy captured perhaps better than any other modern writer the rootlessness that afflicts contemporary America.) With the decline of self-defining Jewish neighborhoods and other institutions that shaped Jewish life, American Jews today are adrift, cut off from bonds that tie them to each other. The most critical need they have is for community, mechanisms to link them to other Jews and the larger Jewish enterprise, to provide them a framework in which they can live their lives. I would further posit that the synagogue can no longer pretend to be merely just another in a web of Jewish institutions; rather, in the search for community, it must become the primary Jewish institution, to which all others play secondary and subordinate roles. It is only through the multi-dimensional capabilities of the synagogue that we can in fact create community.

The centrality of Jewish community is not a new concept. There is a well-known conundrum in the Talmudic tradition that states "Greater is the one who is commanded and performs, then the one who is not commanded and performs." (BT, *Kiddushin* 31a) How are we to understand this? It certainly goes against our contemporary valorization of autonomy, in terms of which one who elects to perform Judaism should be considered superior to one who is compelled to.

Many explanations have been offered for this. My favorite is one that was put forth by a Hasidic master. He observed that the form of the blessings we make is "Who has sanctified us with commandments and commanded us." We utter these blessings as individuals, but express them in the first-person plural. Why? Because the commandments are incumbent on the Jews as a community, not as individuals. Therefore one who is obligated to perform a commandment is doing so as a member of a community, and so is superior to the isolated individual who is performing a commandment on his or her own.

It is in creating and nurturing community that the synagogue will find its future. In such synagogues, rabbis will find their primary roles not as defenders of the faith nor as spiritual counselors, but rather as builder and creator of communities.

Some synagogues are consciously or unconsciously operating in this mode already. But for others, this transition will be a long and difficult road. For them, I would like to share a few principles that I've learned over the years for how organizations can successfully transform themselves from where they are to where they need to be. I will call these the nine rules; for obvious reasons I tried to not have them be ten in number.

First, there has to be recognition of a need for a change before you can begin the process of change. It is hard to believe the remarkable lengths to which organizations and the people in them will go to convince themselves that there is no need to change. John Kenneth Galbraith once wrote, "When it comes to choosing between making change and proving there's no need to change, most people get working on the proof."

Some ten years ago, I had an experience that was so bizarre that two or three years afterwards I was sure that I had imagined it. And then, incredibly, it happened again.

I was visiting a very large company, which was having great difficulties. Its operations were in shambles, and customers were enormously unhappy. Everyone knew this, except for the people in charge at this company. They asserted to me that they had done a customer satisfaction survey and eighty percent of their customers were satisfied. I asked to see the instrument, which in fact offered customers the following response options: satisfied, very satisfied, and satisfied. I am reminded of this when I hear people putting good faces on what are actually dispiriting data about rates of synagogue affiliation.

We must realize that any system, any structures, any organizations that we inhabit are not inevitable. It is not ordained that they must exist in the configurations with which we have become familiar. They are in fact only temporary responses to particular social and economic circumstances, and we have to avoid getting too attached to them.

The second principle is that when one undertakes a major program of change, one cannot expect to know exactly where one is going. This does not say you merely blunder about. You do have to start with a vision, but a vision is very different from a detailed plan. It is said that when Jack Welch took over at GE, he closed down his long range planning organization. People objected, "But if you close down your planning organization, aren't you going to be surprised by events?" He replied, "Of course I'll be surprised by events—but I'll no longer be surprised that I am surprised." Too many people want a strategic plan that lays everything out. Nothing could be more inappropriate. Formulate a direction and a high-level vision, and then get started.

Thirdly, it's critical to have concrete and measurable goals when you begin, because if you can't define success you will never know if you've achieved it.

The fourth principle is that any program of change involves surfacing, questioning, and then changing fundamental assumptions that underlie our systems, assumptions that are almost always tacit and unrecognized. A life insurance company had to redesign the way it worked when it realized that it wasn't written in stone that only salespeople could talk to customers. A bank came to rethink how it handled loan applications when it questioned the assumption that all applications were so complex that experts had to be involved in every one. Similarly, we will need to surface and question many of the assumptions that underlie our current vision of the synagogue.

I am not in a position to identify all the assumptions that need to be changed, but I can provide a few possible examples. For one, that the synagogue is a membership fee institution. This is not inevitable. It has been that way in America, but only for a little while in terms of the long sweep of Jewish history. It wasn't that way in Europe; it's largely not that way in Israel. There are alternatives to envision. Similarly, where is it said that the sermon is the centerpiece of the synagogue service? In pre-war Europe, many rabbis gave sermons only twice a year, and some of their congregants' thought that was too often. Preparing and delivering sermons is an enormously challenging task for rabbis. Perhaps their congregants need to deliver more of the sermons. For another, the idea of a single integrating service for the entire synagogue is an assumption that needs to be called into question. Personally, I'm not a fan of what I call "the bus station school of synagogue architecture," large, drafty halls in which people easily get lost. I think communities are best created in small spaces that are a little crowded, where people sit cheek by jowl and feel each other's presence. That means that larger synagogues will need to offer a diversity of services, targeted at the needs of different constituencies, rather than one. Giving people an opportunity to participate in the service, rather than just be a passive observer of it, is also key to reinforcing community. There are many other assumptions about synagogue life that can also be identified and questioned, and I suspect that different synagogues will resolve these issues differently, but this questioning of assumptions is the very essence of the process of change.

Fifth, we have to recognize that those who are most successful in an existing system are going to be most uncomfortable with any change brought to them. This is not Machiavellian or defensive; it is organic, flowing out of a deeply internalized worldview. People who are deeply attached to an existing system honestly believe that changing it is a bad idea. I have learned at great personal expense that one cannot convince people deeply invested in an existing system of the need to change it; there is no rational argument that will persuade them. Upton Sinclair once wrote, "It is very difficult to get someone to understand something when his salary depends on his not understanding it." One might amend that to say "his or her standing in the community." The management scholar Richard Pascale has written, "It's easier to act ourselves into a new way of thinking than to think ourselves into a new way of acting." You can't persuade people who are embedded in an old worldview; you can only immerse them in a new worldview and hope that their thinking will catch up.

Sixth, our inherited structures and systems will be a problem. When we change private enterprises, their organizational structures, compensation and reward systems, promotion systems, and the like all get in the way, since these were designed with the old enterprise in mind and reinforce it and its values. A similar situation obtains in the synagogue context. Many systems, from how synagogues are governed to rabbinical education, will need to be rethought to support a new model for the role of the synagogue.

Seven, major change is a marathon run at a sprinter's pace. It's not done overnight, but it's also not accomplished by following a Soviet-like ten-year plan. One must start with a long-term vision, and short-term successes are needed to encourage people and to prove the validity of the approach. A common mistake in a long-term program of change is to stop after achieving the first success, thinking that one is finished.

Eight, living in a transition state is full of tension. The synagogue is a stable system today. It may be declining and not functioning very well, but it is stable. Eventually, after a protracted transition, we will get to another stable situation. The problem is that it is very difficult between here and there. An analogy I use when talking to corporate groups is the Biblical story of the Exodus from Egypt. At the beginning of the story, the Israelites are in the land of Egypt, in slavery; at the end of the story, they are in the Promised Land, freedom. It was a wonderful improvement; the only trouble is that between Egypt and the Promised Land there was the desert, which was even worse than Egypt. Like all transitional states, it had neither the advantages of the new nor the familiarity of the old. Getting people to take the first step into the transition is the hardest of all. For a leader to get them to move, a vision of the destination is necessary but is not sufficient. In the Biblical story, Moses had an advantage: it was the army of Pharaoh coming up from behind. A crisis is enormously helpful in motivating people to change. As Dr. Samuel Johnson observed, "Nothing concentrates a man's mind so much as the certain prospect of being hanged in a fortnight." The prospect of failure is a wonderful incentive to change that by itself merely creates despair; it must be combined with a vision of the possible. It is also important to remember that living in a transitional state presents problems that cannot be solved, but can only be endured. There are inherent conflicts and tensions between what we're familiar with, and what we are trying to create, and those problems can often not be resolved in a neat fashion.

Ninth and finally, when making deep change it's important to maintain some continuity with the past, both to help people through the trauma of the transition and to avoid losing one's bearings. The most valuable thing to maintain is a fundamental set of values that root one in the past while when one is creating a future. In our case, rather than chasing after the fads of the moment, the opportunity is to take people's spiritual yearnings and embed them in the sources of our tradition.

Such a traditional source is the Talmudic tractate *Avot*, known as the Ethics of the Fathers. There, Simon the Just says that the world rests on three things: on Torah study, on prayer, and on acts of compassion It is hard to imagine a better recipe for building a new Jewish community or for capturing the future of the synagogue.

THE SYNAGOGUE OF TOMORROW: A NON-PROPHETIC VISION

Rabbi Morris Allen

What I find interesting about the fact that Michael Hammer, Riv-Ellen Prell and I have been asked to participate in this symposium is that each of us albeit with different nuances here and there, have come to our own synagogue life with a similar story. Michael Hammer was involved in the founding of Shaarei Tefillah, in Newton, MA, which traces its origins to a desire on part of an educated orthodox elite in the early 80s to break away from an established synagogue which most of its founders had been attending. It was, in the Orthodox world, not so dissimilar to the drive for a more intimate, shared value community that Dr. Prell speaks about in her book *Prayer and Community: Havurah In American Judaism* and, in truth, it mirrors my own movement to my current congregation, Beth Jacob in Mendota Heights, Minnesota. I could name four *havurot* or *minyanim* that I participated in, or founded, along the journey from Lincoln Nebraska in 1973 when I left home, until I ended up in St. Paul in 1986 as the first rabbi of an embryonic synagogue called Beth Jacob. The fact that each of us has traveled a similar path to this discussion speaks volumes about the evolution of the synagogue. Yet, as in the Talmudic maxim in Tractate *Bava Metzia*, "I am neither a prophet nor a son of a prophet," and so, describing the synagogue twenty five or more years hence is not only a daunting task, but as our participation in this discussion attests, is probably a task that is likely to hinge on societal factors beyond even the most well funded synagogue change operation in the country.

It is always humbling to remember that we are not the first generation that has been concerned with the state of the American synagogue. It might be a good idea to consider what those who spoke about congregational life fifty years ago were thinking. In fact, fifty years ago, at the 1953 Rabbinical Assembly convention, held at the Breakers Hotel in Atlantic City, during Atlantic City's first life, Abraham Joshua Heschel, of blessed memory, delivered a most impassioned speech on the condition of the American synagogue. Listen for just a moment to his words and hear the resonance of his pain in the reality of our own lives today.

> *The fire has gone out of our worship. It is cold, stiff and dead. Inorganic Judaism. True, things are happening; of course not within prayer but within the administration of synagogues. The modern synagogue suffers from a severe cold. Our congregants preserve a respectful distance between the siddur and themselves. An air of tranquility, complacency prevails in our synagogues. What can come out of such an atmosphere? The services are prim, the voice is dry, the synagogue is clean and tidy, and the soul of prayer lies in agony. People expect the rabbi to conduct a service, efficient expert service. But efficiency and rapidity are no remedy against devotional sterility.*

Some twenty years later, at the Rabbinical Assembly convention then being held at the Concord in the Catskills—notice the move of location—a panel was held with six distinguished, self-identifying believers in the *havurah* movement. They spoke on Futuristic Jewish communities. They spoke of the havurah community, of Havurat Shalom, of Farbrengen, of the New York Havurah. They spoke of their sense of loss of belief in the synagogue as the institution that would ever speak to them, and instead were looking for a more holistic approach to the Jewish life—where prayer and study and fellowship, and Tikkun Olam were all interconnected. Among those six panelists were: Michael Strassfield, now the rabbi of SAJ in New York; Richard Siegel, the Executive Director of the National Foundation for Jewish Culture, who is now married to Rabbi Laura Geller who serves as the rabbi of one of Los Angeles' largest Reform congregations; Arnold Jacob Wolf who was then singing the praises of being Hillel rabbi outside the stuffiness of Congregation Solel, and yet who ended his most distinguished career as the rabbi of a congregation in Chicago, KAM Isaiah Israel.

I tell you all of this, because from Heschel's biting critique of fifty years ago, to the spokespeople for futuristic Jewish communities of thirty years ago, what we know to be the case is that the synagogue remains the institution where Jewish lives are created and molded. In spite of the most insightful criticism by Dr. Heschel, in spite of the dreams of six thoughtful and highly committed Jews who offered an alternative vision for American Jewish life, in some ways we are still struggling to respond to these voices of the past. But perhaps we can look at this somewhat differently. The fact of the matter is that Dr. Heschel's analysis of prayer in the American Conservative synagogue was probably one of the reasons why during the 50s and 60s the Ramah Camps experimented with innovation in prayer. It is probably unnecessary to say that the fact that Camp Ramah experimented with prayer during those years helped launch and produce the havurah movement. And it is probably true that the successes, limited but highly significant, of the havurah movement of the 70s and 80s have actually helped transform the synagogue, as we know it today. So in answering this question first and foremost, I would suggest that our analysis at meetings like this, the continued presence of groups like *Hadar* and in Israel *Shira Hadasha* would have an effect on synagogues twenty-five years hence.

As a rabbi who has been privileged to work with a single community, I would just like to add my own thoughts as to what the future holds for us in shul life. Actually while I have had the same title with the same congregation over the past eighteen years, I have probably worked with multiple communities; each called Beth Jacob. The most important factor for synagogue life in the future is going to be whether or not synagogues will be able to project a vision of what it means to be a member of a synagogue. Indeed, we will be blessed with vibrant and vital congregations if every shul can answer the following question: What will a person's Jewish life look like as a result of being part of this congregation? Clearly there are multiple influences on a person's Jewish development, but if a shul holds out a vision of what it is committed to, it can and will have a significant influence in molding that person's *neshama*. Programmatic models aside, what will ultimately attract Jews to synagogues is a sense that the community itself has a compelling message that speaks with pride and honesty.

In order to understand what the future of the American synagogue may look like, it is important to note that a synagogue exists within a larger culture, and if not understood correctly, that culture will undermine any effort of projecting a clear and unambiguous synagogue vision. Let us examine several items.

It is easy to start with demographics. Clearly the most telling statistic is the intermarriage rate. I do not want to use most of my time speaking about this. However, unless there is a massive communal commitment to substantive conversion programs, which address intellectual knowledge of Judaism, experiential understanding of living ones life as a Jew, and a commitment to insuring an ability of a convert to decode Hebrew as should be the case with each Jew, our synagogues will be very different places in 25 years. Here is first and foremost where the broad community must decide to work cooperatively and to seek real dollars for success. It is frightening that last year in a respected reform congregation in a prominent major city, for his Rosh Hashanah sermon the rabbi chose to talk about the need to honor the "members of our community who practice both Judaism and Christianity." Unless there is a massive communal effort undertaken to making conversion available within all streams of the Jewish community, what we will have as synagogues 25 years from now will be a pale resemblance of Jewish life, replaced by a syncretistic religious lifestyle.

Equally important, though, and often times overlooked, and a major issue affecting the future of the synagogue, will be our demographics as it relates to childbirth. It is important to note that while 90% of women in the Jewish community ages 18–24 do not have children, and 70% of Jewish women 25–29 do not have children, 25% of American Jews hold graduate degrees. Is there a correlation? Actually it is quite apparent. Jewish women and couples decide to delay having children while pursuing graduate education. The comparable numbers in the larger American community speak to this fact. Only 6% of all Americans hold a graduate degree. In other words, being Jewish makes you four times as likely to go to graduate school than your non-Jewish neighbor. The implication for our synagogues is quite clear. First of all we need to celebrate this fact. As a community, we need to understand that this is a part of our uniqueness as a people, and one that in all likelihood is not going to change. Thus, unless we create an atmosphere that is not pediatric oriented in nature, young, intelligent career oriented 20s and 30s will not be in attendance. At the same time, unless we attract thoughtful, intelligent people into the rabbinate, not as an alternative choice after law school, but as a primary decision as a result of intellectual commitment, and religious dedication, our ability to speak to this generation 25 years from now will be severely limited. On the other hand, though, let me add one other point that I believe any serious discussion about the future of American Jewry must include, but which is tinged with great political and social overtones. How do we address the issue of moving having children back onto the agenda of our 20s and 30s? It is not as if these people are avoiding serious relationships or at least sexual intimacy. In a 1994 study of American sexual behavioral patters undertaken by the University of Chicago, Jews in their 20s had the greatest number of sexual partners than of any other group in the country. Again, compared to some religious groups the statistics seemed to suggest that Jews sometimes had four times as many partners before marriage than many Christian religious communities. Interestingly enough, we even outpaced those who declared themselves as holding no religious orientation. Again, the researchers attributed this to our desire for graduate education—only I guess they failed to identify the field. Seriously, though, unless there is a serious effort at speaking to the importance of monogamy and of childbearing in the Jewish community, the synagogue twenty-five years hence will be a very different place.

There are three other significant issues that need to be addressed briefly before I describe the heart of the matter. The first is the fact that we live in an age of rapid technological change. The phenomenon of the Howard Dean presidential boomlet speaks to that issue. The ability to use computers and the Internet to create a "community" is appealing, and so appealing that it may even be seductive. Beware. While congregations are going to have to adapt to ever changing technological innovations, and will need to think creatively as to how to use them to supplement our congregational visions, they must remain as supplements and not the main course. Technology cannot supplant the personal. Earl Schwartz, in a wonderful essay entitled the "Oral Torah in an Electronic Age" warns us of the danger inherent in those who see technology as a substitute for interpersonal community. He writes:

> It is of utmost importance to remember that the channels on computer chips may be wide enough for the passage of information, but they are too narrow for the passage of persons. Important information can be communicated through them, but be it baseball scores or Halachic rulings, the function of a medium is to mediate.

Whether one writes with a hammer and chisel or electronic pen, the living memory that makes sense of words can only be found when we open the door and see another human being looking at us. It is, as we have known all along, presence that makes for meaning, and meaning that creates community.

If we are truly serious about creating community, it will not be done through the web. It will only be done through the painstakingly slower method of humanity meeting one another and together meeting God. In an age where disconnect is all too rampant, we cannot allow ourselves to think that the solution to the atomization of the individual, is to reinforce it in our very own religious settings. The synagogue of the future must clearly and unambiguously declare its loyalty to the importance of the human connection, not an electronic substitute. However else we locate and inform people of our existence, the synagogue must be willing to act as a counter-cultural response to the interneting nature of society. There is wonderful music to download from the Internet; there are great CDs of real live concerts; but there is nothing that beats the experience of listening to live music, surrounded by others whose response also touches you. Similarly, there is a great deal of Torah that can be learned through computer programs, there is a wealth of opportunity to master Jewish life on CD-ROMs, but there is nothing that will ever take the place of listening to Torah being read, to Kol Nidre being chanted in the midst of a full congregation, or to the communal celebration of a person's joyous moment, being enhanced by the presence simply of their community.

The second issue is that of Israel. Twenty-five years from now, all demographic studies suggest that Israel will be home to the largest single population of Jews in the world. Unless during the next twenty-five year period there is a shift in the religious tones emanating from *eretz hakodesh*, the Holy Land, Jewish life in the non-Orthodox community will be significantly affected. In twenty-five years, God willing, Israel will be celebrating its 70th anniversary. A continued endorsement of a sole brand of Jewish life will have had a profound influence on how we see ourselves. There is no doubt that the renaissance of Orthodoxy in America can be in part attributed to the linkage between the Israeli Orthodox community and our own. Similarly, if there has not emerged in Israel, a religious alternative to the Orthodox establishment as it stands now, and secularism has run a parallel course unchecked for 70 years, the isolation of the non-Orthodox communities attempting to promote a vision of a religious life in its own voice will be profound. It might even mean that what was once unthinkable would become the reality. Instead of seeing ourselves as one religious community, our denominations would actually become sister religions one to the other. Perhaps the children of our rabbis Hillel will not still marry the children of their rabbis Shamai. And lest you think that this is just a worry for the non-Orthodox community, even in the American Orthodox community, the Israeli yeshiva experience has come under the watchful eye of many "modern Orthodox thinkers." When the best and brightest of the modern Orthodox world come back to America as rejectionists, there is a serious impact on the vitality of the future American synagogue. Sadly, what this has really meant, though, in the short term has been that for those people who are serious about religious life, who are striving to find meaning in prayer and community, Israel recedes from the front pages of their concern. I think it is still a bit early to understand how the growing vile nature of anti-Semitism will affect synagogue life, but it too deserves attention in our thinking about the synagogue of the future.

Back on these shores, Robert Lang, a demographer at Virginia Tech has coined a phrase for the movement of America's population away from the Core City and established first and second ring suburbs. He calls this move the move to the "low SPF Sunbelt," meaning suburbs where the sun isn't hot but the population growth is. In my own home state, the two fastest growing counties are mine—Dakota County and the suburb to the southwest of me, Washington County. Our synagogue is located just over the border in Dakota County and is a first ring suburb to both St. Paul and Minneapolis. These counties are growing because they have cheap, buildable land where young couples and older folk can move. The implications for the Jewish community are real. Hillel Levine has powerfully documented the loss of a Jewish community in Roxbury and Dorchester and its move to Brookline and Newton. However, the fact remains that before people get too comfy in Newton, they had better be looking at Hillsborough county and Rockingham County in New Hampshire. That is, if you want to know where tomorrow's Boston Jewish community might be situated. Clearly, the seriousness of this issue is going to have to be addressed. It would seem to me that each of the religious movements will have to understand this issue in its own way. If patterns of the past are to be a guide for the future, the Orthodox community will remain in its more settled communities longer, because of the need to remain near their congregations. Yet, new congregations will be seeded in these communities, some more quickly by Reform Jews who today seem to be more adept at watching population patterns, but, if the Conservative movement is serious about itself, it too will seed such projects. But let me suggest a possible role in this for established congregations. An urban Chicago synagogue is currently in discussion with a start up group in Mc Henry County that is said to be the fastest growing county in America, to facilitate their emergence into viability. If established congregations understand that it is not their building that is of prime importance, but rather their vision of Judaism that is important, they can see in the work with new congregations an opportunity for insuring healthy congregational development. Suggestions being explored are centralizing purchasing, use of *Sifrei Torah*, shifting *siddurim* and *humashim* to this new site, banking on the good name of the established congregation to identify potential new members for the start up congregation, and utilizing the expertise of the established congregations staff and professionals. Clearly, communal cultural issues are huge between a well-established urban synagogue center and a start up exurban community. It is not an easy thing to negotiate; the playing field is not level in starting the discussions. But if we are serious in responding to this societal trend, this is a notion that needs exploration.

Yet when all of that is said, when all of these issues are addressed, the future of the American synagogue is still up for grabs. And while I am confident that many of the issues that have been addressed in the papers by Dr. David Kaufman and Rabbi Hayim Herring are real and necessary to understand, I am not convinced that they are sufficient to insure the future of the American synagogue. Generational differences have always existed, and different understandings of the world inevitably flow from those differences. As a child during the 60s, I can still hear my oldest brother storm into our home on a break from college and condemn my parent's embrace of middle class morality. His orthodox community today would also be enraged—because of their upper middle class morality. Structural retooling of the congregation and its leadership are important to explore, but before we bank on structural and leadership change, it would demand a communal commitment to establish substantive programs designed to create

COOs of synagogues. I am not sure I see that on the horizon of the community's vision. I would suggest that the rabbi will remain the most important professional in the synagogue. What will guarantee the vitality of the American synagogue twenty-five years from now is not simply structural change or a shift in leadership responsibility, but rather an ethos change about the meaning and the importance of the synagogue. And the first important fact for achieving this is through the ability of a rabbi to articulate a vision not only of his or her rabbinate, but to understand how to share that vision and implement that vision through the prism of the community in which they live. Rabbis are not religious group workers, though group work skills are a requirement. We do not necessarily need to be programmatic geniuses. What rabbis need to be and what congregations need from their rabbis, is a confidence in their own rabbinic vision, and a commitment to operationalize that vision through the interaction with the congregation they are privileged to be a part of. A rabbi must be able to understand the particular culture of the congregation in which they serve, but must also understand how to promote their vision in light of that culture. The first factor that will guarantee vibrant synagogues twenty-five years from now is a renewed rabbinate, willing to offer a counter cultural message against the individualism and rampant glorification of the self, which dominates the larger American culture.

There are three other major areas where synagogues must change if we are to insure vibrancy twenty-five years from now. The first has to do with the "M" word. Money. Money is at the heart of the synagogues' future, and is directly affecting its present. But if we are really serious about creating a synagogue that will be a place that will be attractive to our community twenty-five years from now, addressing the Jewish communal understanding of money is a definite necessity. Synagogues must be accessible to people across an economic spectrum so that they can truly feel part of a community. I am not sure that our children will live lives as comfortable as ours, and in watching the economic arena of American life slowly collapse, I would suggest that unless synagogues redesign their approach to money, so too will they. I would like to address two specific issues with regard to money and congregational life. The cost to participate, and the role money plays in the life of the community as understood through the celebration of Shabbat.

I am in a very special shul; one that I like to joke has as its budget the deficit of probably a much larger Conservative synagogue on the other side of the Twin Cities. In part, it has to do with the culture of the founding of the shul, and in part it has to do with the message that has emanated from the pulpit from day one. People have to be willing to provide a maximalist Jewish education for their children, both in terms of formal education and in terms of informal education. What has this meant? It means that parents understand that part of the culture of our shul is at least the need to seriously investigate day school education for their children. And it has meant that as part of the developing shul culture a maximalist approach to summer camp has also come into vogue. In truth the two go hand in hand. This summer some 60% of all Camp Ramah in Wisconsin campers were day school students. But forgetting the importance of that message for a moment, what does this mean in terms of Jewish life. It means that for a family of two kids, before you turn around you are theoretically committed to $30,000 of tuition costs between day school and camp. That's a pretty tough sell, but one which we have been fortunate enough to figure out how to make possible for families who would otherwise never have this possibility. It means that instead of seeking donors for major projects in the shul, I spend an inordinate amount of time looking for people to help supplement financial aid from an already beleaguered Day School. It means that the message that the day school is the address of the Jewish public school, forces a shul to focus its message on what it expects to produce, regardless of the economic reality of a particular family. I know the Avi Chai studies on the financial picture of Day Schools. I understand the weakening economy. But if a synagogue really wants to demonstrate vibrancy about itself, it will not sacrifice this issue. It will not see all of the answers to Jewish education within its doors, and within its facility. Some shul donors are simply scholarship angels, allowing for kids that they do not know to experience the wonder of a substantive Jewish education. Obviously this benefit does not flow directly into the shul itself. But, I would much rather deal with the fact that there will be tension between day school and non day school kids in a slightly poorer congregation, than eliminate the tension in a more financially secure one. Vibrant synagogues of the future will be partners with their congregants in helping educate their children in institutions other than their own. But that is only part of the equation that insures access to the vision of the shul even at the expense of the shul. But the other piece related to this has to do with dues. Dues are a bad thing, they imply fee for service. We must change that concept. I am not a rabbi of a congregation that expects people to pay for services. In fact, I revel in the fact that we have no dues; rather we have something called an annual sustaining contribution. In intent and increasingly in function, it creates a community that understands that each member has a responsibility to sustain it. As a result, we have had little attrition at the moment of post bar or bat mitzvah. We don't provide services for your dues; we work to create community through your contributions. Along the same lines, there has to be an egalitarian principal invoked here as well. Synagogues need to replicate the biblical notion of the half shekel. In addition to an Annual Sustaining Contribution, synagogues must also emulate the wisdom of Torah and create a fair fee of a half shekel—say $36 or $72. For some it is a simple check to write. For others it will be paid off in 12 installments, but in truth it sends another message that on one level each of us contributes the same to the congregation.

I could continue to analyze the role of money in congregational life, but want to move on to just one other issue. Who owns Shabbat in the synagogue? Until and unless this issue is resolved in American Jewish life, there will be no vibrant American synagogues twenty-five years from now. Here is where I disagree totally with those who proclaim that we should embrace Jews seeking only life-cycle validation. We must do everything possible to withstand the pressure to transform Judaism into a lifecycle circus. What once sustained the Jewish people was the festival cycle, an annual celebration of change and maturation. Now synagogues have begun to cater both literally and figuratively to the life cycle narcissism that exists. For any synagogue that wishes to be taken seriously one of its most important messages is this: if you come on Shabbat or Yom Tov mornings you are treated no differently at the end of the service than anybody else. I grew up in what I thought was a wonderful shul in Denver Colorado. Still, even as a little boy I used to cringe when I heard the rabbi proclaim at the end of the service—"Kiddush for the congregation in the north foyer, for invited family and guests in the social hall." That congregation that had an amazing run in the fifties in the Jewish neighborhood in Denver fell apart in the late 60s and disappeared in the 80s or 90s. I am convinced that it was due in part to the fact that the privatization of celebration created by removing the congregation from the *simcha* sent a message that for all the appearances of community, that synagogue was a glorified catering hall. If Rabbi Herring is correct that this generation now maturing is "universal" in their thinking, then we must take that universalism and utilize it as it relates to most immediate universalistic aspect of their lives, i.e. their fellow shul goers. If congregations send a message that regardless of your reason for being here today, you are equally important to us, synagogue attendance will only grow. This approach will also address a growing vulgarity in Jewish life that if left unchecked for the next twenty-five years, will utterly destroy the Jewish concept of *Zniut* (modesty). If we are serious about ending the vulgarity of conspicuous consumption in the Jewish community, eliminating the private bar and Bat Mitzvah celebration will go a long way in doing so. Instead, our focus must be that this significant moment, like other significant moments in Jewish life, occurs within the context of an open and caring community. A lifecycle celebration does not allow you to claim the deed for Shabbat, but rather allows you the opportunity to share your joy with those assembled.

Pushing the concept of accessibility just a little further let me suggest that communities need to seriously investigate what happens in the synagogue itself. While there is much talk about structural changes as it affects operations, there is often little discussion about the structural changes that must occur inside the service itself. First and foremost, we must see ritual leadership of *davening* as the inheritance of each and every Jew. The legacy of the *havurah* movement, as evidenced by the vibrancy of *Hadar* is the empowerment of the individual to become a *shaliach tzibur*, a leader of the prayer service. If there is any real structural change that is going to have a major affect on synagogue life, it is the idea that those who *daven* and *layn* and chant *haftarot* and often times deliver *divrei torah* are the very people who fill our pews on Shabbat morning. What does this mean for the cantorate? I would think that it means *Klei Kodesh* must see themselves as teachers of *nusach* and trope and *kavanna*. They provide support when necessary, but most often their work will occur outside the Shabbat service itself. If we are serious in creating people who will grab onto the treasure of their Judaism, we must model passion for prayer not by leading the congregation in prayer, but by joining with the congregation in prayer. If in St. Paul, Minnesota, it is possible to create a *davenning* community, where even for the *Yamim Noraim* all *davenning* is congregational led, it is possible to do so in any community. And let me tell you, that vibrant synagogues are praying synagogues; and praying synagogues are the ones that lead to social action, *hesed* and learning, that is all framed within a context of Jewish life. Synagogues must not forget that multiple Jewish institutions are vying for Jews' identification. What we offer that no one else can offer is a path to God through prayer. But, often-times, that path is blocked by well meaning and talented professionals who in facing the congregation in prayer literally push up against the possibility of their own congregants prayer being heard. This issue of accessibility must also be addressed in other ways as well. I have already alluded to the importance of economic accessibility, and I have spoken about religious accessibility.

The third factor is that there must be acknowledgement that people of all ages and families and lives of all varieties are going to find a place in a synagogue. We must work to create synagogues where people across the age spectrum actually interact with one another, where young people are cherished and older people are nurtured. We must do our part in celebrating the importance of partnering, for all who come into our synagogues, and for all we can draw into them. Synagogues must communicate a belief in the importance of monogamous fidelity driven relationships and understand that while the model and ideal might be called *kiddushin,* that we are in need of celebrating those who will not achieve the idealized. At the same time, we must be willing to admit that for some people the age of relationships has passed and for others not yet arrived. Synagogues must also see themselves as the prime place for individuals to gain access to the wonders of Judaism that are experienced in what we might just call Jewish living. Vibrant synagogues will place consistent emphasis on matters relating to how Jews eat, how Jews engage in business practices, how Jews celebrate Shabbat and holy days at home, how Jews create meaningful interpersonal relationships in a world that sees increasingly little value in them, how Jews comfort mourners, how Jews mourn, how Jews give *tzedaka,* how Jews see the landscape of political reality— all of these access issues truly matter. A vibrant synagogue of the future will embrace its responsibility constantly to teach, to remind, to cajole people into living passionate Jewish lives outside the walls of a synagogue building. And a vibrant synagogue of the future will never lose its sense of humor about itself or about its task.

In a time when increasingly we will be dealing with more limited budgets, in a time when other institutions have carved out a respectable niche for themselves, the synagogue must assert its primacy in touching the soul through the strengths it possesses. First and foremost, twenty-five years from now a vibrant congregation must seek a rabbinate that possesses a vision, and is prepared to share that vision with a community in search of meaning. It must underscore a commitment to economic accessibility, both through its dues structure and through its culture of celebration. It must see in the power of prayer an opportunity for allowing for any and every Jew to find significance in religious leadership roles, be it through *davenning, layning* or teaching and it must commit itself to being a place where young and old both are valued and challenged. The synagogue is but one laboratory of Jewish life, but it is the one where lives truly can be and should be molded.

Shortly before his death, Rabbi Hershel Matt, *alav hasholm*, told me a powerful story as we walked home from shul together one Shabbat morning in 1987. It has guided me every day since he shared it with me, and it is a fitting conclusion to this analysis. He told me whenever he felt down about his rabbinate he would go and visit a friend of his who happened to sell blinds and curtains for a living. He would say, "Sam. I think its time for me to get out. I'm tired of the constant struggle that is the rabbinate." Rabbi Matt said, my friend Sam turned to me and said, "Herschel, I sell window dressings for a living. I never touch a person's soul. Every day you have an opportunity to touch a person's soul and to connect that soul to God. I would give anything to have your job." Rabbi Matt walked out of there once again committed to his people and to the craft he so capably understood. I would just say, there is no institution like the synagogue that has such a possibility—of touching a person's soul and in connecting that soul to God, to the Jewish people and to the community that is theirs.

MODELS OF FUTURE SYNAGOGUE LEADERSHIP – HOW DO WE ENVISION AND PREPARE THEM?

Harvey Shapiro

David M. Gordis

Avi Weiss

Scott Sokol

Isa Aron

PROFESSIONAL LEADERSHIP AND THE FUTURE OF THE SYNAGOGUE

Harvey Shapiro

With efforts to transform the American synagogue there is a concomitant desire to restore a more integrated role for professional congregational leadership. This role integration is often manifest in new approaches to team-led change. These change efforts can be improved, however, in a return to a more complex matrix of qualities that can once again be considered essential for any congregational leader—rabbi, educator, or cantor. In fact, the zeal to change synagogues would be well served by recognizing the restorative nature of the intended organizational transformations. With a characteristically Jewish social-ideational dynamic, our "progress" may also be a "return." The return to more complex, holistic roles calls for newly reconstituted professional identities for rabbis, educators, and cantors that, in turn, informs a rethinking of the role of professional preparation and professional development for the synagogue's *k'lei kodesh*.

That the suggested transformations involve returning to and reconstituting traditional functions for leaders and synagogues is evident in the kinds of calls for change that we encounter—the broadening of the role of the *bet t'fillah* to become a *bet knesset* and *bet midrash*, the repositioning of life-long learning at the center of the synagogue's mission, embracing of the more comprehensive role of the synagogue as a *kehila kedosha*, and integrating informal and formal Jewish education.

The very semantics of traditional leadership designations and attributions suggest these complex, integrated functions that are called for today. Jewish texts repeatedly refer to more than one role for the highest levels of spiritual, juridical, and educational leadership. Often expressed as a hendiadys, we do not have to look far to encounter the familiar formulations of *maranan v'rabanan, rav u'moreh,* and the title of *adoneinu morenu v'rabenu.* It is axiomatic that these attributions refer to multiple, integrated roles of individuals, rather than to a kind of division of labor among institutional leaders. I suggest we would be well served by considering the needs for individual professionals to possess these multiple attributes, even as we advocate for a team-oriented approach.

The multiple interdependent competencies and qualities of individual communal leaders are often specifically delineated in the responsa literature. In explaining his recommendation of a communal leader, the *Ribash*[1] relates:

שאלוני הקהל הנכבד ההוא סתם, באיזה רב ומורה הוראה אבחר להם, התם אשר בארץ אפשר לה השגתו. אז עניתים, כי החכם אנביאונה, י"א, יש בו די ורב, לדון ולהורות וללמד לתלמידים ולדרוש ולדבר צחות, בין בכתב, בין במבטא, כאשר הוא אמת. (שו"ת הריב"ש סימן רפז)

> *The honored community asked me which judge[2] I would choose for them, one who is in the land and whom it would be possible to secure. I then answered them that the wise one, Anveona, who is God-fearing, has within him sufficient and plentiful capacities to truthfully adjudicate, instruct, teach students, provide interpretations, speaking with clarity both in writing and orally.*

In one sentence, the individual (a *rav u'moreh hora'ah*—a "rabbi-teacher-judge")—is referred to as *hakham* (wise), *yireh elohim* (God-fearing), with high capacities *ladun* (to render judgment), *l'horot* (to instruct), *l'lamed* (to teach), *lidrosh* (to interpret), and *l'daber tsahot* (to speak with clear precision)—using the modalities of *bikhtav* (writing) and *m'vateh* (oral expression) in conveying *emet* (truth)—a humbling challenge to all who seek to prepare synagogue leaders!

So too, the Mishna Berura,[3] echoing earlier medieval codes, espouses the communal obligation to appoint what might be called an *ish eshkolot* (a multitalented individual) at the helm.

מכאן יש ללמוד גודל החיוב המוטל על כל עיר ועיר בישראל, למנות אלוף לראשם רב מורה הוראה אשר יורה להם במצות התורה ומשפטיה ולהודיעאם את הדרך ילכו בה ואת המעשה אשר יעשון ולא יהיו כעורים המגששים באפלה ... רב ומורה צדק ומנהיג בדרכי ה' ... (משנה ברורה באור הלכה סי' נג סכ"ד)

From here one can deduce the extent of the obligation that is placed on each and every Jewish community, to appoint a rav moreh hora'ah[4] as its supreme head, who will instruct them in the mitzvot and regulations, will exhort them to follow a particular path, to conduct themselves through particular deeds . . . instructing them in justice and leading them in the ways of God.

Even a cantor's more specialized role as a *sh'liach tsibur* is viewed in the context of broader, deeper requirements. Vocal quality and liturgical knowledge are often presented as background requirements, while character, erudition, and seniority are foregrounded.

אין ממנין שליח ציבור, אלא גדול שבציבור בחכמתו ובמעשיו; ואם היה זקן, הרי זה משובח ביותר. ומשתדלין להיות שליח ציבור, קולו ערב ורגיל לקרות (רמב"ם, משנה תורה, הלכות תפילה ח,יא)

Do not appoint a sh'liach tsibur *unless he is prominent among the public in his wisdom and deeds. If he is an elder, this is even more commendable. Try to have a sh'liach tsibur whose voice is pleasant and accustomed to reading Torah.*

Traditional, halakhic voices are also echoed in contemporary calls for education to become a central function of synagogue life. Maimonides reminds us of the familiar dictum that a *Bet Midrash* is a more highly privileged real estate holding than a *Bet Knesset*:

בית המדרש, גדול מבית הכנסת. וחכמים גדולים--אף על פי שהיו להם בעירם בתי כנסיות הרבה, לא היו מתפללין אלא במקום שהיו עוסקין בו בתורה: והוא שיתפלל שם, תפילת הציבור. (משנה תורה, הלכות תפילה ח,ג)

A house of study is superior to a synagogue. The great wise ones— even if they had many synagogues in their towns, would only pray in a place where people were occupied with Torah study. There one would pray with the community.

מותר לעשות בית הכנסת, בית המדרש; אבל בית המדרש, אין עושין אותו בית הכנסת, שקדושת בית המדרש יתרה על קדושת בית הכנסת, (משנה תורה, הלכות תפילה יא,יד) ומעלין בקודש ולא מורידין.

It is permissible to make a synagogue into a house of study, but not to make a synagogue from a house of study because the sanctity of a house of study is greater than that of a synagogue. Increasing the sanctity is permitted—not decreasing it.

The centrality of education is also asserted in Maimonides' statement that professional Torah study will at times takes precedence even over the appointed times for prayer:

מי שהיה עוסק בתלמוד תורה, והגיע זמן התפילה--פוסק ומתפלל;
ואם היתה תורתו אומנותו ואינו עושה מלאכה כלל, והיה עוסק בתורה
בשעת תפילה--אינו פוסק, שמצות תלמוד תורה גדולה ממצות תפילה.
(הלכות תפילה ו,ח)

If one is studying Torah and the time for prayer has arrived, he should stop and pray. If, however, Torah study is his profession and he does not have another livelihood, then if occupied with Torah study at the time of prayer, he should not stop, because the mitzvah of Talmud Torah is greater than the mitzvot of prayer.

Traditional Jewish views of communal leadership, then, suggest that each professional congregational leader should possess an array of interdependent qualities, knowledge, and skills that are all brought to bear on his/her leadership role in the congregation. While teams of professionals are desirable, they should not supercede the integrated roles within any given individual professional k'li kodesh, if we are to show fidelity to this traditional norm for synagogue leadership.

Since the role of educator is embedded in the traditional definitions of rabbi and of cantor, isolating the educational function in one individual (i.e. the "educator") would represent a significant departure from the tradition. If, however, we consider the educator's role, in part, as working with the rabbi and cantor to let their sometimes eclipsed educational roles shine forth, we may suggest a different kind of team approach.

What better person is there to advocate and guide others in their educational functions than one who has extensively studied Jewish education and its role in Jewish life? Part of the educator's role is thus to assist, even to guide the rabbi and the cantor in putting their educational functions into a foreground—reminding them, again and again, that to teach means more then to instruct—that it means to engage in a meaningful way, to nurture growth, and to foster not only the acquisition of information, but the increased capacity for judgment and application in Jewish living and learning.

So too, the rabbi and cantor, might divest themselves of a kind of exclusivity in their respective roles and specializations, in the interest of working with the educator to serve as a spiritual leader, adult educator, interpreter of the vast corpus of Jewish knowledge, and representing the congregation before God.

A rabbi's role may be then, in part, to draw out the aspect of educator that is *rav*. If this is the case, then the rabbi should not only delegate technical educational responsibilities to the educator but should engage the educator in aspects of their own Jewish scholarship, working with them to inspire and engage others in spiritual meaning, and to provide congregants with religious guidance.

There are prominent examples in *halakhic* literature of qualifications given for a leader without reference to a technical, specialized role of rabbi, cantor, judge, or teacher. Turning to Maimonides again, we see the assertion that spiritual leadership involves challenges for change, not merely meeting congregants "where they are."

וכן כל הנביאים הוכיחו לישראל, עד שחזרו בתשובה. לפיכך צריך להעמיד בכל קהל וקהל מישראל חכם גדול וזקן וירא שמיים מנעוריו ואהוב להם, שיהא מוכיח לרבים ומחזירן בתשובה. (הלכות תשובה פרק ד, ב)

> *Since all of the prophets admonished Israel until they repented, the community should appoint a* hakham gadol *(a greatly learned person), an elder and God-fearing person from his youth, who is beloved to them, who can cause them to repent by publicly admonishing them.*

Education is fundamentally not a therapeutic activity; it is often even unsettling. The educator's role is thus not only to meet congregants' felt needs but also to challenge their current habits of mind and conduct. There is no education without change. The synagogue educator thus bears a constant responsibility to challenge others in their learning and growth, reminding one's fellow synagogue leaders that even as we shepherd, we challenge. Perhaps the triangulation of shepherding, challenging, and representing the congregation before God can form a useful, authentic, integrated set of capacities in all of our congregational professionals.

Endnotes

1. Rabbi Isaac Ben Sheshet Barfat, 14th century Spanish Talmudic authority

2. Though *rav moreh hora'ah* is a technical juridical designation, the semantic educational resonance of *moreh* and *rav* should not be overlooked.

3. The Mishna Berura is a Jewish legal work by Rabbi Yisrael Meir Kagan (who was also known as the Chafetz Chayim), published in early 20th century Lithuania.

4. See note 2.

RABBINIC EDUCATION FOR AN
EVOLVING COMMUNITY

David M. Gordis

The creation of the new Rabbinical School at Hebrew College has provided the occasion for serious reflection on the Rabbinate today, as a career, as a sacred calling, and as a principal shaper of the Jewish community. Challenges to creating a new rabbinical training program are imposing but clear: they include historical, ideological and practical considerations.

The principle that guides my thinking on developing a program to prepare men and women for a career in the Rabbinate, is that one must be concerned both with what the Rabbi **is** and what the Rabbi **does.** The title Rabbi carries with it a historic resonance, suggesting an authentic grounding and a degree of mastery of Jewish tradition and continuity with a calling that has existed for two millennia and that though constantly evolving has sustained a commitment to competence, scholarship, and tradition. At the same time, the evolution of the profession and the settings in which rabbis are called to serve has been extraordinary. Training must be appropriate to the broad range of skills and competencies which rabbis will require in successfully meeting their calling. Institutions are differentiated by type. While many rabbis will serve in synagogues, increasing numbers of rabbis are functioning as educators in schools, as chaplains in hospitals and social service agencies, as mentors and program directors on college campuses and as Judaic resources for other agencies and institutions. And the synagogue itself no longer represents a single institution, if it ever in fact did. Synagogues are differentiated by ideology, formality or informality of services, size, staffing, range of programs and strategic objectives. It follows that even in training rabbis for synagogues, the challenge of sustaining the continuity of the rabbinate against the background of the diversity of the synagogue is significant. In my view, an acceptable resolution of this dilemma is only achievable through a program that combines a shared core of Jewish competence and scholarship, a common skill set and a core program of religious and spiritual development, with a differentiation of training appropriate to the specific ideological and career path goals of students.

Rabbinical schools have historically failed to differentiate between their roles as graduate schools of Jewish studies and professional schools. They have often opted for a model that would be appropriate for individuals who were preparing for an academic career in Jewish scholarship and only grudgingly included considerations of the skills required by the contemporary rabbinate. Most often this created programs that neither trained scholars nor adequately prepared rabbis. Graduates of the major seminaries who wished to pursue careers in academic scholarship generally moved on to other institutions for formal academic training, though linguistic and textual skills acquired at the seminaries were very helpful. Rabbis often entered the field feeling inadequately prepared to face the demands of the careers on which they had embarked, and much of what they learned about functioning as rabbis was self-taught.

Scholarship is a full-time occupation, and it is too much to expect every rabbi to be a scholar in the sense of the professional who devotes his or her entire career to teaching, research, and publication. Scholarly attainments on the level of those expected from the full-time scholar cannot realistically be expected from the rabbi who is pursuing an active professional career. But rabbis must have a thorough grounding in the texts, ideas and central features of Jewish tradition. They must be able to access classic Jewish texts, Biblical, Talmudic, post-Rabbinic, medieval and modern, and speak and teach authoritatively from the tradition. If not professional scholars, rabbis must be **scholarly.** The shared core of rabbinic education must therefore focus on developing this competence in the Jewish tradition.

What rabbis **do** is now far more complicated than it used to be. In traditional settings not very long ago the function of the rabbi was to deliver two major discourses each year, a *halakhic* discourse on the laws of Passover on *Shabbat Haggadol,* the Great Sabbath before Passover, and an ethical discourse on *Shabbat Shuvah,* the

Sabbath of Repentance between Rosh Hashanah and Yom Kippur. The Rabbi also provided guidance in matters of *halakhah*, Jewish law. Synagogue Rabbis now typically perform a wide range of functions including preaching, teaching, counseling, managing, spearheading volunteer social-action efforts, overseeing diverse educational programs serving pre-schoolers and seniors and everyone in-between. Rabbis also serve as religious and spiritual mentors both through active engagement with congregants individually and communally, and through role modeling and mentoring.

Synagogues are only one setting in which the active presence of rabbis is sought. Hillel Foundations on campus most commonly seek rabbinic leadership for their programs; elementary and secondary day schools seek rabbinic presence and expertise; Jewish social service providers increasingly see their role as including the nurturing of Jewish continuity and often seek to include rabbis on their professional staffs, and the growing network of non-formal educational initiatives including but not limited to summer camps and youth groups are more and more frequently seeking significant rabbinic presence. Each of these settings requires an array of professional skills for effective functioning, which must complement and not take the place of the fundamental Jewish expertise we've described, and which must also form a major part of rabbinic education and training. While a range of skills including teaching, preaching and public speaking, counseling, ability to guide individuals and families at significant moments of transition must be a part of the core training of all prospective rabbis, it is not possible within a five year program to adequately cover all the areas that a rabbi will need in his or her work. Two implications: Beyond the core, differentiated programs of study need to be developed appropriate to the career goals of individual students; and students must emerge from their studies leading to ordination with the conviction that study and preparation for the career do not end at ordination but must be considered lifelong pursuits to which high priority must be assigned even within busy and demanding schedules. Furthermore, modes of study and skills must embrace more than the classroom, but should include mentoring, internships and practical experience in community and institutional settings.

A number of additional components of Rabbinic education should be mentioned. As already stated, today's synagogue is not a single institution, but represents a range of institutions which share a core of religious services but differ widely in size, range of programs, interests of members and availability of staff resources. Beyond the present "variations on a theme" which the contemporary synagogue represents is the reality that the synagogue is a dynamic institution in a living and evolving community. Rabbis must develop leadership skills, preparing them to work with members who are most often no less sophisticated than their rabbis in crafting and guiding positive change. Leaders must be willing to assume risks, think boldly, and be both good listeners and active participants in processes of change. There must be openness to differing views; an awareness that Jewish texts speak with multiple voices and that we will differ from one another in the voices we choose to hear most clearly. Leadership skills are a combination of aptitude and training. Not all rabbis will be natural leaders, though those should be prime candidates for the rabbinate. But leadership has been studied extensively and many leadership skills can be taught and acquired in such fashion as to enhance leadership skills significantly.

Finally, there are intangibles involved both in the selection of candidates for rabbinic training and in the training itself. Future rabbis must bring a love for Jewish life and the Jewish people, excitement about Jewish learning and Jewish experience, and a commitment to Jewish religious tradition. Future rabbis must bring selflessness, a love for people and a desire to serve. Rabbis for today and tomorrow must nurture receptivity to diverse beliefs, values and behaviors among their congregants. Rabbinic education may begin in Rabbinical School but it must be viewed as a life-long undertaking. Entering rabbinical students must be committed to a life of learning, a life of service, and a life of continued intellectual, religious and spiritual growth.

I recall many years ago reflecting on rabbinic education to a group of leaders at one of our major seminaries. I commented then and restate my conviction that rabbinical schools undertake to do the impossible and then somehow manage to come close to achieving their goals. I know of no perfect rabbinical schools; there are too many ingredients of this remarkable and complex calling to allow perfection. But in our efforts we will work to come as close as possible, and with God's help our work will be a blessing for the Jewish people.

Though I have suggested that rabbis will increasingly be called upon to serve in other than synagogue settings, I remain convinced that the synagogue will remain the central point of engagement for

Jews with Judaism and the principal institution in which rabbis will serve. While most observers would agree with this observation, it seems clear that the community approaches the synagogue with a degree of ambivalence. Coupled with the conviction of the synagogue's unchallenged centrality, is the sense that it is an institution in need of change, transformation or renewal. Rabbis must be prepared both to be accepted by synagogues, but also to assume roles as change agents, working with members and other professionals to bring about change. This leads me to make some observations about the reality of the contemporary synagogue and the challenges its rabbis, leaders and members will face in the coming decades.

In our conversations at this conference, we have had much talk about modernism, and the notion that one of modernism's central features, the "Sovereign Self," is a newly emerging adversary of tradition and continuity. Does the authoritative tradition as received from the past stand threatened by the "Sovereign Self?" Is this a tension between diametrical opposites? I would argue that the answer is no. This notion of the tension between the self and the community is not something new, not something that was invented by modernism. Great figures of religious leadership are always both traditional and subversive; they are those who find a balance point between the dominance of the community; and the assertiveness of individual moral and intellectual judgment. Correctly understood, the tradition should not be understood as standing firm against change, but rather as a tradition of continuity and change in balance.

The community, the synagogue and its leaders must seek a balance point between the affirmation of the tradition and its continuity and the willingness to stand up and be subversive when it may be important to assert that Sovereign Self. Another way of talking about Sovereign Self is not in opposition to community, but as the assertion of personal freedom and responsibility. Individuals and groups will pursue this navigation between the poles of continuity and change differently, but in my view, is a feature of Jewish life for all synagogues and all denominational and ideological expressions, and rabbis must be well prepared to actively participate and lead.

Rabbi Gordon Tucker has asserted that there are different kinds of Sovereign Self. There is a narcissistic self-indulgence that claims to be an expression of Sovereign Self, and that type of self-indulgence must be rejected. But, the voice of reason that encounters tradition and seeks answers when we face crises of belief is a positive embodiment of that Sovereign Self and should be nurtured.

The contemporary problem for many Jews, and I include myself among them, is that in traditional liturgy we are often called upon to affirm repeatedly formulations that are no longer consonant with what we actually believe. A variety of strategies are adopted by those that deal with this problem of inconsistency, but for many, no persuasive approach to a liturgy that no longer speaks to them has emerged. That is one of the reasons why quite a number of people are alienated from the Synagogue though the community would like to attract them and they themselves see no alternative point of Jewish engagement for themselves. This is an area where experiments with renewal must be undertaken and in which rabbis must be prepared to play an active role.

It has been suggested that the Synagogue need not be the Jewish institution for everyone; there are other Jewish institutions to fill other needs. I understand the argument but see no viable alternative to the synagogue as the focus of Jewish engagement. Only the synagogue can serve as the address for the process of exploration and engagement with the spiritual dimension of life. It is the only arena that we have where that search for meaning drawing on Jewish traditional sources, and connection with Jewish tradition and Jewish community can take place. But the synagogue needs to be better prepared to assume that role, and rabbis need to be prepared to lead.

If the synagogue will continue to be the only viable address for Jewish engagement, what we do about those who find increasing levels of discomfort with traditional formulations is a critical challenge. This includes many who define themselves as secular or somewhat secular, are alienated from the synagogue yet seek to engage Jewish tradition and Jewish community and are on a search for responses to issues of core meaning within Jewish tradition and culture. My sense is that adjustments will need to be made both by synagogues which will need to find ways of welcoming and meeting the needs of these non-traditional Jews, and by these self-defined secularists who will need to overcome their inhibitions about entering and engaging the synagogue. Rabbis need to be prepared to guide this process, understanding the problems created for some by traditional liturgical formulations and usages and reshaping the synagogue to be hospitable to a more ideologically diverse population.

I have put forward a number of the shaping considerations about the rabbinate and the synagogue that moved me to propose the establishment of the new Rabbinical School at Hebrew College. It remains now only to comment on why we've opted for a trans-denominational approach to rabbinic training. Clearly, as a *klal yisrael* institution, Hebrew College would move to establish a program serving the entire Jewish community. But the decision goes beyond that. We have argued that the historic roots of the rabbinate when juxtaposed with the diversity of the contemporary Jewish community, requires a program that combines a shared core of study in Judaica, religious and spiritual development and acquisition of skill sets with specialized and individualized programs superimposed on the core. Our program seeks to contribute to reinforcing the sense of a single Jewish people while sensitizing our students to the diversity of the community. Whether our students are preparing to work in the institutions of one of our denominational/ideological synagogues or institutions or are preparing for a career in a communal institution that transcends ideological lines, it is important that as a community we not exacerbate denominational divisions. We seek to contribute to overcoming fragmentation. Our program seeks to balance appropriate training in our diverse ideologies with a stress on commonalities. This is achieved not only in curricular content but in the relationships which are created in communal worship and in the *bet midrash* studies which complement more conventional graduate school courses. We make no claim that this is the only acceptable mode of rabbinic training. But we feel that this model is a promising one for preparing students for their rabbinic careers and strengthening a Jewish community for which diversity can be source of blessing rather than a threat.

THE SYNAGOGUE AS A HOME AND THE ROLE OF THE RABBI

Rabbi Avi Weiss

I have been asked to reflect upon how my model of synagogue relates to a model of a rabbi and how that influences my notion of how we should train rabbis. The model of synagogue with which I am most comfortable is a model that I call "The Bayit." We affectionately call our synagogue, the Hebrew Institute of Riverdale, "The *Bayit*." Whenever someone comes in we say, "Welcome to our Home." It follows that the congregation housed in that *bayit*, in that home, is nothing less than *mishpacha*, it is family.

In the Torah portion of *Vayetze* (Gen. 28. 10 ff) Jacob has a dream of a ladder, anchored on earth that was going heavenward, with the Angels ascending and descending on it. Upon rising he takes a vow "*Vayidar Ya'akov neder leimor* (Jacob takes a vow saying), *Im yihyeh Elokim imadi*, (If God will be with me) . . . *V'shavti besholom el **beit** avi*, (And I will return in peace to the house of my father) . . . *V'ha'evan hazot asher samti matzeva* (and this stone which I've established here as a monument) *Yehiyeh **beit** Elokim* (will be the house of God)." (Gen. 28: 20–22)

The careful reader of the Biblical text is always sensitive to redundancy of words. The word that is repeated in this lengthy passage is the word *bayit*, house. Many commentators are troubled, because it sounds like his commitment to God is conditional, *Im yihyeh Elokim imadi*, as if to suggest a deal—If you'll be with me, I'll be with you. I would like to suggest that what Jacob is really saying to God is—if you will be with me, I will do something that heretofore has never been done in the history of the Genesis narratives: If you will be with me, I will create for you a ***Bayit***, a house, a *Beit Elokim*, a house of God.

Up to this point, Bereshit was a book of selection. Of Adam v' Chava, only the descendants of Seth make it, his descendants were of course Noah, and his family. Of Noah, only Shem is the ancestor of Abraham and Sarah. Of Abraham, Isaac is the heir, Ishmael is not. Of Isaac and Rebecca, it is Jacob who is chosen and not Esau. At this point in the Torah, Jacob says to God, "God if you will be with me, no more selection"—our people will be a community of inclusion. No more choosing one child and casting away the other child. If you'll be with me God, I will create for you a *Bayit*, a home, my whole family will be counted in, no one will be excluded.

That really is the human story of the Book of Genesis, a story of fragmented family in desparate need of unification and common purpose. Even Jacob, who makes this deal, has a family that fragments. The family becomes whole at the end of the Book of Genesis in chapters 49 and 50, when the children of Jacob are standing around him, and all receive *brachot*, blessings. At that point, when all elements of the family are whole, it is only then that the nation can be born.

Only when the family is whole can the nation evolve. The Book of *Shmot*, Exodus, that tells the story of nation building, comes on the heels on the Book of Bereshit. What is true about nation is true about my vision of community and about Synagogue. Similarly the synagogue is our home and our congregants are our extended family.

This model is manifested in a number of ways. First, just as families are intergenerational and our synagogues are an expression of family, so too they should be intergenerational as well. There is a tendency these days to compartmentalize and divide into generational groups when, in fact, intergenerational communities are most conducive to spiritual striving. As families are inclusive, not withstanding the differences between siblings, and certainly siblings may have different ideological bents, but nonetheless, without blurring distinctions, every family member in a healthy family is welcomed, so too, with the extended family—the synagogue.

The second element of family is inclusivity. Being inclusive means to encounter and to engage. Encounter means everyone; the less observant, the more observant, the less involved, the more involved, the less knowledgeable, and the more knowledgeable, all have something to offer to our community. Just as families embrace the infirm, the needy, the sick, the strong, the healthy; so too our congregational family embraces those of various strengths and differing needs.

The test of community is not the way a community reaches out to the most powerful; that is very, very simple. Rather, the test of community is the way we reach out to the most vulnerable. In every family, every member has moments of strength, and moments of vulnerability. The question is not, will we become vulnerable, but rather when will be become vulnerable, and how will we, and how will our larger family, handle that vulnerability? That is why for me, a synagogue is architecturally beautiful if it has ramps. If it is accessible, it is beautiful. If it is not accessible, and I mean accessible to the *Bimah*, accessible to the Ark, it means that something is lacking.

This model of family, of *bayit*, of intergenerational inclusivity in Genesis is only half of the picture. After all, Jacob adds a word: I will build for you not just a bayit but rather a, *beit Elokim*. Not only is the model of synagogue a home, but it is a Godly home. It is a place of *beit Elokim*. It is a place of Jewish spirituality.

Spirituality means many things to many people, but for me, it means reaching beyond the self to feel the presence of God. That's a simple definition. Reaching beyond the self to feel the *Elokim*, to feel the presence of God.

The movement in reaching beyond the self to feel the presence of God has three elements.

The first element is to delve inward, to kindle the spark of God in each of us. This reach, as taught by the late Rabbi Avraham Yitzhak Hacohen Kook, is the gateway to prayer; it is the gateway to *avoda*, worship. Indeed the synagogue, the *beit Elokim* is known as a *beit tefillah*, house of prayer. "Once kindled," says Rav Kook, "Once our souls are aflame in the softest way, our souls can soar to connect to the infinite God above."

The second direction of this spiritual flame, the spirituality is also directed horizontally, not just inward but horizontally to the other in whom the image of God resides. This reach is the gateway to *g'milat hassadim*, to interpersonal kindness, the role of the synagogue as a *beit knesset (a house of assembly)*, and the greater the need of the other, the greater the act of kindness.

Then there is the third direction of the spirituality towards God, not within, in the *beit tefillah*, or outward the *beit knesset*, but upward, to God above. This reach is the gateway of the Synagogue as *beit midrash*, where the upward values of Torah are taught, the system of ethical monotheism, even, when that system conflicts with and challenges contemporary culture.

All of this is within the framework of *bayit. Beit tefillah*, the inward movement to God; *beit knesset*, the horizontal movement towards the God in the other; *beit midrash*, the upward movement, all are critical elements to what Jacob calls, the *beit Elokim*.

Now, when one considers the Synagogue as a *bayit*, as a home, as a *beit Elokim*, as a spiritual home, fascinating possibilities for roles of the rabbi begin to surface. First of all, there is the role of Rabbi as what I would call, "*the Moreh* or *Moreh Rebbe*." *Moreh* is the teacher, one who teaches and imparts cognitive knowledge. The *Moreh* is intellectual, sharing the wisdom of the mind, offering objective information and teaching what in midrashic literature is called the *aish shachor*, the black fire of the letters of the Torah. When you look into the Torah, you can see the black letters, and that is the *Moreh*, the one who imparts intellectual or cognitive information.

The *Rebbe* takes it a step further. The *Rebbe* is one who can combine the intellectual message with spiritual meaning. It is the teaching that comes from the heart, not just from the head; it is the teaching that comes from the soul. It is what in midrashic literature is called the *aish lavan*, the white fire; those white empty spaces between the black letters. That soulful teaching is best taught by example. You look at the *Rebbe*, and you could feel his, and I would now add you could feel her, soulfulness. For the *Rebbe*, what counts most is not only what the *Rebbe* says, it is not just the sermon, it's not just the divrei Torah; it's what the Rebbe does.

I would like to suggest the role of rabbi as *abba* or as *ima*, as a father or as a mother. What is a role of rabbi as *abba* or as *ima*? It is the role of the parent, one who leads with unconditional love, as a parent loves no matter what. As a Rabbi, I may not like everyone in my congregation, but a good Rabbi loves everyone in his or her congregation. I may not like them, I may not even respect them, but in fact, I love them. I love them deeply as people, and I have a relationship with, and a responsibility towards them.

The paradigmatic rabbi is the one who is *abba* and/or *ima*, and built into that is one who is also *moreh*, and *Rebbe*. This is the image with which I identify. If this model of rabbi is one who is *abba* and *ima* of a congregational family then it follows that his or her style should be much like a parent's relationship to an older child—nonjudgmental.

The paradigmatic rabbi is the one who is *abba* and/or *ima*, and built into that is one who is also *moreh*, and *Rebbe*. This is the image with which I identify.

How do you develop such rabbis? Let me set out several suggestions. First, we must do better when it comes to recruitment. We have to say very clearly that we need to encourage the best to enter the Rabbinate. In that same sense we need to find the best rabbis who can be a living expression of holiness.

We ought to begin recruiting early on, and generate a culture that becoming a rabbi is the greatest blessing. Remember John F. Kennedy's famous idea that serving one's country is the greatest honor. We have to begin developing that culture in our Jewish community by telling our young men and women that serving the Jewish people as spiritual leaders is a great honor. This value ought to be inculcated early on in Hebrew schools and day schools as well as in our high schools. This really requires a fundamental change of vision that is not just a technical correction but is really an adaptive change, which means changing all of our culture. We must do better in recruiting.

Secondly, as we design and implement programs in our rabbinic seminaries, I would suggest that we ought to have in mind the *abba* and *Moreh Rebbe* roles. To train our young men and young women, however old they are, to become a *Moreh* or a *Morah*, one must have a body of knowledge. In my case, it is imparting what I call open orthodoxy, and that has certain inherent dangers. Normally in my community learning the minutia of *halacha* leads to ideological closedness. The challenge in my seminary, Yeshivat Chovevei Torah, is to be fully committed in one's commitment to orthodoxy, but yet remain ideologically open.

To walk the delicate balance between legal commitment and openness and inclusivity, to become a Rebbe, to soulfully lead by example, that is much more difficult. One needs to understand one's self.

I am proud of the fact that in our institution each year rabbinic students engage in process groups, which is unheard of elsewhere. Beyond process groups there are classes in didactic psychology. If I am going to lead by example, I have to come to an understanding of who I am. I must come to understand leadership skills; how I lead, how one leads, and yet allow for process within my congregation.

In order to become an *abba* and *ima*, our children, early on, must be filled with two words, with the spirit of *ahavat Yisrael*, the love of their fellow Jews. If you ask me what is the most important dimension of being a rabbi, it is a person who loves people, and has a special love for the Jewish people, although no one can love all people equally since that would mean that we are not human.

The second concept is *arvut*, responsibility. One needs a special feeling of *ahavat Yisrael* that motivates one to assume responsibility and act on that *ahavat Yisrael*. You know who does that does that well? Although I have great differences with Chabad, on messianism, on soulful superiority and the centrality of the Rebbe, one must recognize that they are successful around the country because from day one they have been inculcated with the spirit that to be a rabbi, and in their case to be a rabbi's wife as well, is the greatest thing. They've been inculcated with this message of *ahavat Yisrael*. Like dedicated members of the Peace Corps, they have been told, and correctly so, that they have a responsibility to go out. Our seminaries must develop that sense of Jewish responsibility in addition to academic achievements.

Finally, in order to really develop rabbis one needs all of the cylinders working in a synchronized manner; a rabbinical school is not enough, communities have to be shaped. When we graduated our first class, I faced the obvious challenge. Rabbis have to be placed in communities, but are these communities ready for these rabbis? You know what kind of work that is, to begin shaping community attitudes to receive rabbis and to work with them properly. If, somehow, the mentality of a community is not shaped so that there is a framework that is conducive to the rabbi's work, then why should our new rabbis enter the rabbinate? We must do better when it comes to shaping community values or our efforts to train them may be wasted.

But there is one additional critical element. We not only need the seminaries, we not only need the communities; we need the input of rabbis in the field who will be senior mentors because some things can't be learned from the book or even the classroom; they can only be learned by sitting at the feet of a seasoned and experienced rabbinic mentor. The key is for the mentor to have the confidence to step back, so when there is an intern, assistant, or associate Rabbi working with you to give him or her a sense of ownership. That builds confidence and pride. The more one steps back, the more recognition and space one gives to an associate, or an assistant, the more regard it brings to the senior rabbi. All of these cylinders have to work.

To conclude as I started; Jacob says, *Im yhiyeh Elokim imadi,* "If you will be with me o' God," if you will be with me, I'll build you a beit Elokim. And the future of this Beit Elokim will be, as he says *"V' ze yehiyeh sha'ar hashamayim,* "And this [place] will be a gateway for heaven." May we be blessed so that our Batei Elokim, our synagogues, indeed become gateways to heaven here on Earth.

THE CANTORATE: HISTORY AS PRECEDENT FOR EVOLVING ROLES

Scott Sokol

There's an old Yiddish proverb that goes something like this:

איינער איז א מבין אויף א פשטל, דער צווייטער אויף חזיר-האָר,
אָבער אַלע זענען מבינים אויף א חזן.

*One is an expert on scholarly discourse, while another is an expert
on boar's bristle, but everyone is an expert on cantors!*

Although the saying is certainly funny on its face, I think we
can get more out of a proverb than simply a good laugh. Specifically, this proverb opens a window into Jewish attitudes about cantors. One of those attitudes appears to be that the status of
hazzanut lies somewhere between rabbinic discourse and knowledge of pig's hair (hopefully a bit closer to the former than the latter). Another is the assertion that all Jews have a stake (as well as
apparent expertise) in what it is that cantors do.

As a point of departure then, I'd like to ask how and why have
these attitudes developed? Answering this question requires us to
look historically at the role of the *hazzan* and the evolution of the
cantorate. Once reviewing the past history of the cantorate, we can
begin to examine the possible futures that the profession may yet
have.

A Brief History and Some Terms

In its earliest days, the religion of Judaism focused on the sacrificial cult, and was administered largely by the Kohanim or Priests.
Temple singers were an important part of this cult, embellishing
the sacrifices and supporting them liturgically through the singing

of Psalms, usually accompanied by instruments. The Temple musicians generally were from the tribe of Levi, and the grand Levitical choirs that they formed served as the template for all future choral music in the synagogue and church.

Sometime between the Restoration of the Temple in the 6th century B.C.E. and the time of the Hasmoneans in the middle of the 2nd century B.C.E., a system of satellite, supplemental worship developed, known as *ma'amadot* (recounted in Mishna Ta'anit 4:2). Basically, each Jewish town or village was included in a rotation that sent representatives to Jerusalem to assist the Priests in the sacrificial rites. While the Temple service was going on in Jerusalem, other representatives back home met in the local *knesset* to study scripture and (if a Kohen was available) recite the Birkat Kohanim. With the organization of these *ma'amadot* and the establishment of the *knesset* as the community meeting place, the synagogue as an institution had begun, as had its primary goal of facilitating communal worship. At about this same time, we first encounter the term *hazzan* in connection with the *Knesset*. Its two elected officials were *rosh ha-knesset* and *hazzan ha-knesset*, although at this point the latter term likely indicated an overseer of sorts, rather than a prayer leader.

Terminology

There are a variety of opinions as to the derivation of the term *hazzan* and how it came to be associated with the position of the cantor as we normally understand it. Other Near Eastern roots are consistent with a definition of "overseer," which may well be linked to the Hebrew term חזון meaning "vision" or according to some, "prophecy" (perhaps because music itself is often linked to prophecy in scriptures, cf. The Psalms of David).

As for understanding the current meaning of *hazzan* as the clergyperson responsible for prayer-leading, we need to consider a good deal more about the evolution of prayer in the synagogue. During the Talmudic period and up until the early Gaonic period, the prayer canon was limited. As such, volunteers who were liturgically knowledgeable could serve as the leader for the prayer service. Such an individual was referred to as the שליח צבור — messenger of the community. It was certainly an honor to be chosen for this service, but the leader was not considered a "professional" in the sense that we would use today.

By the time of the codification of the Mishna and Talmud, much of the current *matbeah tefillah* or prayer canon was established; however, there remained a great deal of variation in how the required themes were to be liturgically realized. Around the 6th century, the number of prayers grew and became more complex. Furthermore, written prayer books were rare (many authorities in fact deemed them non-halachic), and familiarity with Hebrew became less and less common. As a result, a need arose to have a highly trained individual who was not only well-versed in the emerging liturgy, but who could contribute to that efflorescence, crafting liturgical poetry for special occasions and holidays. These individuals came to be known as *hazzanim*, and their poems as *piyutim*. The *piyut* developed into an important Jewish literary art-form, and more and more communities felt the need to hire their own professional *hazzan* to render these as well as the required *tefilot*. The concept of *hidur mitzvah*, the fulfillment of mitzvot in ever more beautiful ways, became the *raison d'etre* of the *hazzan*. What emerged then was an individual whose talents, knowledge and piety, permitted him to render the service carefully, beautifully and creatively.

Qualifications of the Hazzan

One of the most fascinating aspects to the study of the cantorate involves examination of the qualities that *hazzanim* are expected to possess. This study itself goes a long way towards understanding our initial proverb. The Mishnah states the following about the qualifications of the "reader" (prayer leader):

עמדו בתפלה, מורידין לפני התבה זקן ורגיל, ויש לו בנים, וביתו ריקם, כדי שיהא לבו שלם בתפלה.

One who stands to pray before the ark should be mature ("old and regular"), have children, but his home should be empty so that his heart is full of prayer.

The implication is that a *hazzan* should be an inept breadwinner! The Talmud Ta'anit elaborates on this, and mentions other necessary qualities:

. . . he be burdened by labor and heavy family obligations but have not enough to meet them, one who has his labor invested in the field, and whose house is empty, whose youth was unblemished,

who is meek and is acceptable to the people, who is skilled in chant-ing, with a pleasant voice, and possesses a thorough knowledge of Tanach, *who is conversant with the* Midrash, Halakhot *and* Agadot *and all the Benedictions.*

Interestingly, of these the matter of the pleasant voice appears of somewhat ancillary importance. Later codes, however, do spend some more time on the vocal qualifications. The *Aruch haShulchan* states the following:

מי שזיכהו הקב"ה בקול נעים, ירנן להקב"ה בשמחה
של מצוה ולא שאר רננות.

He who the Holy One Blessed be He has endowed with a pleasant voice, let him sing to the K"BH at festivals in honor of the fulfill-ment of a mitzvah, rather than at secular festivities.

Having a good voice, however, is seen by the rabbis as merely a necessary characteristic for being a *sheliach tsibbur*; it is certainly not a sufficient one. In fact, the *Mishnah Brurah* states quite clearly:

ויניחו אותו להתפלל משום נעימת קולו,
אין הקב"ה מקבל תפילתו

If one is allowed to serve (as sheliach tsibbur) by merit of his voice alone, God does not accept his prayers.

Indeed, the halachic requirements of a *sheliach tsibbur* are extensive, and interestingly do not seem to apply to other individu-als such as rabbis. In addition to listing a large number of neces-sary attributes, the *Mishnah Brurah* tells us that a *sheliach tsibbur* must be a "suitable person," and who is considered suitable? One who is free of sin and whose reputation was not defamed, even in his youth. Along these lines, we learn that even a single congregant may protest and attain the dismissal of a *sheliach tsibbur* of whom a continuous defamatory rumor is circulated.

The obvious question here is why? Why do our codes spend so much time on the requirements and characteristics of the *sheliach tsibbur*? There are several answers to be sure, but I'd like to enter-tain just a couple.

The qualities sought by the Mishnah to my mind are among the most interesting. The necessity that the *hazzan* (as this indi-vidual was later called) be old, have children and have experience with the difficulties and burdens of providing for one's family all seem to go to the desire that the one who represents the *kahal* be able to empathize with the common man. A youth does not understand responsibility, a rich man cannot understand physical toil the way a farmer might, and one without children may not understand what it truly means to be relied upon. In fact, the 13th century *paytan* Rabbi Meir of Rothenburg emphasized that the more a *hazzan* had suffered, the more acceptable he became as a cantor, since "the Lord prefers the prayers of a person broken in spirit." Ultimately, the rabbis want their *sheliach tsibbur* to truly be able to represent their needs before the Heavenly court, and so require that the *hazzan* at least share them. This is a remarkable insight on their parts, and sets the Jewish precentor quite apart from many other faiths in which the clergyman has an almost divine status. The *hazzan* needs to be part of *amcha*.

That said, the community still wants to look up to their *shaliach*. As a result, the rabbis instituted a set of moral requirements that frankly are hard to imagine fulfilling. Which of us has had a pristine moral record even as a youth? Nevertheless, the ideal in this arena is given as a benchmark against which an individual may be compared.

Finally, the *hazzan* needs to be well-versed in Jewish text and law. This aspect of the cantorial package will be discussed at greater length below, but for now it is sufficient to state what should be obvious. Namely, that without proper grounding in and appreciation of Jewish text, a *hazzan* would not be able to bring much authenticity to the rendering of a liturgy which itself is so often a product of intertextuality, that is, derived from other primary text sources such as the Tanach. Furthermore, as with all matters of Jewish practice, there is a great deal of *halacha l'ma'aseh* that is essential for the leading of prayer, and one needs to be sufficiently schooled in these laws to carry out one's duties with authority.

The Power of Music

I'd like to digress a bit for a moment to mention one other likely locus for the myriad moral and experiential requirements placed on the *hazzan*, namely the seemingly magical powers of music to reach inside our very souls. The great twentieth century Jewish philosopher Abraham Joshua Heschel wrote a seminal essay entitled "The Vocation of the Cantor." In it, Heschel speaks at length about the spiritual powers of music.

The only language that seems to be compatible with the wonder and mystery of being is the language of music. Music is more than just expressiveness. It is rather a reaching out toward a realm that lies beyond the reach of verbal propositions.

And then he states:

Listening to great music is a shattering experience, throwing the soul into an encounter with an aspect of reality to which the mind can never relate itself adequately.

And just in case one were not sure of the primacy that he ascribes to music, he goes on to say:

I am neither a musician nor an expert on music. But the shattering experience of music has been a challenge to my thinking on ultimate issues. I spend my life working with thoughts. And one problem that gives me no rest is: do these thoughts ever rise to the heights reached by authentic music?

Heschel's words are poetic and moving in their own right, but in addition they speak to a core truth about the ability of music to touch the spirit in ways which words, even liturgical words are unable to do alone. The power of music is in this respect almost akin to magic or sorcery. Indeed, people have often associated unusual musical talent with divine or sometimes satanic powers. Nicolo Paganini, surely one of the greatest violin and guitar virtuosi of all times, was in fact required to make a statement swearing that his musical ability did not derive from the devil, so unbelievable were his talents and their ability to move people.

The rabbis, I think, were clearly aware of the ability of music and song to move the spirit. Perhaps the most obvious example of this is the concept of *kol ishah*, the proscription against hearing women's voices in the synagogue and in public. According to certain authorities women's voices are thought to be too alluring for men to resist, and therefore must be avoided in both prayer and secular settings. (Of course, this thought is not unique to Israel; the Sirens of classical mythology offer another example.)

In Judaism, prophecy is also clearly linked to music, though such a discussion falls outside the purview of this paper. In essence, it appears that the detailed restrictions and regulations that the rabbis place on the *sheliach tsibbur* are at least in part a result of their discomfiture with the intimate powers of the voice, at least when properly channeled. These *halachot,* then, serve as a system of checks and balances to prevent undue control from someone who could be of suspect character.

Evolving Roles

Although the *hazzan* has been a veritable fixture of synagogue life since the beginning of that institution, his roles have undergone some interesting and important changes over the centuries.[1] In almost all periods, the *hazzan* had an extremely varied and extensive set of responsibilities, despite generally low financial compensation and status. Landman put it well in his historical survey of the cantorate when he said:

> *Neither the low salary scale of cantors nor their low status prevented the communities from demanding the services of the cantors in numerous communal activities. Their duties seem endless. The scope of their activities were boundless. The cantor seemed to be the catch-all for all communal activities for which no one else had been designated.*

Primarily of course, *hazzanim* were expected to lead services. This has been true since early Gaonic times till the present. The exact boundary of this service was not always the same, for example, did the *hazzan* lead all services on all days, or was their leading limited to specific services (e.g., Musaf) or holidays (e.g., Festivals and High Holidays)? During the Middle Ages, it was not uncommon (as today) to engage one *hazzan* for the bulk of the calendar year, but to seek a special candidate for the High Holidays. At this critical time of the year, the "specialness" sought was more likely to involve a degree of perceived piety than vocal ability. This is, of course, different from current practice where the High Holiday cantor is generally chosen for his or her voice more than any other single quality.

The *hazzan* was also the primary individual responsible for insuring that a *minyan* was available for services. At various times, this requirement might have involved combing local pubs and inns or going out to the fields to recruit Jewish men. This practice is alive and well today, although soliciting congregants' *minyan* participation via cellphone has for the most part replaced walking up and down the streets in search of an unsuspecting tenth.

Due to the level of musical and scriptural skill required, *hazzanim* have often been responsible for daily, weekly and seasonal

Torah reading, as well as the chanting of the more obscure *megillot*. This part of the job is well in line with typical cantorial training, though in the previous generation it was often seen as a bit unseemly for the cantor to have to chant from the Torah.

As early as the Gaonic period, there were other accompanying duties to reading Torah including the prerogative of deciding who would be called for *aliyot*. Also, it was the cantor's duty to recite a prayer on behalf of the *oleh*. In some communities, these responsibilities led to conflict as certain individuals felt that they resulted in too much power for the cantor and could lead to corruption. There is at least one recorded instance of bribe-taking on the part of a cantor in order to call an individual for an honor.

The *hazzan* also recited specific prayers for the sick during the Torah service, as today. Hazzanim were also called upon to perform other ritual tasks during the holidays, such as blowing *shofar*, lighting the Hanukah candles, or making the Sabbath *kiddush*.

In the Middle Ages, additional responsibilities were often given to the cantor that were not religious in nature. One was town crier. It was up to the cantor to make communal announcements, perhaps due to his louder trained voice, but also presumably due to the respect and recognition he was given by the community. The *hazzan* was the individual responsible for announcing upcoming events such as weddings and circumcisions. In some communities, this town crier role was extended to matters involving communal sentencing, such as when an individual was placed in *herem*. Legal resolutions were also announced by the *hazzan* in a public forum. This role of the *hazzan* was not always an enviable one as you can imagine, since people have a tendency to "shoot the messenger."

An important additional responsibility fell to many *hazzanim* as early as the Gaonic period, namely to preach to the congregation. In many instances, the *hazzan* was in fact the primary preacher due again in part to his "stage presence" and his ability to project his voice. Rabbis were certainly the legal scholars and well-versed in Talmud, but may not have been gifted in oratory. Also, at times when Torah study itself was banned (such as during the Justinian period), skillful *hazzanim* wove Torah learning into their *piyutim* and thus served as pulpit teachers to the congregation when rabbis could not. Even in modern-day synagogues, it is increasingly common for *hazzanim* to have some designated times to offer sermons and *divrei Torah* to the community, such as on *Shabbat Shirah*.

Again, as is true today, the *hazzan* has for centuries been an integral—and sometimes sole—participant in life-cycle events for his community. The personal high and low moments such as birth, circumcision, marriage and death saw the *hazzan* as officiant or co-officiant. For weddings in particular, it was felt important for a cantor to be present. Indeed, in some Spanish communities there were *takkanot* written to require the presence of the cantor at all weddings. This was likely not only in pursuit of *hiddur mitzvah*, but also a reflection of the fact that it was usually the cantor who announced the original betrothal and knew its particulars.

In the 16th century, it became customary for cantors not only to officiate musically at funerals, but also to eulogize the deceased. A related role was played by *hazzanim* of the Gaonic period during the period of *shivah*. The law required that during this period, the usual conventions of discourse be suspended, and individuals visiting the mourners were not allowed to initiate conversations with them. Rather it was up to the mourner to do so if s/he felt up to it. Oftentimes, though, this was difficult for the mourner, so it became customary for the *hazzan* to be the "ice-breaker" on all conversations. Since mourners were visited at all different times, this required the *hazzan* to be present with the mourner for most of the day, a situation which itself no doubt offered additional comfort.

In addition to all these roles, cantors have historically taken on a great number of others including *sofer* (ritual scribe), *mohel* (ritual circumcisor), *shochet* (ritual slaughterer), teacher and community entertainer. The combination of *hazzan/shochet/mohel* was especially common throughout the Middle Ages into the 20th century. Following this longstanding tradition, modern cantorial schools have sometimes made *milah* programs available to students interested in this important communal function, and as a result, today some of our most skilled *mohelim* are also *hazzanim*.

Status of the Hazzan

A good deal could be written on the topic of the evolution (and occasionally devolution) of the *hazzan's* community status throughout the centuries. The topic, however, falls a bit out of the purview of this paper. Interested readers should consult the Landman volume (see bibliography). I'll simply state that the status of the *hazzan* has often been quite high in the community, but at its height there has usually been a backlash, sometimes from rabbis and sometimes from the community as a whole. As an example, during the Gaonic and early Middle Ages *hazzanim* enjoyed a very high status. Their names were typically included in the list of dignitaries saluted by the Geonim in their epistles to communities, in deference to their position. In community processions, they were often the first or second in line even before the *parnas* who was viewed as the community leader. In many communities in the Middle Ages, cantors were provided a special seat of honor, elevated and near the place from which he conducted services. This practice still exists at several synagogues.

The exalted position of the cantor, though, often coexisted with significant opposing sentiment. The famous 13th century Jewish satirist, Judah Harizi showed the cantor as a bumbling idiot, at the same time exalted and revered, but upon closer examination one who stumbled over most ordinary words in the prayers, confusing consonants and mistaking vowels resulting in the cantor not knowing what he was chanting and the people not understanding what he said. Another Yiddish proverb sums up this often tacitly-held assumption: *chazonim zenen naronim* (cantors are fools).

Despite these longstanding negative attitudes towards cantors, there have throughout the ages been *hazzanim* of exceptional quality who have effected large-scale and important changes in the Jewish landscape. Again, space constraints prevent discussion of these individuals here, but it is worth acknowledging this fact.

Modernity

The early nineteenth century was an important period of time for the cantorate, and marked to a large extent the beginning of its modern professionalization. Prior to this period, there was little if any written documentation of the *hazzan's* most important tool: *nusach hatefilah* (i.e., prayer chant melody). This changed with the nusach collections of several prominent *hazzanim* and Jewish musicians, in particular Salomon Sulzer in Vienna, Louis Lewandowsky in Berlin and Samuel Naumbourg in Paris (the first and third of this trio were their communities' *hazzanim*). Not only were these individuals well-versed Jewishly, but were regarded as peers within the broader community of musicians. For example, Sulzer was a good friend to Franz Schubert, and actually hired Schubert to write a setting of the Psalm for the Sabbath in Hebrew. At the same time, Sulzer was one of the most celebrated interpreters of Schubert-*lieder*.

There were of course exceptions of musically tutored Jews prior to this time (most notably the Italian Jew Salamone Rossi who lived during the sixteenth and seventeenth centuries), but it was the nineteenth century that for the first time saw the emergence of a highly trained cantorial corps.

During the late 19th and early 20th centuries, many of these European *hazzanim* émigrated to the United States where their roles as community leaders and entertainers were sometimes as important as their roles as spiritual leaders. Out of the American Jewish yearning for cultural art forms of their own emerged what is generally regarded as the Golden Age of the Cantorate. In this time period (perhaps a fifty year span beginning in the early 20th century), *hazzanim* were the dominant musical and cultural outlet for growing numbers of Jewish immigrants. The dividing lines between the synagogue, the concert hall and the Yiddish theater were crossed easily and to great success. Many *hazzanim* emerged as film stars as well (e.g., Moishe Oysher), and it is no mere coincidence that the first successful 'talkie' film, "The Jazz Singer," featured a plot about a cantor and his son, as well as cantorial music.

The great success of the American cantor as cultural impresario gave rise to renewed animosities with rabbinic counterparts who saw the cantor more often than not as a highly paid minstrel rather than a sacred singer. This perception (although no doubt accurate in many cases) was unfortunate and a gross oversimplification. As always, the great majority of successful cantors of the day were pious and well-versed in Jewish text and law.

Professional Education

Despite the great amount of knowledge and training that professional *hazzanim* must possess to perform their duties successfully, until quite recently most *hazzanim* trained for their craft by means of a journeyman approach. Only in the past couple of decades have the larger professional organizations of cantors (specifically the American Conference of Cantors and the Cantors Assembly) expressed in their policies and practices a preference for the cantorial school route. No doubt, part of this shift has been the result of the dwindling influence of many older *hazzanim* who resisted a paradigm that went counter to their own experience. Equally important, though, was the emerging desire of *hazzanim* to professionalize their calling.

As early as the turn of the 20th century, there was an outcry for a professional school to train *hazzanim* that would convey upon its graduates not only the requisite knowledge to serve the modern cantorate, but also some degree of legitimacy as regards the academic (and rabbinic) world. It was not until after the Holocaust, however, that enough impetus existed for the formal launching of such a school. In 1947, the School of Sacred Music was founded at Hebrew Union College, initially as a training ground for all cantors regardless of movement within Judaism. Klal *yisrael* would not be so easily served, however, even among cantors. In 1951, the Conservative Jewish Theological Seminary founded its own cantorial school: the Cantors Institute (CI, now the HL Miller Cantorial School), and in 1954 Yeshiva University followed suit with its Cantorial Training Institute (CTI, now the Belz School of Music). The schools of HUC and JTS remain the dominant training ground for today's professional *hazzanim*.

In more recent years, several other options for cantorial education have asserted themselves. Since 1992, the Academy of Jewish Religion (AJR) has offered a transdenominational cantorial ordination program in New York and has recently added such a program on its Los Angeles campus. AJR's ordination programs (both rabbinic and cantorial) were the first to allow part-time study. Gratz College has partnered with the Reconstructionist Rabbinical School (RRC) to offer cantorial training and investiture, and the Aleph Alliance for Jewish Renewal now offers their own cantorial ordination track which includes a good deal of private study and mentoring. Finally, Hebrew College began a paraprofessional cantorial arts certificate program several years ago that has recently been expanded and developed into a full ordination program (see below); like AJR, Hebrew College's program is transdenominational. In general, each of these schools or programs requires a Bachelor's degree (often in Music or Jewish Studies) for admission. Programs typically require four or five years of full-time study, and in the majority of cases result in a Masters degree (usually in Jewish or Sacred Music) along with cantorial investiture/ordination.[2]

As *hazzanim* have enhanced their educational background and religious commitments, they have become much more on par with their rabbinic colleagues. This should be good news for the cantorate, as well as for the congregations in which these *hazzanim* serve, but interestingly these educational changes have not gone as far as one might imagine to quell the rivalry (and sometimes out-right animosity) between rabbis and cantors. Indeed, to some extent they may have exacerbated the situation. Whereas once rab-bis could comfortably believe themselves on a different educational level than their cantorial counterparts (perhaps justifying the not infrequent condescension mentioned above), with greater educa-tional and religious authority placed in the hands of *hazzanim*, the difference in professional attainment has became more apparent than actual. Thus, rabbis may feel more threatened than ever by their cantorial colleagues, and cantors for their part may be assert-ing their professional independence to a much greater degree than in the past.

Emerging Paradigms

As educational paths have changed for the modern *hazzan*, so have expectations and opportunities within the Jewish professional world. Whereas most of the 20th century saw the primary role of the *hazzan* as vocal artist, more modern sensibilities require a far broader portfolio. To be sure, the *hazzan* remains primarily a musi-coliturgical specialist, but this specialization is reflected in an increasing number of roles both as educator and spiritual leader. Hazzanim in large synagogues probably spend upwards of 75% of their time teaching, with the majority of that devoted to training *b'nei mitzvah*. As a result of their close work with youth, cantors are often the single most important synagogue agent for Jewish conti-nuity at this critical age. Their success or failure with a bar/bat-mitzvah student often predicts the degree to which the child continues along a Jewish life path.

In addition, the *hazzan* is expected to devote a good deal of attention to adult education and spiritual guidance of congregants. Pastoral counseling as well as chaplaincy are integral to the can-tor's clerical roles. Of course s/he is still responsible for musical and other cultural programs, and increasingly for interfaith pro-gramming (e.g., Thanksgiving concerts, Holocaust commemora-tions). Finally, the expectation remains that the *hazzan* will be an officiant or co-officiant at major lifecycle events.

Cantors and rabbis. Given the broad range of current responsibili-ties, one might wonder about whether the roles of rabbi and cantor are on an intersecting course. The answer is yes and no. To be sure, more rabbis and cantors are receiving training and experience in what were once considered each others' purview. For example, many rabbinical students study *nusach* and song-leading, and *halacha l'ma'aseh* is part of most cantorial curricula. However, I believe that for most rabbis and cantors, there will remain important differences in training and emphasis. What the increased training affords, however, is the opportunity for rabbis and cantors to be sole practitioners when needed, as well as more appreciative and able collaborators when they have the good fortune to work under the same roof.

On this issue, I should note that several codes of Jewish law consider the situation in which a congregation cannot afford both a rabbi and a *hazzan*. In most cases, the codes prefer the hiring of a rabbi (which is perhaps not surprising since the codes were themselves written by rabbis . . .); however, this is not always the case. A congregation whose main charge is providing worship services for its community might be better served by hiring a *hazzan* rather than a rabbi when a choice needs to be made. An alternative would be to hire a rabbi who could serve as a competent *sheliach tsibbur*.

Interestingly, despite the large number of synagogues that find themselves in the position of being able to afford only one synagogue professional, there are very few rabbis who receive cantorial investiture or *hazzanim* who are ordained rabbis. The most likely reason for this lack of composite professional is the great amount of time it would take to train in both areas successively (and successfully). Also, the requisite mix of abilities is probably rare. Nonetheless, modern rabbinic and cantorial schools would probably do well to consider whether some sort of composite degree would be feasible or desirable. An intermediate training program for "Spiritual Leader" would also seem a viable solution for many. In fact this idea has begun to receive attention in the Jewish renewal world, specifically in the Aleph programs, which include a category of Rabbinic Pastor that shares some but not all of the requirements of the rabbinic and cantorial ordination tracks.

On the topic of spiritual leadership, it should be noted that an increasing number of *hazzanim* are co-opting this term (myself included) from their rabbinic colleagues. The rationale for doing so seems relatively straightforward—it is the *hazzan*, often more so even than the rabbi, who is concerned with matters of the spirit such as prayer. Finding a rabbinic colleague willing to relinquish this title is more difficult. It obviously requires self-confidence in ones own strengths and areas of expertise, and appreciation for what a fully engaged *hazzan* can bring to congregational life. I consider myself very fortunate to have such a colleague in the community I currently serve (Rabbi William Hamilton at Congregation Kehillath Israel).

Another way to consider titles and roles is by classifying the duties and responsibilities that are typically carried out by one professional versus another. In my own synagogue, consideration of this question led the rabbi to propose a structural system that divides the tasks and programs of our synagogue into one of several clusters: *Torah, Avodah, G'milut Chesed, Kehillah and Terumah.* Within this scheme, the rabbi is the *"rosh"* of the *Torah* cluster, whereas I as the *hazzan* am *rosh* of the *Avodah* cluster and the synagogue administrator is *rosh* of *Terumah*, etc. (This is actually an oversimplification of our system, but true in its essence.)

Cantors and synagogue educators. In addition to the possibility of simultaneous training for the rabbinate and cantorate, a second emerging paradigm for the modern cantorate is the "cantor-educator." In this model, a *hazzan*-to-be works simultaneously on cantorial investiture and a higher degree (usually a Masters) in Jewish education. Upon completion of his or her education, such a cantor is able to serve many additional roles including (when needed) educational director. Again, the economic advantage of such training to synagogues is obvious: namely, being able to hire one individual rather than two, at least in a congregation whose program is small enough to allow such a composite to be manageable. However, this hybridization is more than economically advantageous. It acknowledges the emerging reality (noted above) that the modern-day *hazzan* spends a significant proportion of time in the role of educator, broadly conceived. It therefore would seem critical for cantors to receive a significant amount of training in pedagogy, whether or not they end up serving as classroom teachers or educational directors.

We at Hebrew College are the first to offer this dual training in a fully integrated program. In the Fall of 2004, we welcomed our first class of students into the Cantor-Educator Program (CEP). Successful completion of this five-year, full-time program will result in cantorial ordination and a Masters in Jewish Education, with targeted professional coursework addressing not only each field individually, but their intersection (e.g., B'nei Mitzvah Pedagogy, Jewish Music Education).

The Influence of Contemporary Music

A final area that cannot be ignored when considering the present incarnation of the cantorate is synagogue music itself. It is, after all, not only enhanced educational opportunities that have altered the relative weight of cantorial duties. Changes in musical sensibility have been just as critical. Specifically, during the "Golden Age," the successful cantor was a vocal showman precisely because such skill was necessary to properly realize the elaborate and often operatic settings preferred in that day. Although participation has virtually always been a part of Jewish prayer experiences, the level of desired participation has changed dramatically over the past thirty or so years. No longer are congregations content to listen to the beautiful prayer renditions and cantorial recitatives of their *hazzanim*. Rather, they are requiring that their cantors are as much song-leader as song-singer, helping them to reach their own musical moments through communal singing.

As a result of this desire (or in concert with it), the dominant musical genre in the synagogue is more folk-oriented than ever before. The huge success of Debbie Friedman and those like her in the liberal streams of Judaism, and Reb Shlomo Carlebach and Chasidic songsters in the more traditional streams have given rise to musical idioms that are far more spiritually and musically accessible to many congregants. As a result, curricula at cantorial schools have had to shift from a purer *nusach*-oriented approach with overlaying recitative, to one more musically flexible and contemporary. Although one could argue that the dwindling of the cantorial recitative is perhaps not so great a loss (though I might personally disagree), the loss of *nusach* as a foundation for tune-smithing is nothing short of tragic. This is, to be sure, the subject for another discussion, but suffice it to say that as we abandon the primacy of *nusach* in our synagogues (something which frankly is happening across the movements and especially in the Reform and Orthodox streams), we run the risk not only of losing century-old melodies, but also the calendrical and "midrashic" associations that those melodies once coded.

This assertion on my part though, is of course just that: a personal view (albeit a very strongly held one). As a *hazzan*, I need to remind myself that my own perceptions cloud my view of this enterprise just as surely as those of all the other *mevinim* who may judge me. This thought of course brings us full circle to our proverb and its flipside, namely the expertise of the *hazzan* him/herself. The *hazzan* after all is also a *maven,* specifically an expert on prayer, and has been invested thereby with a great deal of authority and responsibility to represent the community before G-d. Yet prayer is ultimately a personal enterprise, and as a result a *hazzan* must be careful not to impose himself or herself too heavily on the prayer practices of individuals, remembering instead that what and how a person prays is truly sacred.

A cogent reminder of this fact can be found in the *Sefer Hasidim,* a pietistic work of the eleventh century attributed to Rabbi Yehuda HaHasid, in which a story is told of an Israelite herdsman who did not know how to pray.[3]

> *Each day he would say, "Ribono Shel Olam, Master of the Universe, it is obvious and known before You that if one had cattle for grazing and gave them to me to protect, I would be paid for my services. But for You, I would guard Your herd unpaid because I love You so dearly."*
>
> *Once upon a time, a sage of Torah went on his way and found the herdsman praying, "Ribono Shel Olam . . ." (in the manner that the herdsman would pray everyday). The sage balked: "Fool, don't pray that way." So the herdsman inquired, "How then should I pray?" The sage agreed to teach the herdsman on the condition that he no longer pray that which he had been accustomed to each day. And so the sage taught the herdsman the blessing before and after the Shema, the Shema and the Amidah.*
>
> *Unfortunately, after the sage left, the herdsman forgot everything the sage had taught him and ceased praying—even that prayer which he had been accustomed to say. For he was afraid: the sage had forbid him from uttering the prayer of his heart. That night, the sage had a dream and a voice said to him, "If you do not tell the herdsman to say that which he had been used to saying before you came to him . . . if you do not go to him, know that evil will find you. For you have stolen a soul from the world to come."*
>
> *Immediately the sage went out and asked the herdsman, "What are you praying?" The herdsman answered, "Nothing, for I have forgotten what you taught me, and you also forbade me from saying my own prayer." The sage recounted his dream to the herdsman and said, "Say that which you were accustomed to pray."*
>
> *Behold, the herdsman had no great learning or deeds to his credit, but thought well of G-d and so he was raised to greatness. For G-d desires the heart.*

Bibliography

Heschel, A.J. *The Insecurity of Freedom.* New York: Schocken Books, 1972.

Landman, L. *The Cantor: An Historic Perspective.* New York: Yeshiva University Press, 1972.

Levine, J.A. *Synagogue Song in America.* Crow Point, IN: White Cliffs Media Company, 1989.

Slobin, M. *Chosen Voices: The Story of the American Cantorate.* Urbana and Chicago: University of Illinois Press, 1989.

Werner, E. *A Voice Still Heard: The Sacred Songs of the Ashkenazic Jews.* University Park and London: Pennsylvania State University Press, 1976.

Endnotes

1. Apropos this sentence, one of the most important of these changes is that the pronoun "his" no longer includes all hazzanim.

2. Note that the terms investiture and ordination are generally synonymous, although investiture was the preferred term for a time. In the eyes of civil law, ordained or invested cantors are considered clergymen with all the rights and privileges implied (such as the ability to perform marriages, tax benefits of parsonage, etc.).

3. I thank Rabbi Matthew Berkowitz for sharing this teaching with me.

THE ROLE OF THE EDUCATOR IN THE PROCESS OF SYNAGOGUE TRANSFORMATION

Isa Aron

In good Jewish tradition, I'd like to begin with a *mashal:*

Back in the 1960s, when I was in college, undergraduate programs were pretty clear about their mission, which could be stated very simply: to select the most able students and to offer them excellent academic courses. In the intervening decades this clear, but somewhat narrow, sense of purpose has been continuously enlarged. Today my alma mater seeks, in addition: to create a microcosm of American society, with a diverse student population; to assure that students adhere to the norms of civil discourse; to offer academic, psychological and career counseling; and these are but a few examples.

This broader mission is based on a number of assumptions:

- Education consists of much more than coursework.
- There should be a continuity between the curricular and the extracurricular, and between school and work.
- Students exposed to diversity in college will be better able to appreciate diversity in a democratic society.
- Rather than imagining that students all conform to an idealized template, the college must understand how students differ in terms of both abilities and needs.
- How selective a college is, is less important than how engaged its students are.
- There is no immutable ideal of the perfect college; rather, colleges need to change continuously, in response to changing social issues and ideals.

But while many of the college's stakeholders shared these assumptions, they were still surprised, and somewhat dismayed, by their practical implications. For example, both the board of directors and the parents who paid the bills were astounded by how much it cost to provide the academic, social and psychological support systems that enabled a more diverse student body to be truly engaged in learning. Individual faculty members, for their part, were unhappy with the increasing demands on their time. In addition to being productive scholars and engaging teachers, faculty members were now expected to be role models, counselors, and active participants in communal events.

Now for the nimshal:

Like liberal arts colleges, many American synagogues have broadened their mission, sometimes slowly and unconsciously, at other times deliberately and dramatically. David Kaufman has written the definitive study of how the turn-of-the-century *beit t'fillah* became (or at least aspired to become) the "shul with a pool," which served as a *beit midrash* and a *beit knesset* as well.[1] Since the 1950s, the heyday of the synagogue-center, synagogues have continued to enlarge their spheres of activity, undertaking outreach to the unaffiliated, more intense adult learning, and spiritual and social support for those with chronic illness, to cite just a few examples.

While the mission of the synagogue is different from that of a liberal arts college, there are striking parallels between the assumptions which undergird both kinds of transformation:

- *Torah, avodah* and *g'milut hasadim* are the practices of a lifetime. Jewish learning is not just for children; social action is not just for the social action committee. Rather, the goal is for *everyone* to participate in worship, study, building and caring for the community, and working to make the world a better place.
- If Jewish living is to be more than a series of isolated activities, these core Jewish practices must be intertwined. Study should be part of worship, worship a part of study, and so on.
- The Jewish community is much more diverse than we once imagined. Synagogues must reach out to all Jews, not just the declining percentage of intact, upper middle class, heterosexual families.

- Rather than simply offering an array of set programs with a take-it-or-leave-it attitude, synagogues must practice *keiruv*, meeting their marginally-affiliated members "where they are at," and finding ways to bring them closer to the Jewish Tradition.
- The size of a congregation, its standing in the larger community, and the public profile of its clergy are much less important than how engaged its congregants are in living a Jewish life.
- And, finally, no synagogue can afford to rest on its laurels. There are no *transformed* congregations, only *transforming* ones.

But much as we affirm these assumptions in theory, we may find some of their implications difficult in practice. As synagogues aspire to reach more people in a variety of new ways, they find both their budgets and their professional staff strained. This paper looks at the new demands placed on congregations that are undergoing a transformation, with particular focus on the role of the educator.

What Kind of Professional Staff Does It Take to Lead a Transforming Congragation?

Being a rabbi, cantor or congregational educator has always been a demanding job. But as synagogues attempt to live up to the assumptions outlined above, these demands grow even larger. To live up to the mandate of a transforming congregation, the professional leader must be:

- fully grounded in the Jewish Tradition, yet able to meet those on the periphery "where they are at;"
- both inspirational and responsive;
- both idealistic and pragmatic;
- clear about his or her own vision, yet open to hearing the vision of others, and skilled in working with others to create a shared vision.

Only rare *individuals* possess all of these qualities, which makes this list of qualifications seem daunting and unrealistic. But if we think of synagogue leadership as residing in a *group* that works *collaboratively*, the impossible becomes eminently possible. This shift in perspective is in keeping with some of the latest thinking about leadership in the worlds of business, government, and education.

*Historically, leadership has been conceived around an individual—
the leader—and his or her relationship to subordinates or followers. . . . As a result, the leadership field has focused its attention on
the behaviors, mindsets, and actions of the leader in a team or
organization. This paradigm has dominated our thinking in the
organizational behavior field for decades. In recent years, however,
a few scholars have challenged this notion, arguing that leadership
is an activity that is shared or distributed among members of a
group or organization. . . . [This change] has largely to do with
shifts in how work is performed. For example, today the fastest
growing organizational unit is the team and, specifically, cross-
functional teams. . . . Each member of the team brings unique perspectives, knowledge and capabilities to the team. At various
junctures in the team's life, there are moments when these differing
backgrounds and characteristics provide a platform for leadership
to be distributed across the team.*[2]

When professional leaders work collaboratively, they can brain-
storm together, pool their talents, critique and support one another,
and, not unimportantly, help one another avoid being swallowed
up by the immensity of their tasks. When lay leaders are added to
the mix, professionals benefit from the skills they bring in marketing, administration, teaching, facilitating, grant writing, etc. Working collaboratively with lay leaders, especially lay leaders drawn
from different sectors of the congregation, keeps the professionals
from being isolated and "out of touch." There is a second reason
that collaboration with congregants is so critical. A change in the
synagogue's culture, which is the goal of many transformation
processes and projects, cannot be mandated from above; it can only
evolve slowly, in ever-widening circles. A broad coalition of lay leaders gives the process a momentum it would otherwise lack.

The Role of the Educator

Within a collaborative group of lay and professional leaders, the
educator becomes much more than the principal of the religious
school. A holistic vision of Jewish life, in which *torah, avodah,* and
g'milut hasadim are interconnected, implies that learning for all
ages is a part of most (if not all) synagogue activities. The pre-
school, the day school (if the synagogue has one), the religious
school, bar/bat mitzvah preparation, the high school, family education and adult education (as well the day camp and the youth

group) must all be seen as parts of an integrated "delivery system," which also includes Torah study at Shabbat services, in committee meetings, before mitzvah day, and so on.

Of course, no one educator can be responsible for directing all of these learning venues single-handedly. Thus, it is not surprising to find that synagogues aspiring to become Congregations of Learners end up hiring several professional educators on their staff, if they can afford them. Family educator positions are now fairly common, especially in Boston, where Combined Jewish Philanthropies' subsidies have stimulated their creation. More recently, synagogues have begun to hire coordinators for adult learning. And, as the interest in alternative models of the religious school grows, congregations are finding that they must hire coordinators for these new programs as well.

But even the wealthiest of congregations cannot afford to keep adding highly paid professionals to their staff. This leads to a second shift in the educators' role, which now goes far beyond the hiring of a small number of teachers in August or September. Finding appropriate teachers and facilitators for a Congregation of Learners requires (to quote one educator) "a continual man-hunt." The educator must identify, entice and cajole members from every sector of the congregation—avid adult learners, seasoned religious school and day school parents, innocent but eager preschool parents, exuberant college students, and young adults engaged in a spiritual search—to teach, whether as volunteers for a single study session, or as paid teachers of an ongoing class (and everything in between). But the educators' responsibilities do not end here, for after recruitment comes training, mentoring and support. Thus begins a second, more selective, "man-hunt," for the congregants who have professional expertise in teacher training and mentoring, to lend a hand in devising a workable system.

As if this kind of *professional* pressure were not enough, the educator's role in such a congregation now requires a larger communal presence as well. Whereas once it was common for the educator to say: "I work here, but it is not *really* my community," keeping this kind of distance no longer seems appropriate. As learning becomes a more prominent feature of congregational life, creating a sense of community now becomes a more important part of learning. Likewise, the educator can no longer say "Sorry, I don't lead services." If members of the congregation can learn to teach Torah, surely the educator can learn to lead services and give sermons. The collaboration with other professionals require the educator to participate with and, at times, substitute for the rabbi and the cantor. How better to model holistic Jewish living than to have the educator davening on Shabbat and serving meals at the homeless shelter?

Finally, education professionals must be an integral part of the ongoing process of transformation, even if that process focuses, initially, on worship or community building, rather than learning. Most transformation processes require that a task force or a board engage in visioning exercises; some include, in addition, parlor or town hall meetings. Educators have many of the skills required to design and facilitate these exercises and their professional networks give them access to a range of new ideas and programs that merit consideration and adaptation.

None of these changes are particularly easy for either the educator or the congregation: Members of the congregation may have difficulty understanding why they need to hire additional members of the professional staff. Both the educator and his or her professional colleagues may have difficulty adjusting to this expanded role, and learning to work collaboratively. And educators themselves will find it quite challenging to be directing existing programs, even as they are examining these programs critically, and envisioning newer and more engaging alternatives. In the words of one educator: "Since the task force process has begun, working in my congregation is like driving a car while changing the tire—not for the faint of heart."

In fact, a few of the educators in congregations participating in the Experiment in Congregational Education decided, along the way, that the process of change *was* too unsettling, and resigned their positions. And, in a few other cases, the congregation realized that the educator was not capable of handling the new responsibilities his or her role entailed. But for every educator that has been overwhelmed, three or four have been energized, and five, six or seven have applied for the newly created positions. For these educators, working in a *transforming* congregation has been a welcome professional challenge, an opportunity to bring their visions and dreams to life.

Finally, since this conference is under the auspices of a college with a venerable school of education, I should add that as the role of the educator changes, so must the school of education. We professors of Jewish education must nurture within our students visions of changing congregations and equip them with the skills to facilitate the change and bring their visions to life. Over and above these changes to our curriculum, we, like both the liberal arts college and the contemporary American synagogue, must be prepared to enlarge our mission.

In my own institution, the Rhea Hirsch School of Education at HUC/JIR we decided, twelve years ago, that rather than simply training educators for the field, we should also prepare the field to be worthy of our graduates. Thanks to generous grants from generous foundations, we created two change projects, the Experiment in Congregational Education, and Jewish Day Schools for the 21st Century. With over 25 congregations and a dozen day schools in our orbit, the synergy between the academy and the field is richly rewarding. The synagogues and schools who are our partners challenge us to improve our academic and clinical programs. And our graduates, in turn, challenge the synagogues to keep changing.

Endnotes

1. David Kaufman, *Shul with a Pool: The "Synagogue-Center" in American Jewish History* (Waltham, MA: Brandeis University Press, 1999).

2. Craig Pearce and Jay A. Conger, *Shared Leadership: Reframing the Hows and Whys of Leadership* (Thousand Oaks, CA: Sage Publications, 2003), pp. 1–2.

Models of Lay Leadership: A Symposium

Jerome M. Epstein

Lee M. Hendler

Terry Rosenberg

RABBI JEROME M. EPSTEIN

No matter what you think about it, or what your opinion might have been, the recently held California recall vote teaches us a great lesson about leadership. The people of California recalled the governor that they had elected only eleven months earlier. But, the real story is the impetus for the referendum and the momentum that developed because Gray Davis was doing so poorly in the polls. That is what inspired others to move against him. He was elected on his *long-term* record; he was recalled because of *short-term* concerns.

The recall initiative gained momentum because the Governor was not doing what the people wanted him to do; and, in a sense this goes to the perceived need for leaders today, in many situations, to reflect the popular will of their constituency. This creates great pressure for politicians. It forces politicians to seek popularity in order to keep their jobs. But, that raises the real issue: what *is* the job of the leader? Is it to follow the will of the people or to lead based upon the vision that he or she develops and helps to formulate? The question is: should the leader do what the leader thinks is popular or do what is in the best interest of the organization or institution which that person is charged to lead?

I want to be clear; I think the role of the leader is to lead based upon a vision, but not necessarily a vision which the leader alone crafts. Rather, the vision must be one that the leader crafts with his/her constituency.

Now, not everyone who is called a leader actually leads. In synagogue life we often confuse leadership with other synagogue roles and we use the term "leader" rather loosely. In so doing, I think we, in effect, cheapen the role and the title of "leader."

For instance, on our boards of directors we have many workers. They serve on committees; they do what they're told for the benefit of the cause; they work very hard. What they do is important. But they may or may not be leaders! There are managers—committee chairs—who work together to get a particular job done and they coordinate the efforts of the workers. They provide the oversight, but they, too, may not be leaders. The reality is that a board of directors may not be comprised of leaders. Because the board is a representational group, it is charged to represent the will of the congregation. But, boards also have the responsibility to lead those who they represent and that is a real challenge.

I was intrigued by a recent survey that was on a website for nonprofit organizations called, boardsource.org which is a wonderful resource. The survey noted that boards, especially non-profit boards, spend considerable time on major policy questions—thirty-three percent. Thirty-two percent spend considerable time in planning for the future. But, sixty-one percent of boards say they *never* devote time to minor management issues.

As I read this data, I wanted to ask myself the question, how many of our Synagogue boards can say they *never* devote time to minor management concerns? The truth of the matter is, that many Synagogue boards devote time to small issues that should be the concerns of the workers and the managers; but not necessarily the concerns of the leaders. The net effect is that governing boards' involvement in minor issues often results in bad leadership. It's not fulfilling; it doesn't give people a sense of gratification at the end of the meeting.

In contrast to the board, which is made up of workers and managers, the Synagogue Executive Committee is composed of officers. Key officers are the leaders of the congregation. They must lead the community; that is what they're elected for. Their challenge is not to merely say, "We should do this because, in dialogue with congregants, we have determined that this is what they want." It isn't through being aloof and deciding what others need that the best results are obtained. Rather, effectiveness comes through dialogue with congregants to determine "felt needs." Leaders must then challenge themselves to remain steadfastly focused on what the mission and what the vision is.

It is imperative that we redefine the role of leader. Warren Bennis describes four common traits for all leaders that I think are important to consider.

The first quality is, the management of attention—the ability to communicate a sense of vision that attracts followers. It is important to have a vision. But that is not sufficient. The true leader is able to communicate that vision to attract followers.

The second trait is the management of meaning—the ability to create meaning with clarity emanating from the actual vision. A vision is something that is nebulous. The leader, therefore, must concretize that vision so that it has meaning to the people when it is communicated.

The third trait is the management of trust—the ability to convey consistent integrity relating to the vision or mission. The leader is in charge of conveying that consistent integrity and being tied to that integrity no matter what other pressures arise.

The fourth quality is the management of self—the ability to know oneself; one's strengths and one's weaknesses. The leader knows how to capitalize on his/her strengths and to compensate for weaknesses. No leader will have all the needed skills and experiences. But the true leader knows where his/her shortcomings are and is able to compensate through utilizing other resources and other people.

How do we recruit and train for the type of leadership we need? I think that leaders will only lead if they see value in leading. It will not come out of duty nor obligation. People lead because they see value in the task. The implication for us, however, is that we have to help make Synagogue leadership a meaningful job. We have to empower an increasingly large group of leaders to help shape the vision and mission of the congregation, even if these decisions are not those that we would have chosen.

Let me propose four points that are a frame of reference for real leadership:

First: In creating more leaders, more power is shared. When you create more leaders you share more authority. In most political decisions, in which synagogue boards and officers are involved, there are multiple truths. We cannot tolerate a structure that permits a leader to say—"it's my way, I'm the President." Our task must be to help people shape their leadership role by sharing their power. Rabbis, cantors and educators have to learn that as well. Leaders must be willing to share the responsibility of leadership, and, in doing so we must accept the fact that decisions may not turn out exactly the way we want.

We require leaders who will invite others to participate in shaping the vision. A vision that has the investment of others is a much stronger vision than one that is "privately" owned. What we currently have in many congregations is "sphere" leadership. The rabbis have their spheres. The chazanim have their spheres. The educators have their spheres. The officers have their spheres. What we need to develop is shared leadership, a shared effort to implement the vision.

Second: It is critical to attract leaders to synagogue life who will represent the held vision. We have not been forthright about expectations. An organization with a development mission, such as a federation, would not accept a leader who did not give meaningful "gifts" to its cause. One cannot be the leader of a federation if he/she articulates, "I don't believe in giving *Tzedakah*." To be a leader one has to identify with the vision and mission.

The synagogue's mission is religious living. We must begin to foster the expectation that synagogue leaders will live that mission. Leaders must want to lead because they are committed to the mission. Personal practice must become an expectation. It is not sufficient to have leaders who are only involved in the administration of the synagogue because the synagogue can only be run like a business if we remember what business we are in. The synagogue is a religious institution, and, therefore, our leaders must have a sense of what the religious vision is.

It is also important to train people to communicate. That communication may take place through words, but it can also take place through being an example. We can be effective role models for congregants. In many cases lay leaders may even be more effective models than the clergy, because the rabbi is "expected" to live Jewishly. When I was serving a pulpit, nobody said to me "isn't that great the rabbi is observing Shabbat or isn't it great that the rabbi is observing kashrut?" When the synagogue president was a model for Shabbat and kashrut observance, it made a statement; it was noticed.

Third: We must begin to train leaders to communicate through two-way communication. It is much easier for one to send out a memo, write a bulletin article, or give a speech than to dialogue on an issue, because in one-way communication you don't have to be concerned with challenges to the ideas you present. But, where there is dialogue, the communication is much more effective.

Finally, I want to suggest that we have to "raise the bar" and recruit new leadership. We have to be willing to say that being a leader is an important task with real expectations. I have observed may nominating committees at work. When nominating committees often invite people to join the board and the prospective board member asks, "What's expected of me?" The chairman of the nominating committee usually says, "Well, not much. You just have to come to a meeting." I think that we have to be forthright with people in saying "being a leader is a sacred task" and we must communicate that they have an opportunity to shape the congregation. Unless we are honest and forthright, we do our cause and ourselves a disservice.

Creating the leadership we need must become the priority for the synagogue community. It will not be an easy task but I am convinced that not only is it "do-able," it is mandatory. For, only through meeting this challenge, will synagogue life fulfill our dreams.

LEE M. HENDLER

I love the world of ideas and abstractions and my assignment was a really interesting one: "To discuss the role of lay leaders in charting the ideological and programmatic course of a synagogue rather than focusing upon management and human relations skills." With the added caution. . . . "The interaction and the relationship of lay leadership with the professionals deserves a significant but not a dominant comment." But as I thought about it, I realized that as a lay leader I just couldn't think about synagogue lay leadership in this way.

I don't think it is a lay leader's responsibility to chart the ideological and programmatic course of a synagogue and I don't think the interaction and relationship between lay leaders and professionals is incidental to the course a synagogue charts for itself. Synagogues are places that provide contexts within which Jewish visions can be created; visions that enable Jews to discover who they were, who they are, and who they want to be. It occurs through prayer, study, acts of loving-kindness, day in and day out. It happens from cradle to grave, in the parking lot and the class room, in the chapel, and the board room, the social hall, the gym, the bathrooms, the basement, the sanctuary, the rabbi's study, the executive director's office, the nursery school playground, the adult *beit midrash*, in the hallways, at the cemetery and the *shiva* house; under the *chuppa and* at a baby naming, and in the hospital waiting room. The lay leader has to get this first before anything else. This is what synagogues can do that no other institution in the Jewish world can. We can provide the contexts in which life happens. Whether synagogue dweller or spiritual seeker, the yearning to make meaning out of our lives prevails; the need to connect with other human beings in community persists. It doesn't go away and synagogues are there when the need is most present. So when I think about a vibrant shul like the one I belong to in Baltimore, I don't think about ideology and programs in terms of the things we've lead and dreamt of in the past decade and the things we need to do in the coming decades, I think of contexts.

How did we create the contexts for serious study to occur? How did we establish the framework for transformative social action programs, engaging worship experiences? How do we think about the ways in which people connect to one another in a community as complex as ours? What do lay leaders have to know in order to envision those contexts? We have to see ourselves as agents for helping to create these contexts by being personally responsible for them. We have to study ourselves. We have to learn about and participate in cutting edge social action work. We have to understand and care about worship and go out and worship in other places too. We have to hold ourselves and our congregations to a standard of conduct that mirrors the kind of sacred community we want our members to experience. We must consider the extent to which we uphold and live by the values of values like *brit, k'vod ha'briyot, sh'- leymut, hachnasat orchim, shalom bayit.* We have to hold ourselves accountable at every level to a standard of excellence that radiates confidence and competence as we drive ourselves forward with a healthy institutional restlessness. In synagogues more so than in any other institution the work must be done collaboratively by lay- men and professionals. How can we possibly suggest that God needs us as partners in the creative work of world building if lay- men and professionals do not need one another as partners in the world building of our own synagogues?

What good lay leaders bring to the synagogue is the freshness of alternate perspectives, the vitality of worlds "other than." Our job as leaders is to translate, interpret and apply the outside knowledge we possess to the context of the synagogue because the synagogue world tends to be way too insular and precious, much like the world of academia. It is ridiculous to respond to many of its chal- lenges as if they've never been encountered elsewhere. We lose a lot of wisdom that way and disregard the lessons of our own his- tory. In my case, those other worlds happened to be fundraising, mission statement development, board management, strategic and financial planning skills, along with a fairly strong pedagogical background. The synergy when properly managed can be enor- mously beneficial not only to the synagogue but to the leader. Don't forget the growth of the leader. When the leader grows, the insti- tution is likely to grow too.

What is the model of leadership that we need? In the end I think it is pretty simple, perhaps deceptively so. Doing it well is a lot harder than it sounds and takes much more time than anyone ever imagines. You get really good people together who understand what the purpose of "the" synagogue is and who have a shared understanding of the purpose of that particular synagogue and you start to create contexts. When the contexts are rooted in a mission they enable multiple visions to emerge. If each vision is about excellence it will be exciting—not to everyone (it rarely is) but to enough people to matter—for enough Jews to see their better selves in it, to begin to see their Jewish stories in it—which will attract the resources that vision needs to get off the ground. That is another part of the leader's job, which is to make sure you have the resources you need, whether it is people or money. Pretty soon you've got multiple contexts and multiple visions—each authentic in its own way because leaders have nurtured them from within the community, understanding the particular needs and culture of that community. And before you know it you've got a synagogue that has the capacity—without compromising its integrity—to appeal to both dwellers and seekers because you're creating contexts for life, not just ideology and programs.

I believe that we have lots of untapped talent in the Jewish community, but it is a risky business to tap it. When God recruited Abraham and Moses, He got a little more than he bargained for. He got leaders who argued with Him, who challenged and provoked Him. Real leaders must have a gift and the guts for recognizing that kind of talent. My Rabbi, Joel Zaiman was willing to take a chance on me, willing to make space for me. There are hundreds, maybe thousands of us all over the country who are hungry for what Judaism has to offer us; hungry to give of ourselves, but we're demanding and difficult and perhaps even a little dangerous. Status quo and "It can't be done" are phrases we do not understand. We bring skill sets and expectations that are often foreign to the synagogue world. We make work, lots of it, but we do work. As I've traveled around the country I've heard the lament. . . . "We couldn't possibly do what you did at Chizuk Amuno; you had Rabbi Joel Zaiman, you had you," to which I generally respond, "Nonsense." It took vision; it took perseverance; it took hard work; it took love; it took conviction. It also took a commitment to excellence, that which Rabbi Herring called it in his paper "the lonely task of setting standards."

If there's anything I think we suffer from in Jewish life it is mediocrity. One of the joys of working with Larry Hoffman, Ron Wolfson and the rest of the S2K team has been seeing the results of their steadfast insistence on excellence in everything we do. There is too much mediocrity in synagogue life and the saddest part for me is listening to all the excuses I hear for conceding to it. We're a stiff-necked people, not a complacent one. True, we have to do our full measure of whining but we do finally get through the wilderness and accomplish magnificent things. We have the courage to choose freedom, the wisdom to choose Judaism. We build tabernacles in the desert, we conquer lands overrun by giants. We rebuild temples and when others destroy them we have the genius to replace them with new expressions of Judaism that create new contexts in which Jews can still experience our relationship to God and one another. Surely we can do this! We can create sacred places, communities, homes where Jews can discover the meaning of our lives and we can find ways to nurture the particular kinds of leaders we need to do it. It's not about ideas as much as it is about will and conviction. Ideas and programs are easy, a dime a dozen. What matters is having the kind of professional leaders who actively seek strong lay leaders as partners to create the enduring contexts in which those ideas and programs can take root.

TERRY ROSENBERG

The journey I have traveled since reclaiming my Jewish soul a decade ago is due, in no small measure to many people who made it their business to save the lives of those, like me, who were lost in the desert, their birthright unclaimed. Today, I am a committed Jew who has dedicated herself to Jewish study and community building. How did I manage to return? I would love to say that it was the appeal of my synagogue but, in fact, my synagogue had initially been a deterrent to my reentry to Judaism. The Yiddishkeit from my parents, my childhood Jewish education including one summer at Camp Ramah surely helped, but that alone did not tip the scales. The tipping point was more subtle. A few people, some familiar, some not, merely invited me to have a conversation. I must have been ready to listen, but their voices ultimately resonated with my deepest longings. These conversations were even more powerful because through the support of Boston's Combined Jewish Philanthropies and Hebrew College, our synagogues are undergoing a renaissance of learning and revitalization. Any influence these individuals had on me was reinforced at the communal level.

My journey back to Judaism began when I agreed, with great reluctance, to a friend's invitation to attend a synagogue retreat. I can't remember the details of the day, but at some point I experienced a moment of awakening, the realization that there was indeed a birthright for me to claim and the chance to claim it. It was then that I committed to what has become a serious and passionate engagement with Judaism through the study of its texts, traditions and rituals, and as a lay leader in my synagogue and in the larger Jewish community, both nationally and locally.

Over the past few years I have come to feel responsible for the thousands of others who are still waiting for someone like me to reach out and invite them to reclaim their birthright. Will we be able to marshal the creativity and the innovation, the vision and the

hard work that is needed? With all due respect to the many scholars, Jewish professionals and clergy who wrestle with this issue,
the answer really depends upon each one of us, professional and
lay leader alike.

I appreciate the questions that Rabbi Herring raises when he
asks how we can make our synagogues more spiritually relevant in
light of the tension between the synagogue's adherence to tradition
and spirituality's need for freedom of expression and individual
autonomy. When we ask—how can individual spirituality be nurtured within community, it begs another question, which is: what
does it mean to be a spiritual community? Are synagogues merely
places where people design their own unique forms of religious
self-expression?

Contemporary spirituality is well grounded in Jewish tradition.
It is not removing oneself from the world and speaking to God on
a mountaintop. Moses did not invite the children of Israel to go up,
he brought the tablets down. Contemplative practices may be valuable and enriching but they are not for everyone. Spirituality is not
a philosophy or a theology, limited to a well-crafted narrative about
the nature of God, nor is it the immediacy of God in one's own
experience, either through prayer or other forms of ritual, including study. To be Jewishly spiritual is to be deeply concerned about
the way we live and whether our living truly reflects God's presence
on earth. To be spiritual is to know that how you listen to others,
how you treat the stranger and how you conduct both the private
and public parts of your life is terribly important. Spirituality lives
not only in the privacy of one's soul but also in our communal
expressions of compassion and justice. Spirituality is *Torah, Hesed*
and *Tzedek* in real time.

So how do we manage the tension between the communal life
of synagogues and individual quests for spiritual meaning? I think
the tension will take care of itself if synagogues of whatever form
provide meaning, value and a sense of belonging. If synagogues
have a chance of attracting the disaffected among us, then authentic, spiritual engagement must include a deep questioning of our
beliefs and practices. The real challenge of synagogue life is to
make room for these conversations without feeling threatened.
Can we welcome the stranger in our own midst? Can we open our
hearts and minds to questions that on the surface appear to shake
the very foundations of our tradition, but really have the true pos-

sibility of transforming both us and our communities into communities of meaning and purpose and engagement? Do we truly listen to each other or are we content to listen only to those voices with whom we agree or are we willing to become multilingual? Do we embrace opposing views, asking ourselves what is right about what that person is saying, rather than what is wrong? Do we welcome the stranger, or politely close the door in his/her face?

Our styles and structures may change but our fundamental values of *Torah, hesed* and *tzedek* endure. Each of us has the choice to embody and manifest those values at each moment; in our homes, with our friends, in the boardroom and the hallways of our shuls, at weddings and at funerals, at the brit and the Bar and Bat Mitzvah. But as much as each of us must act individually, ours is ultimately a collective task. The covenant at Sinai was made not with one individual or subgroup, but with the entire Jewish people. To move from our individual journeys to *k'lal Yisrael* we need to build meaningful dialogue with each other. Our sages always knew that the questions were more important than the answers. Judging by the numbers of unaffiliated Jews, for this is the largest growing segment according to the 2002 National Jewish Population Survey, the greatest threat to our future existence is not dissent, but the ignorance and apathy of those who are orphaned from history and are searching for meaning in a world that feels increasingly dangerous and fragmented.

Synagogues will continue to evolve as they always have, but, what is important to understand is that what our synagogues look like and feel like now and in the future, is reflective of how we think, how we believe and how we behave. Our physical and spatial boundaries and constructs are manifestations of our mental boundaries and constructs. Therefore, if we are able to be successful in effecting a change that is transformational and not merely additive we must begin with ourselves. We need to span, not just for new ideas but also for a new inner Jewish experience.

Abraham Joshua Heschel suggested the goal of adult education is that every Jew becomes a representative of the human spirit, and that these insights and experiences must become embodied in our personalities. As leaders, we need to open our arms, and our hearts, and invite others into the process, encourage their leadership, and give them the autonomy, and the authority to make the journey with us, respecting that it will be in their particular way and style. As we change, the change is reflected around us, in the design of our physical space, our rituals, our organizational structure, the content and style of our conversations, our habits, and our practices. Ultimately, the change becomes institutionalized and it moves again into the background where it takes its place as the normative context until the next cycle of change begins. But, this is so much easier said than done.

Anyone, who has been involved in any kind of transformational change initiative, knows that change is difficult and not for the faint of heart. The reason for this is because we personalize our ideas so that they become not just what we think, but who we are. Our ideas are based on unexamined assumptions about how the world works and how people work. We approach learning situations thinking that we are open, believing that we are open, when so often we are only able to translate what we hear into an improved version of what we already know.

I'm not accusing us of closed mindedness or parochialism, but our time tested beliefs and world views are not like clothing that you can just put on or take off at will. We don't have perspectives; we *are* these perspectives. If we are serious about real transformational change then we must have the courage to put these assumptions at risk. It's not that we're asking ourselves to give up our cherished opinions, just our certainty about them.

As Dr. W. Edwards Deming, statistician and management consultant says, "Nothing happens without personal transformation." And personal transformation is risky business. As a religious community that respects boundaries and privacy, transformation is only possible in environments where there is safety, trust and where learning is valued.

Peter Senge, author of "The Fifth Discipline," and popularizer of the term "Learning organization," identifies three obstacles to developing communities of learning. He calls them, "fragmentation, competition, and reactiveness."

First, we're a culture that likes to break things apart and analyze them. Fixing one part, however, invariably causes a problem somewhere else. Synagogues are systems where the parts are interdependently linked. There is usually no single, "right" answer, but a multiplicity of perspectives and possibilities that require creative, systemically based solutions. Analytic thinking, which is our strength, and our tradition, is effective, but limited. Challenges, like more engaging prayer services, inspiring Torah classes, or increased membership involvement, resist these analytical approaches.

Second, competition is healthy and it can be great fun inspiring creativity and new ideas. But competition without an equivalent amount of collaboration and cooperation is problematic. Collaboration requires a different skill-set, a different mind-set. It requires the discipline of thinking beyond the desires, needs, and concerns of the single person, committee or organization, and it seeks to find common concerns and shared goals.

Perhaps, the process of developing leaders is more like gardening then long-distance running, more like dancing than sparring. To be brutally honest, we sanction behaviors that minimize the threat from opposing voices. The one with the loudest and most argumentative voice usually wins.

For example, in some synagogues the motto is, "don't contradict the majority," or "there's no point in bringing that up because the rabbi is just going to do what he/she wants anyway." People hold their untested beliefs as their private certainties. There may be voices or challenges of dissent among the brave and adventurous in meetings, but it is nothing compared to what you hear in the hallway where the real meeting takes place. Real collaboration puts these background conversations, as I call them, on the table where they can be challenged in a spirit of openness and mutual respect.

Third, and last, Senge defines reactiveness as the tendency to want the shortest, most direct route for solving the problem. A good example is the development of a vision statement. We all understand the need for a vision, but if we see it as a problem to be solved we treat it as a product to be developed, and disseminated. It ends up on a wall, or in the Synagogue bulletin, and that is where it dies and fossilizes. Need more spirituality in the boardroom, add a D'var Torah to the agenda, which is often the first thing to be eliminated if time is short. But, seriously what could be more important than words of Torah. We may be learning how to speak words of Torah, but are we learning how to think from Torah?

A vision that has life comes not from a reactive mode but from a creative process that is internally driven and reflective of people's deepest, most intimate desires and dreams. When our Jewish values are front and center in the discussion, both the vision and Torah come alive.

How do we create a culture that minimizes fragmentation, competition and reactivity and maximizes unity, cooperation and creativity? I indicated previously that everything flows from the individual and communal contexts in which we live. If we are serious about real, systemic, transformational change, where our communities are bursting with a spirit of creativity and partnership, then we need leaders who are bold, Jewishly literate, learning –centered and committed to their own personal transformation. One skill that is needed above all is the skill of listening.

Surely, good leaders have many qualities, but I would like to focus for a moment on listening. We are a culture that values speaking, and we are good at it. No one would argue that our verbal and oratorical skills are highly developed, and should be valued. Yet our Jewish texts contain many examples where listening was a critical element of the story.

Consider the story of Abraham. Before Abraham can act, he **hears** the call. It wasn't something that others heard. His capacity to hear what others couldn't turned him from a worshipper of idols to a believer in one true God. God's first words to Abraham, "*lech leha*," translated as go forth, literally mean, "take yourself." A midrash interprets this to mean go forth to find your authentic self to learn who you were meant to be. Abraham's physical and spiritual journey begins with listening.

When Jacob becomes Israel, whose name we carry, the core image of his wrestling with the angel is his engagement in self-listening, or personal reflection that ultimately leads to his transformation from Jacob to Israel. Self-listening and reflection are part of the rhythm of living a Jewish life, especially during Rosh Hashanah and Yom Kippur. Martin Buber tells us that when we encounter another, when we listen deeply, and experience the other person for who they are, the divine is present.

So, what does it mean to listen? It is interesting that there is no real discipline or serious literature on the topic of listening. Amazon.com lists over 1,700 books with listening in their titles, although only one serious philosophy book stands lonely, and mostly unread on the shelves. Listening is of great concern in many fields, but rarely is it given serious attention. Our common sense understanding is that listening is about receiving and processing messages, and this is the problem. We use tape recorders and computers as the model, and we believe that listening is primarily an intellectual process happening in our minds. I want to challenge this understanding and offer an interpretation that I believe can support our vision of interdependence, cooperation, and community.

First, we are always listening to something. Listening is mostly an automatic process, happening not by choice but by the ongoing workings of our biological, neurological and psychological systems. Listening is shaped by our history, and experience, individually packaged.

Second, listening doesn't happen just in the mind, it's a whole body experience involving our moods, our emotions, and our intellect. And, third, while listening is also a linguistic process, it is more than that; it is also a state of being, rather than doing. It encompasses more than understanding words and analyzing concepts. If we try to listen, our attempts usually take us out of the experience, rather than help us to remain present *in* the experience.

As you can see, listening happens on many levels and although it is difficult to pinpoint we can greatly improve the quality of how we listen to ourselves and to others. Here are just a couple of prerequisites: Good listening requires humility. Good listeners are open to new possibilities in life, and to changing the course of their lives. Good listening is transformative; people who listen well are trained observers of their own emotions, and the emotional state of the person, or people to whom they're listening. They listen to the music of the message, as well as the words, or the content.

If we are serious about cultivating communities of meaning, caring, and spirituality then we can't ignore our need to develop the art and practice of good listening. We as leaders need to train ourselves to speak in ways that open rather than close possibilities. We need to learn to cultivate moods of curiosity and enthusiasm, and environments of caring, trust, and safety. We need to welcome conflicts and controversy as expressions of deep commitment, and work in partnership to find solutions. We need to encourage individual initiative, balance pragmatism with sacred mission, and celebrate our failures as learning opportunities. We need patience and compassion for ourselves as leaders and for those in our community who share our passions, and frustrations.

We are not just leaders; we are healers and guides, teachers and learners, shunning the comfort of Egypt for the dream of a promised land, knowing that the transition through the desert will test our convictions, and fortitude. As lay leaders we need to develop Jewish language in our thinking and our speaking. We need to recognize that we're partners as well as leaders, more comfortable with answers, but nevertheless committed to asking new questions.

A word of caution: Being open to listening to all points of view does not mean abdicating one's personal position. My friend and mentor, Rabbi Larry Hoffman reminds me that good leaders need more than good vision, good listening, compassion, empathy, and tolerance for disagreement. He says and I quote, "Good leaders must also rise to the occasion by demonstrating that they are men, or women of spirit." "They convince us that they are doing God's work, not just seeking greater power, more attention, or self aggrandizement." Good leaders consult the people but they also consult their conscience. They are able to convince because we sense their conviction and in the end we follow because as much as we believe in their ideas, we believe in them.

Sh'ma Yisrael, the fundamental mandate of our religion is to listen. In hearing the call we are choosing to invent ourselves newly, engage in the creation of new selves and new synagogue communities. As lay leaders we become engaged in sacred partnerships with God, our rabbis, cantors, educators, our fellow congregants, and all the agencies and organizations around us that are committed to a vibrant and sustainable Jewish future.

The work before us may be challenging, exhausting, inspiring and aggravating, but, if we respond to the call, we have the opportunity to inspire a whole generation of wandering Jews, who like me, are searching, yearning to come home. Regardless of how we draw the denominational lines or to what degree we retain our traditional norms and practices, if our synagogues are communities where God's presence is revealed in the conversations and practices of its members and if true spirituality is present, they will come.

Epilogue

David M. Gordis

RE-ENVISIONING THE SYNAGOGUE:
SOME CLOSING REFLECTIONS

David M.Gordis

A n evolving institution for a diverse and dynamic community—this is the picture of the contemporary synagogue
that emerges from the essays presented in this volume.
Fundamental questions emerge: Is the changing synagogue a
response to the changing dynamics of the Jewish community or
has the synagogue itself generated that dynamic, at least in part? Is
the synagogue best left to transform itself through the changing
demands made upon it by its constituents, or should systemic and
systematic attempts be undertaken to transform it? Can the synagogue be made into a more effective institution than it is now, preserving the creative vitality of the Jewish people and enhancing the
quality of Jewish life? And further, should the synagogue be reaching out to new constituencies, or should it be content to serve the
needs of those who choose to join its ranks?

The contributors to this volume, representing a range of professional backgrounds, lay leadership roles and ideological perspectives, agree on the centrality of the synagogue as the unrivalled
point of Jewish engagement for the vast majority of Jews who
choose to affiliate formally with the Jewish community. They differ
on how effectively the synagogue is meeting its potential, and
exchange views on how its functioning can be enhanced. These
historical, conceptual and analytical perspectives are meant to
deepen our understanding of how the synagogue has functioned in
the past and might be sustained and enriched in the future.

A number of contributors see the key to synagogue transformation both in its reconceptualization and in the development of new forms of leadership for a reconceptualized institution. Some suggest that the synagogue's role as educational and communal center must be enlarged to embrace populations who may not be drawn to the strictly religious and ceremonial functions of the synagogue. New forms of rabbinic, cantorial, educational and lay leadership are proposed as critical to the broadening of the synagogue's role in Jewish life. The implication of these observations is that absent the emergence of new forms of leadership, the synagogue will in all likelihood remain stagnant and may even decline in its capacity to attract Jews to itself, a process which some see as already beginning to occur. Results of recent studies of the Jewish community certainly suggest a diminution in communal allegiance and commitment to the synagogue, and it seems appropriate to inquire as to whether that process can be slowed or even reversed. But where does leadership fit in? Do leaders transform institutions, or do transformed institutions themselves generate new forms of leadership? Or do institutional change and evolution of leadership types develop simultaneously and work synergistically? Further study and experimentation on leadership development and function appear warranted.

Finally, though a number of the contributors to this volume have engaged the core question of how an institution that exists to transmit traditional norms and beliefs can navigate and serve a culture dominated by autonomy and self-definition, this question remains unresolved. As the repository of traditional beliefs and practice, how can the synagogue both fulfill its historic function and be responsive to a community increasingly disinclined to be shaped by externally imposed norms of belief and practice? Can the synagogue find ways of reaching out to this diverse and increasingly "inner-directed" community?

Our intention in offering this volume has not been to provide ultimate answers but to contribute to the discourse concerning this vital institution of Jewish life. We attempt to do this by providing analysis of core issues, suggesting a variety of approaches and directions, and offering the perspectives of a broad swath of professionals, leaders and "end-users." Our hope is that the observations and perspectives presented in this book will lead to the strengthening of this central institution of Jewish life and through it of the fabric of Jewish life in general.

THE CONTRIBUTORS

RABBI MORRIS J. ALLEN has served as the spiritual leader of the Beth Jacob Congregation in Mendota Heights, MN, since 1986, and is recognized by his peers for his vision and skill in encouraging observance in a supportive environment and for offering creative programming and educational opportunities.

DR. ISA ARON is Professor of Jewish Education at Hebrew Union College-Jewish Institute of Religion in Los Angeles where she teaches courses in pedagogy, philosophy of education and organizational change. She is the founding director of the Rhea Hirsch School of Education's Experiment in Congregational Education (ECE). Dr. Aron's publications include *Becoming a Congregation of Learners* and *The Self-Renewing Congregation: Organizational Strategies for Revitalizing Congregational Life.*

RABBI JEROME M. EPSTEIN, is Chief Executive Officer/Executive Vice President of The United Synagogue of Conservative Judaism. Before assuming his national position he served as a congregational rabbi and regional director for the USCJ. He is a spokesman for Conservative Judaism and a guide and mentor to its lay leaders.

DR. DAVID M. GORDIS, President of Hebrew College since 1993, is Professor of Rabbinics and Director of the National Center of Jewish Policy Studies, successor to The Wilstein Institute of Jewish Policy Studies. An ordained rabbi, he is widely regarded for his classic Jewish scholarship, his communal leadership and his extensive writings on Jewish Life in America and Israel. He previously served as Vice-President of the University of Judaism in Los Angeles and as Executive Vice President of the American Jewish Committee.

DR. MICHAEL HAMMER, an exponent and a practitioner of organizational change, originated the ideas of reengineering and process management, ideas that have transformed the operations of corporations and non-profit organizations around the world. He is the author of numerous articles and four books, including the international bestseller, *Reengineering the Corporation.* Dr. Hammer is President of Hammer & Company, a management education firm, and was previously a professor of computer science at MIT. Currently, a Fellow of the Business School at Oxford University, he is also a Senior Lecturer at the MIT Sloan School of Management.

RABBI ZACHARY HELLER, Associate Director of The National Center for Jewish Policy Studies (successor to the Wilstein Institute) at Hebrew College since 1996, is editor of this volume. Before coming to the Center he combined a career in the rabbinate with national and international Jewish communal leadership and is the author of articles in the fields of Jewish policy and bioethics.

LEE MEYERHOFF HENDLER, a past president of Chizuk Amuno Congregation in Baltimore, is the author of *The Year Mom Got Religion,* an autobiographical memoir of mid-life learning and transformation. She serves on a number of boards including Johns Hopkins University, Hillel International, the Institute for Christian and Jewish Studies and Synagogue 2000, and is a well-known speaker on family philanthropy and the initiator of "Freedom's Feast," a unique civil ceremony for Americans to conduct around the Thanksgiving table.

DR. HAYIM HERRING is Executive Director of STAR (Synagogues: Transformational and Renewal) whose mission is to promote the renewal of the American Jewish community through congregational innovation. He previously served as rabbi of Beth El Synagogue in Minneapolis and then worked with the Minneapolis Jewish Federation. Rabbi Herring has conducted studies and published articles in the areas of Jewish continuity, Jewish adolescence, Jewish identity-formation in postmodern American, Conservative Judaism, new organizational models of the American Jewish community and professional development for congregational rabbis.

Dr. David E. Kaufman is Associate Professor of American Jewish Studies at the Hebrew Union College-Jewish Institute of Religion in Los Angeles. His publications include articles on the social, religious and architectural history of the American synagogue; a history of the Teachers Institute at JTSA; and a full-length study of early 20th century Jewish communal institutions, *Shul With A Pool: The "Synagogue-Center" in American Jewish History* (UPNE 1999). As lead researcher for a study of the contemporary trend in synagogue transformation, he co-authored the Wilstein Institute's Report to STAR (2000).

Rabbi Richard Marker serves professionally as an independent philanthropic advisor to foundations and philanthropists and as Senior Fellow at NYU's George Heyman Jr. Center for Philanthropy. He has been a writer, speaker, and consultant on synagogue change and over the years, has served as both a lay leader and rabbinic scholar in residence at synagogues throughout the United States.

Dr. Riv-Ellen Prell, an anthropologist, is Professor of American Studies at the University of Minnesota. She is the author of *Prayer and Community: the Havurah in American Judaism*, which was awarded a 1990 National Jewish Book Award, and *Fighting to Become Americans: Jews, Gender and the Anxiety of Assimilation*. She has written extensively on American Jewish culture and community, and is the author of a study of two Conservative synagogues that was included in *Jews in the Center* edited by Jack Wertheimer. She serves on the academic boards of a variety of Jewish institutions and has consulted widely in the American Jewish community.

Terry Rosenberg is an organizational consultant specializing in leadership training. Since 2000, she has been National Chair of Synagogue 2000's Advisory Board and recently joined the Board of Governors of the Hebrew Union College-Jewish Institute of Religion. She holds many leadership positions in the Boston Jewish community including Combined Jewish Philanthropies and Hebrew College and her synagogue, Temple Beth Elohim in Wellesley, MA. In 1999 she was honored with the Deborah's Legacy Award by the Women of Reform Judaism.

DR. HARVEY SHAPIRO is Associate Professor of Jewish Education and Dean of the Shoolman Graduate School of Jewish Education at Hebrew College. He holds a Ph.D. in Jewish Education from Hebrew Union College. His research interests and publications are on subjects relating to the place of Israel in Jewish education, educational change in Jewish life, American pragmatism and intellectual history of Jewish education. Dr. Shapiro serves as the Hebrew College liaison to The Avi Chai Foundation for the development and dissemination of the NETA project on Hebrew language education and teacher training for Jewish day high schools throughout North America.

DR. SCOTT SOKOL is the Dean of the Jewish Music Institute and Director of the Cantor-Educator Program as well as the Program in Jewish Special Education at Hebrew College. He also serves as Hazzan and Spiritual Leader at Congregation Kehillath Israel in Brookline, MA. Dr. Sokol has been a leading figure in the Jewish choral movement and is the editor of the *Journal of Synagogue Music*. He has also published extensively in the field of neuropsychology and behavioral medicine.

DR. DAVID B. STARR is Assistant Professor of Jewish History and Dean of Me'ah at Hebrew College, overseeing its curriculum and pedagogy. An ordained rabbi, he earned his doctorate in American history and modern Jewish history from Columbia University with a dissertation entitled *Catholic Israel: Solomon Shechter, a Study of Unity and Fragmentation in Modern Jewish History*. He has held fellowships at the Hebrew University in Jerusalem, Columbia University and Harvard University.

RABBI AVI (AVRAHAM) WEISS, Senior Rabbi of the Hebrew Institute of Riverdale, is founder and Dean of Yeshivat Chovevei Torah, the open Orthodox Rabbinical School in New York City, where his stated mission is to place 100 rabbis in synagogues in the coming decade. An activist Jewish communal leader, he is President of Amcha—The Coalition for Jewish Concerns. Known for his willingness to challenge entrenched ideas, he has written widely and is the recipient of numerous awards.